International Relations Theory
and the Third World

International Relations Theory and the Third World

Edited by Stephanie G. Neuman

St. Martin's Press
New York

ISBN 0-312-17299-0 (cloth)
ISBN 0-312-17706-2 (paper)

Permissions

Permission granted to reprint 4 lines from Muhammed Iqbal, *Poems From Iqbal,*
John Murray Publishers Ltd., 1995.

Permission granted to reprint 11 lines (p. 246) from 'The Vultures' by David Diop,
translated by Gerald Moore from *The Penguin Book of Modern African Poetry* edited
by Gerald Moore and Ulli Beier (First published as *Modern Poetry From Africa*
1963, Third edition 1984) copyright © Gerald Moore and Ulli Beier, 1963, 1968,
1984. Reproduced by permission of Penguin Books Ltd.

Permission granted to reprint 13 lines (p. 97) from 'Footnotes to the Book of the
Setback' by Nizar Qabbani, translated by Abdullah al-Udhari from *Modern Poetry
of the Arab World,* translated and edited by Abdullah al-Udhari (Penguin Books,
1986) copyright © Abdullah al-Udhari, 1986. Reproduced by permission of Penguin Books Ltd.

Library of Congress Cataloging-in-Publication Data

International relations theory and the Third World / edited by
  Stephanie Neuman.
    p. cm.
  Includes bibliographical references and index.
  ISBN 0-312-17299-0 (cloth)   ISBN 0-312-17706-2 (paper)
    1. International relations—Philosophy.   2. Developing countries—
Foreign relations.   3. Developing countries—Politics and
government.   I. Neuman, Stephanie G.
JZ1242.I58 1997
327.1'01—dc21   97-13407
                                                  CIP

Internal design and typesetting by Letra Libre

First edition: February 1998
10 9 8 7 6 5 4 3 2 1

Contents

The whole machinery of our intelligence, our general ideas and laws, fixed and external objects, principles, persons, and gods, are so many symbolic, algebraic expressions. They stand for experience; experience which we are incapable of retaining and surveying in its multitudinous immediacy. We should flounder hopelessly, like animals, did we not keep ourselves afloat and direct our course by [these] intellectual devices. Theory helps us to bear our ignorance of fact.

—George Santayana, The Sense of Beauty:
Being, the Outlines of Aesthetic Theory

Acknowledgments

The idea for this book has germinated since 1981 when I first began teaching a Third World security studies course at Columbia University. To my disappointment, the International Relations Theory I had studied and taught for so many years proved inadequate to explain much of the behavior of non-Western states in the international system, and there was little other theory to take its place. Why was this so? Why was the conduct of the myriad less powerful states so generally ignored by International Relations theorists?

But time constraints for a researcher dependent on soft money, such as I, meant that a book dealing with these questions would have to wait while other projects took precedence. And so the idea for this book remained relatively dormant until 1993–1994 when, as a Visiting Professor at West Point, I simultaneously taught International Relations Theory and Third World security courses. The theoretical gap between the two areas and the scant attention it continued to receive from most IR theorists reignited my interest in this project. In 1994 I contacted several political scientists who were also questioning the applicability of mainstream IR paradigms in non-Western settings to discuss the possibility of collectively addressing the issue in an edited volume. And so this book was born.

The essays in this volume passed through several stages of development. The initial drafts of all but the Introduction and Conclusion were presented at the annual meeting of the International Studies Association held in San Diego in 1995. Subsequently, using the criticisms and suggestions received at that meeting, the essays were substantially revised and in several instances entirely rewritten. Some additional revisions were later made during the editorial process. The contributors, in turn, made useful substantive suggestions that were incorporated into the final draft of the editor's Introduction.

This volume would not have appeared without the encouragement and support of many people. The authors and the editor owe them an unusual amount of thanks. Colonel Daniel Kaufman, the Director of the Political Science department at West Point, encouraged me to go ahead with this endeavor and not wait any longer. Once the project was launched, Kristina Mani Clark, a Ph.D. student at Columbia University, provided invaluable research and organizational assistance. She served as liaison between the contributors and me during the period I resided in Sweden, and at times provided emergency editorial support and yeoman's service in the library. The library staff at the Stockholm International Peace Research Institute (SIPRI), where I was housed as a Fulbright scholar for three and a half months, worked unstintingly to provide me with reference material with which to check quotations and footnote citations. No publication was too difficult for them to find. I am particularly grateful to Christer Berggren, Nenne Bodell, Gunnie Boman, Olle Persson, who took turns fulfilling my frequent requests and to Sten Wiksten and Gerd Hagmeyer-Gaverus who patiently bore with my computer illiteracy. I am also thankful to Billie Bielckus, who lent her editorial expertise to one of the chapters and to Adam Daniel Rotfield, the Director of SIPRI, who extended warm hospitality during my tenure there. Thanks also belong to Robert Jervis, at Columbia University and Jean Pascal Zanders at SIPRI who took the time to read and constructively comment on the Introduction.

I also acknowledge, with enthusiasm, the stimulating intellectual climate provided by my colleagues at the Columbia University Faculty International Relations Seminar and by the many excellent students, graduate and undergraduate, who it was my privilege to teach. I learned much from them. Their comments, queries, and insights contributed to the genesis of this book.

The authors and editor owe a special debt of gratitude to Karen Wolny, our editor at St. Martin's Press, who so efficiently shepherded this manuscript through its various complicated production phases.

Stephanie G. Neuman
Columbia University

List of Abbreviations

ASEAN	Association of Southeast Asian Nations
CENTO	Central Treaty Organization
IR	International Relations
LDC	Less-developed Countries
MTCR	Missile Technology Control Regime
NAM	Nonaligned Movement
NATO	North Atlantic Treaty Organization
OAS	Organization of American States
OAU	Organization of African Unity
SEATO	South East Asia Treaty Organization
UN	United Nations
UNAMIR	UN Assistance Mission for Rwanda

ONE

International Relations Theory and the Third World: An Oxymoron?[1]

Stephanie G. Neuman

During the Cold War, scholars focused obsessively on the challenges of the U.S.–Soviet confrontation, paying little heed to the role of the Third World in international politics. Such attention as it did receive was within the context of the East-West struggle. As the hostilities of the Cold War began to fade in the 1980s, so apparently did the creative energy of International Relations (IR) theorists. Since then, in spite of major global change, no new theoretical revolutions have occurred and no radical reorganization of the field has taken place.[2] Aside from a few notable contributions, mainly by the authors in this volume, the role of the Third World in international politics remains relatively unexplored in the literature. If anything, changes in the international system in general, and in the Third World in particular, seem to be outpacing developments in International Relations Theory.

The Relevance of IR Theory for the Third World

The idea for this book was conceived while I was teaching a course on Third World security at Columbia University. The course concentrates on the foreign and defense policies of Third World countries. Students are asked to take a worm's-eye view of relations among states: How do less powerful states perceive their position in world politics? How do they plan for their defense? What factors explain their foreign and defense policy choices? Which set of internal or external factors most influence those choices? To answer these questions we examine numerous concepts, approaches, models, and theories drawn from the IR literature that focus on the importance of, for example, military, bureaucratic, organizational, political, economic, and psychological factors, alliance behavior, and the structure of the international system.

To the surprise of both the students and myself, however, theory has never quite been borne out by events in the Third World. Some paradigms appear to explain some cases but not others. Amitav Acharya, for example, notes in chapter 7 that conflicting theories declaring the stabilizing or the destabilizing effect of the bipolar system can both be supported in the Third World. This is true for much of mainstream IR Theory. Even central concepts such as anarchy, the state, sovereignty, rational choice, alliance, and the international system are troublesome when applied to the Third World. Most perplexing, however, have been the unstated normative and empirically unsubstantiated assumptions that underlie much of what is written in the field. As many of the contributors to this book observe, mainstream IR Theory—(classical) realism, neorealism, and neoliberalism—is essentially Eurocentric theory, originating largely in the United States and founded, almost exclusively, on what happens or happened in the West. If the published record is any measure, then most IR theorists believe that studying the Western experience alone is empirically sufficient to establish general laws of individual, group, or state behavior irrespective of the point in time or the geographical location. Few look to the Third World to seek evidence for their arguments. It is the Eurocentric, normative character of the literature, and its claim of universal relevance, that are considered in this work.

Concepts That Do Not Fit

Many of the most common concepts in the IR nomenclature are at issue here. When applied to the Third World, they have little apparent reference to objective reality and evidence a normative stance in which Western ideas and institutions are not only considered to be universal but, implicitly, also to be superior to the political concepts and arrangements in other parts of the world. In most respects, Western IR theorists seem to envision a very different world from that of many non-Western leaders and scholars. The examples of conceptual misfit, discussed later in this chapter, are representative of an entire set of Western ideas and assumptions that serve as the foundation for mainstream International Relations theories.[3] Realism, neorealism, and neoliberalism are under attack from many quarters on many grounds, but the apparent fissure between theory and empirical reality in the Third World remains virtually unexamined. Even the so-called critical theorists, whose assaults on IR Theory have been the most vigorous, have all but ignored this issue.[4]

Anarchy

The assumption of an anarchical international system, for example, is particularly difficult to apply to the situation of most less developed countries (LDCs). Realists, neorealists, and neoliberal scholars hold that anarchy exists in the international system because there is an absence of central rule—often interpreted to mean the lack of a central government with the power to curb the aggressive ambitions of others.[5] International politics, in their view, is a self-help system whereby states must rely on their own capabilities to defend themselves against the aggressive acts of other states; it is a competition where "each is the equal of all the others," where none can command and none must obey.[6] Such stability as does exist in the world is attributed to the balance of power. As several analysts in this work and elsewhere observe, however, while these assumptions about the nature of the international system may describe relations among the major powers, whether they reflect the situation of lesser powers, who perceive the international system to be ordered and regulated by the few Great Powers in it, is open to serious question.

Carlos Escudé contends in chapter 3, for example, that it is not anarchy but hierarchy that constrains the external behavior of most Third World states, and that this is how their leaders and intellectuals see it. Alexander Wendt and Michael Barnett take a middle position in the debate, arguing that the international system is existentially anarchic but is overlaid by informal hierarchical "authority structures" they call "informal empires" that are not anarchic for the dependent political units within them.[7]

Similar questions of relevance are raised by the assumption of domestic order in states. If, as Kenneth Waltz claims, the difference between domestic and international politics "turns on the distinction between politics conducted in a condition of settled rules and politics conducted in a condition of anarchy,"[8] is it theoretically or empirically credible to assume that order rather than anarchy prevails within states whose greatest single problem is to establish "a condition of settled rules"? For many LDCs, then, the realist focus on a sharp boundary between domestic "order" and international "anarchy" may be applicable, but in reverse. It is the hierarchical structure of the world that provides them with an ordered reality, and a "condition of unsettled rules" that afflicts them at home.

The International System

Even more daunting are the issues raised by the assumed unitary nature of the international system in IR Theory. As David Singer puts it: there is only one international system "on and around the planet Earth,"[9] but if the international system is less anarchical, or not anarchical at all for the majority of states in it, is it not then logical to wonder whether there is, in fact, only one international system? Perhaps two or more worlds of international politics exist that follow different political norms and practices.[10] If a system is characterized by its interconnectedness and the sensitivity of each unit to change within and among other member units, does this concept apply to an international system that includes the Third World?[11] Do weak states significantly affect the security interests of the principal units in the system? In fact, neorealist theory maintains they do not.[12]

In the view of some critics of systems theory, the very requirement of interrelatedness among the separate parts of a putative international system, empirically excludes the Third World from it. They see it rather as yet another Western construct that may be relevant for "the core" but not for "the periphery."[13] It is, they maintain, the lack of connectedness to the core that marks the distinctiveness of LDCs in interstate relations.

Yezid Sayigh, for example, observes: "a distinguishing feature of developing countries generally is their position in international politics and the world balance of power. There is a consensus that they are 'seen as not belonging to the central East-West arena' . . . developing countries which accept that they have a separate status in the international community are, therefore, a 'self defining group of states.'"[14] Similarly, Max Singer and Aaron Wildavsky envision two very distinct international systems: "The key to understanding the real world order is to separate the world into two parts. One part is zones of peace, wealth, and democracy. The other part is zones of turmoil, war, and development."[15] Seth Carus believes that there is now a division of the world into two separate spheres based on the large differential in military and industrial capabilities of the North and the South. As a result, he concludes, Third World wars will be fought on a different level than those of the developed world, with little probability of war between the two camps.[16] According to these scholars, separateness rather than interrelatedness distinguishes the Third World in international relations.

This view is not unanimous, however, even among analysts who focus on the Third World. Mohammed Ayoob avers that not only is the Third World an integral part of the international system but that it also plays a significant role in it. In chapter 2, he dismisses the claim by some IR theorists that the weakness of the periphery has made it unable to have a major impact on the security concerns of the major powers or on the stability of the international system. On the contrary, Ayoob argues that because of the ever-increasing interdependence of the globe, it is "wishful thinking" on the part of the industrialized world to think it can be insulated from the problems of disorder in the Third World. He sees one international system and challenges the idea that the "zone of peace" can be, even conceptually, separated from the "zone of conflict."

Irrespective of their differences, these analysts are expressing their dissatisfaction with the fit between observed evidence and traditional IR Theory with respect to the position of the Third World in international affairs. As one social theorist remarks, "A theory that ignores existing evidence is an oxymoron. If we had the equivalent of 'truth in advertising' legislation, such an oxymoron should not be called a theory."[17]

Rational Choice

"Rational choice theory" has also proved problematic as an analytic tool in a non-Western setting (and to some social scientists in the Western setting too).[18] It assumes that any chosen behavior can be understood as optimizing material self-interest. In class, many of my students and I wondered how we could make the assumption that all human decisions and acts are a means to a self-interested, material end in all cultures. How does one know this empirically? Is the behavior of a Japanese kamikaze pilot to be considered rational or irrational? From whose perspective? Would it be judged in the same way by an Asian, an American, an African, or a European? Is what is rational in one culture irrational in another and does it need to be explained differently? Intuitively, we felt that the strength of a body of theory that ignores cultural variety is suspect. It was important to know whether variations in a society's order of normative preferences, such as fairness, respect, honor, and humiliation matter and whether they might dictate deviations from rational choice predictions about human behavior.

Joel Larus, in a compelling study of precolonial Indian military history, wonders about a pattern of behavior that to the Western mind is inexplicable, if not irrational. Why, for example, did India never become a naval power? It sat astride the ancient world's major maritime trade route (between the Persian Gulf and the Red Sea in the west and the South China Sea in the east). Its long coastline of 3,750 miles and its abundant resources would seem to have made trade and conquest attractive options for the ancient Hindu kingdoms. Yet unlike the Greeks, Romans, and other early Mediterranean peoples, precolonial India never produced a navy or a class of overseas merchants that could have advanced its power in the ancient and medieval world. Larus found that the complex Hindu religio-caste system was a critical factor explaining not only the absence of an Indian naval tradition, but other unique historical patterns of Hindu military behavior that, in his view, are not explainable in terms of the rational actor model or the geostrategic situation of India at that time.[19]

Unfortunately, our questions about the relationship between cultural values and foreign policy behavior remained largely unanswered. It was surprising how little we were helped by the rational choice literature and how little cross-cultural research had been done. In general, we found that rational choice theorists have given scant empirical attention to the issue of non-Western cultural differences and their possible relevance to rational choice constructs.

The State

The same problem attends even so central a concept as the "state" in the Third World, where the features normally associated with it are often absent. Generally identified with Western, democratic, constitutional political institutions, an effective government, inviolate geographical boundaries, and a monopoly over the use of force within those boundaries—the concept of statehood does not fit easily into most non-Western settings.[20] The arbitrary boundaries drawn by external powers are often unacceptable to warring ethnic groups that reside within them and the ruling central government is frequently perceived as a threat to be challenged. According to Donald Puchala in chapter 6, these borders are unacceptable to many Third World radical intellectuals "not only [because] they are meaningless in cultural, tribal, geographic or economic terms, but [because] *they were drawn by the imperial powers* and are imperialism's lingering, insulting legacy." In many parts of the Third World, Western-inspired governments exert only tenuous control over sometimes large areas within their territorial jurisdiction for extended periods of time. Laws and regulations, such as they are, cannot be enforced with confidence and are not always complied with. In some countries, at differing time periods, a condition of anarchy exists.[21] Zaire, Somalia, and Albania are only three examples.

As the authors in this book eloquently describe, Western attempts to refashion the world in its own political image have not been noted for their success. Other scholars, such as Eli Kedourie, declare that these efforts did not bring political freedom, did not increase prosperity, and have not been conducive to peace. On the contrary, he says, they have "created new conflicts, exacerbated tensions, and brought catastrophe to numberless people. . . ."[22] Yezid Sayigh also observes that: "In many cases this 'crisis of statehood' forms a connecting thread between the problems faced by developing countries in achieving social, economic and political progress and those posed by the problems of managing their external environment."[23] Barry Buzan's seminal work on this issue suggests that if indeed most Third World countries are to be considered states, they must be thought of as belonging to an identifiable separate class of state, with little connection to the established Western concept.[24] In other words, large and observable differences between Western and Third World political behavior suggest there is an important disjunction between the empirical reality of political organization in the Third World and the idea of the state as we know it.[25] There is, however, little consensus among scholars on what, if anything, might take its place.

Sovereignty

Other concepts closely associated with statehood, such as sovereignty, are equally troublesome. The term sovereignty, for example, is defined in so many different ways by different analysts, Stephen Krasner is prompted to complain that it is mired in "hopeless confusion."[26] Most commonly, sovereignty is defined as freedom from external control.[27] Since the Peace of Westphalia in 1648 and its legitimization of the state system, the term has been linked to the concept of state autonomy. Sovereignty resides within the state, and all states then, by definition, are endowed with it regardless of their relative capabilities.[28] Both realists and liberals take this as given; autonomous states are the basic units in the international system and vary only according to their power capabilities. Although sovereignty is a central assumption of most major International Relations theories,[29] the nature of sovereignty itself has not been a subject of comparative empirical study.

In reality, there has always been tension between theory and practice. Even in the seventeenth century, when the power of the sovereign state was considered absolute and intervention by an external power implied the violation of that sovereignty, "the principle of nonintervention applied only to relations among European states and not to those between European states and the less civilized people outside the international system."[30] By the twentieth century, however, this distinction between fully sovereign states and other less sovereign or nonsovereign units was no longer acceptable under international law. All states, recognized as such by the international community were to be considered sovereign and equal. But the disparity between what states said and what they did about the norms of sovereignty and nonintervention was growing larger, especially with regard to the Third World. Intervention by the major powers in countries such as Afghanistan, South Vietnam, Cambodia, and Chad, to mention but a few, are testimony to the increasing divide between theory and major power behavior.

Even the UN has been inconsistent on this issue. Despite UN officials' reluctance to push the organization into actions that override the principle of national sovereignty, intervention in the internal conflicts of Third World states has in recent years been the rule rather than the exception. International human rights, humanitarian law, and international regulatory agreements are further pushing the envelope of conceptual meaning, particularly when foreign military intervention is justified in their name. To some in the Third Word, even the divide between peacekeeping and intervention has grown increasingly murky.[31] A senior Congolese official, for example, commenting on his Government's refusal to meet the demands of the United Nations on the treatment of refugees and other issues related to the UN's peacekeeping mission, said that his Government suspected an international conspiracy of sorts to use the refugee issue in the United Nations to destroy President Kabila's Government and replace it with leaders more amenable to the West. A Foreign Ministry official explained: "The history of our country and the United Nations is a history of a failed romance. . . . At independence in 1960 the United Nations banned our own Prime Minister from the radio, and a U.N. peacekeeping force took sides in our civil war. We have reasons to suspect the worst."[32]

The traditional definition of sovereignty then is challenged by overt intervention in the Third World but, according to some, it is under siege from other less visible sources as well. In their view the dependence of most LDCs on the major powers for military technology, economic assistance, foreign troops to protect them from internal and external challenges, and for political support in regional and international forums, casts significant doubt on their ability to act independently from their benefactors.

In chapter 8, Buzan takes the position that sovereignty exists for Third World countries because "they claim them [all of the functions of self-government] and these claims are in nearly all cases accepted by the other members of the system." In the eyes of the international community all states are equally sovereign. But Escudé and others in this book suggest that this is not so. It may be that the major powers and the elites in the Third World do give lip service to the legal principle of sovereignty but, they argue, in reality sovereignty is denied to many countries, particularly Third World countries that are extensively penetrated by major powers.[33] In other words, these authors contend that the rules are not the same for all units nor are they really accepted as such.

Xavier Alcalde Cardoza, in his book *Development, Decay, and Social Conflict,* also complains about the myth of Third World sovereignty. He maintains that even the concepts designed to economically and politically restructure Third World societies originate in the developed world. "The choice of development by the Third World did not involve, as in the case of the Industrial Revolution and Western economic progress, an autonomous historical process. The evolution of the idea of Third World development has . . . taken place primarily in the North."[34] The South's contribution, he argues, has been mostly limited to the technical implementation of a Western concept of development.[35]

Alcalde is not alone in challenging the assumption of Third World sovereignty. Puchala claims that *dependencia*—a neo-Marxist theory linking economic underdevelopment in the periphery to the penetrative, exploitative policies of the capitalist core—is regaining popularity among Third World radical thinkers.

Once discredited (in part due to the fall from fashion of Marxist economics in the 1980s) the capitalistic West and the international institutions it dominates are seen once again as the exploiters and perpetrators of poverty in the Third World. Puchala notes that in late 1996 one of the major demands of the Tupac Amaru guerrillas in Lima, Peru, was the abandonment of the governments' [Western-inspired] economic reforms as the price of releasing their hostages. To most Third World radicals, then, Western domination did not end when formal political independence was achieved. In their view, Puchala writes, it "continues today in the form of quisling elites manipulated by outsiders, international institutions controlled by the West, imposed doctrines like 'parliamentary democracy' endorsed by the West, and interventions by Western-dispatched 'peacekeepers' and the ever-present CIA."[36]

Given the extent of ideological and material penetration from the West, few Third World analysts believe their country to be "free from external control." This is true even for less radicalized intellectuals. Yezid Sayigh, for example, declares that the history of most Third World countries is one of subjection, not only to the military power of Western states, but to their economic, political, and cultural dominance as well.[37]

The empirical inaccuracy of the "sovereignty" model is evidenced not just by Western behavior in the Third World, but also by the analytical corollaries derived from it. Because the term *sovereignty* has been tied so closely to the concept of statehood, IR Theory expects physical threats to sovereignty to originate outside the political boundaries of a state. In many Third World countries, however, competing claims to sovereignty are taking place within those boundaries, further weakening the governments' putative authority and increasing their vulnerability to outside pressures. In this context, the idea of sovereignty can have only abstract theoretical meaning for most LDCs.

In spite of its poor conceptual fit, few theorists have attempted to redefine sovereignty to reflect the objective situation of most Third World countries. Even the neoliberals, such as Joseph Nye and Robert Keohane, do not challenge the term's classical meaning, claiming instead that in the twentieth century it has been eroded by economic interdependence, revolutionary technologies, and democratic politics. States, they believe, are no longer autonomous because they can no longer control their borders and are less able to achieve their policy objectives;[38] but even the concept of erosion suggests that sovereignty existed originally, an assumption that, if it applies, it applies largely only to the core states. During the colonial period of the eighteenth and nineteenth centuries, Third World polities could hardly be considered "autonomous," even for abstract theoretical purposes. In the end, the debate between neoliberals and neorealists over whether sovereignty has or has not been eroded is conducted within the same Eurocentric framework that characterizes so much of mainstream IR Theory.

Krasner claims that ("Westphalian") sovereignty has always been a myth since few states have ever enjoyed total domestic autonomy. He cites numerous examples where the sovereignty of Western states, including the United States, has been violated.[39] Others contend that worldwide communications and information networks have made the concept of borders and government control over the activities of its citizens within them ever more tenuous for all states.[40] Empirically, this may be true, but from a Third World perspective clearly some states have more autonomy than others.[41] Theodore Couloumbus, for example, contends that powerful nations can afford to be "more sovereign" than weak nations. In his study of Greek history he concludes that "time-honored principles of international law such as sovereign equality, independence, noninterference in the domestic affairs of nations could appear at best as utopian goals for the future rather than characteristics of an observable international system of behavior."[42]

Although there is much controversy regarding its relevance in the twentieth century, a realistic assessment of the nature of sovereignty and its conceptual utility awaits systematic empirical analysis. Rather than being an absolute concept, either present or absent, sovereignty may prove to be a relative variable that applies in some cases and not in others, or exists in varying degrees in different countries during different time periods in diverse parts of the world.

Alliances[43]

Alliance theory, in general, is a less developed part of International Relations Theory. With few exceptions, what does exist focuses almost exclusively on the alliance behavior of major states.[44] In the tradition of realism and neorealism, alliance theory assumes that changing alignments are a response to changing power configurations in the international system. They are a means by which states add power to deal with perceived external threat, and it is the distribution of relative capabilities among states that explain their alliance behavior, whether it be balancing or bandwagoning.[45]

In their chapters in this book, both Kalevi J. Holsti and Amitav Acharya declare this body of theory irrelevant for developing countries. They point out that there have been few alliances in the Third World, particularly between weak states. According to Michael Handel, historically the Great

Powers can be found even behind the few putative alliances among weak states.[46] Moreover, those alliances initiated by the superpowers during the Cold War, such as SEATO and CENTO, were not notable successes. Alliance theory provides little guidance as to why this should be so.[47]

Steven R. David, too, finds alliance theory wanting. He believes it does not capture the motives for alignment or the alignment behavior of Third World countries because it ignores the internal threats that preoccupy many of them. In an earlier article in *World Politics,* he offers omnibalancing as an alternate concept, holding that alignment in the Third World often reflects the governments' attempt to balance against internal rather than external enemies.[48] The crux of omnibalancing is that leaders will align to deal with those threats that endanger their survival, be they internal or external. It is the more likely and more potent internal threat that alliance theory ignores.

Most weak states, by their very nature, must rely on external sources of strength to deal with threats. Yet, traditionally, weak state alliances have not been prominent, lasting, or successful[49] even in the face of danger. It is interesting to note that this may be true in the precolonial Third World too. Larus finds that despite frequent invasions from the north, the various early Hindu kingdoms did not form alliances to protect themselves from attack and repeated defeat. To Larus the answer can be found in the particular Hindu religious culture,[50] but the persistence of this behavior in modern times suggests the need for a more general explanation.

In fact, Third World behavior generally denies the expectations of IR alliance theory—that in response to structural changes in the international system the balancing behavior of states will alter.[51] During the Cold War, for instance, much of the Third World either maintained a posture of "neutrality" or was aligned with one or the other of the superpowers. Alliances between Third World states were fragile and short-lived.[52] Most IR theorists explain this behavior in terms of bipolarity and the balancing response of the superpowers to it. In other words, from the perspective of the major powers. In a bipolar system, they hold, the greater the tension between the superpowers the more they will compete for the allegiance of weak states. During the Cold War, a primary interest of each superpower was to extend its own bloc among small and uncommitted states at the expense of its rival and prevent the other superpower from expanding its influence among them. Both the Soviet Union (for example, in Afghanistan) and the United States (for example, in Vietnam) were willing to pay a relatively high price to prevent defection to the other side.[53] Waltz declares that "In a bipolar world there are no peripheries. With only two powers capable of acting on a world scale, anything that happens anywhere is potentially of concern to both of them."[54] Because the superpowers were preoccupied with balancing each other, some analysts claim, neither was considered a serious threat by their small allies. Even if a Third World state were threatened, it could expect to be protected by the other superpower. Alignment, tacit or not, was primarily seen by most Third World states as a means to obtain aid and protection against a local rival[55] or a threatening superpower.

Dramatic changes in the structure of the international system, however, such as those that occurred at the end of the Cold War, should, according to the theory, precipitate changes in patterns of alignment as well.[56] As Waltz contends "the theory leads us to expect states to behave in ways that result in balances forming."[57] Theoretically, this should be true for all states, including weak states, for whom these structural changes have important security implications.[58] Handel and others observe, for example, that as competition between the major powers declines, so, too, does the value of Third World alignment and the major powers' incentive to pay for it.[59] In the absence of a countervailing source of support and protection, and unable to balance by defecting to the other side, weak states now appear to be not only more vulnerable to internal and regional threats, but to pressure, penetration, and potential intervention from the West as well.[60] If a bipolar system served as some protection from these threats, then its demise, in theory, should elicit some change in the balancing behavior of Third World states. Yet the response of the Third World to these global shifts has been remarkably muted. Other than some former Communist bloc countries, there has been little movement toward alliance. Curiously, given the combination of threats facing most Third World states—their comparative weakness, persistent internal instability, regional conflict, and the growing disinterest of the major powers in their affairs—the question is why Third World states have not sought to increase their strength through alliances, particularly with one another? It is a puzzle for which IR Theory provides few answers.

Conceptual Linkages

When these and other IR concepts are strung together to create general theories or paradigms of human behavior, it is not surprising that they prove poor predictors of outcomes in the Third World. Alcalde, for example, contends that Western theories maintaining a positive linkage between economic development, political stability, democracy, and world peace have been proven wrong in the Third World. These linkages, he argues, "crumble at the most cursory confrontation with historical reality."[61] Events since World War II demonstrate, in his view, that economic development has not conditioned the political system in the Third World toward democracy and stability. On the contrary, Third World leaders chose to regard political stability as a precondition for economic growth, and in many cases opted to guarantee both with increased authoritarianism.[62] Alcalde contends that neither the vision of world peace or even the more modest goal of reduced conflict have materialized. "[Western] ideas of development and peace, have represented a vast utopia."[63] Domestically conceived measures and autonomously implemented efforts appropriate to the circumstances of the individual societies are, Alcalde believes, the solution. It is a view that differs significantly from universalistic Western conventional wisdom.

In chapter 7, Acharya, too, finds many of the conceptual connections in IR Theory spurious, curious, and ethnocentric. Pointing to the theoretical linkage between stability and conflict, he notes that the polarity-stability debate in the United States equates stability with the absence of war among the Great Powers. If this is so, he argues, then ironically a "stable system" still permits any number of non–Great Power wars, or "limited wars"—that again raises the question of the "interconnectedness" of the international system.

Acharya also decries the conceptual linkage between democratization and conflict in much of Western literature. He points out that throughout the Third World many cases of democratization have been remarkably peaceful. "Multiparty democratic elections led to the replacement of existing regimes in Zambia, Madagascar, and Cape Verde. Internationally monitored elections saw the peaceful return of the governments of Seychelles, Guinea Bissau, and Kenya."

This discussion, then, has identified some of the conceptual weaknesses that plague IR Theory. The noblesse oblige attitude of so many IR theorists and policy analysts is, therefore, all the more puzzling to scholars studying the Third World. This "we know best what is in your interests" stance, despite the lack of empirical evidence to support it, pervades the debates over economic growth, political development, human rights, peacekeeping, arms control, and nuclear proliferation that take place principally within Western forums. Non-Western members of the "international system," comprising some three-quarters of its membership, are generally considered objects of Great Power policies rather than independent, autonomous players in the system. Unlike their more sanctimonious Western benefactors, Third World analysts believe power, rather than Western theoretical wisdom, drives North/South relations.[64] Ironically, like the realist theorists they often condemn, Third World thinkers have adopted realism's basic premise.

The Birth of a Book

These concerns about IR Theory led to the birth of this book. I invited scholars who had already expressed some dissatisfaction with various aspects of IR Theory in earlier publications to write papers on the relevance of IR Theory for the Third World for a panel to be held at the International

Studies Association Conference in San Diego, California, in April 1996. Each was asked to address a series of questions: Does IR Theory accurately describe, explain, or predict the behavior of Third World states in international affairs? If not, what are its deficiencies? If yes, what are its strengths?

The following chapters, for the most part, are the edited and revised versions of those papers. Buzan's critical chapter, based on his verbal commentary at the conference, and this introduction were written expressly for this book. When I organized the panel, I hoped that the book derived from it, whether or not there was consensus among the authors, would broaden the debate on IR Theory and enrich our understanding of interstate relations and foreign policy decision making, particularly in the Third World. International Relations Theory informs and motivates policy as it filters down into government and political circles. It is the lens through which policymakers see the world and make decisions. It is, therefore, important that the assumptions upon which these theories are built realistically reflect the nature not only of Great Power political-military relations but the interactions between the core and the less powerful periphery as well. The ongoing debate in the United States among IR analysts about whether or not the Third World matters is a clear indication that sound theoretical thinking is lacking on this issue.[65] Even within this relatively narrow conceptual sphere, the indeterminacy of IR Theory as a policy guide has meant that conflicting and often diametrically opposed claims are tendered, sometimes by scholars within the same theoretical school of thought. Commenting on this Michael Desch observes: "Realists share the same core assumptions about the international system yet many come to different conclusions about whether and how the Third World matters."[66] It is interesting to note that the debate over the significance of the Third World is carried on almost exclusively in the United States and from the perspective of United States policy interests: what is sound strategic policy for the United States in the Third World? It illustrates the extent to which an ethnocentric focus pervades almost every level of IR theoretical discourse.

The role of the Third World in international politics remains a "theoretical" puzzle, presenting us with "observable outcomes for which existing explanations seem insufficient or erroneous."[67] The response of Third World governments to international events continues to surprise us as do the persistently high incidence of internal war,[68] the huge loss of war-related lives,[69] and the tenacious poverty and suffering in many of these countries. These observable "realities" defy our theoretical models and so we are unable to understand or agree on their significance for world order. Until we do, policymakers will obtain little guidance from IR Theory. James Rosenau believes puzzles are the precursors to theory: "To have a theory is to think you know how things work, to be puzzled is to wonder why and how they culminate as they do?"[70] The contributors to this book describe their puzzlement and offer tentative explanations as to why and how they are relevant to global interstate relations.

Consensus and Disagreement

As it turned out, the contributing writers do not agree on the best approach to understanding the role of the Third World in international politics, nor is there complete accord on the issue of the relevance of IR Theory for the Third World. Steven R. David, for example, makes a case for the ability of the neorealist model to explain some forms of conflict in the Third World. Although neorealism requires broadening to include domestic threats, he argues that key neorealist concepts, such as balance of power and the security dilemma, are as applicable to internal wars in anarchic states as they are for interstate conflicts.[71] Escudé, too, finds elements of classical realism and neorealism relevant to Third World foreign policy behavior, but offers amendments in the form of "peripheral realism." In his view, hierarchy (not anarchy) in the international system combined with the norms and preferences of society determine Third World external behavior. Similarly, Acharya maintains that although much of the polarity-stability debate contributes little to understanding the security experience of Third World states, he believes the Deutsch-Singer model of multipolarity is a relatively accurate predictor of future conditions in the post–Cold War Third World.

Holsti, on the other hand, contends that the main International Relations paradigms, neo-realism, as well as neoliberalism, have little relevance to the Third World. Because International Relations Theory, whether of the eighteenth- or nineteenth-century variety, assumes the existence of a state, in his view they explain neither the internal nor external conflict behavior of Third World actors. Puchala agrees, but on different grounds. He believes that Western IR Theory is so focused on power that it ignores the strength of cultural and ideational explanations of Third World behavior: "Contemporary Western thinking about International Relations has had little to offer to explain, or to evaluate the significance of, the embittered tone, the complex motivations, the mythological underpinnings, or the historical dynamics of North-South relations." In Puchala's view, it is another world out there that does not fit easily into Western conceptual categories and for which Western IR theories offer few guidelines.

Ayoob, too, concludes that IR theories are limited in their ability to explain the workings of the international system because they ignore the behavior of the majority of non-Western members of the international system, and therefore fail to provide adequate explanations for the causes of conflict or guides to its management and resolution. He, too, maintains that neorealism and neoliberalism do not provide an adequate map of international reality and offers his own theory of "subaltern realism" instead. Several contributors focus on the continuing armed violence in the Third World. They, too, differ over the implications for the future. David believes that although the prognosis for peace and stability within new states is bleak, with better conceptual tools, internal war could be successfully ameliorated, managed, and resolved by resolute outside powers. He is, however, pessimistic about the willingness of outside states to do what is necessary to stop internal wars.[72] Ayoob, on the other hand, sees war as part of the state-building process. He supports Charles Tilly's position that "war makes states." To Ayoob state-making and internal wars are two sides of the same coin. Until the process of state-making is completed, conflict will continue to characterize International Relations in the Third World. By implication, he believes, order in the international system cannot be achieved until the process of state-making is completed. Acharya, is more optimistic. He sees hope for diminished Third World conflict in a less bifurcated, multipolar world. Escudé implicitly concurs on other grounds. He submits that a hierarchical order imposed by the Great Powers severely limits the options of "peripheral" states unwilling to pay the costs of rebellion. Thus the power relationship between those that command and those that submit establishes a form of order in an otherwise anarchical international system that lessens the likelihood of international conflict. Puchala, too, observes: "for the next several decades the struggle between the non-West and the West is likely to be most intense, and consequential, *within* societies rather than between states, because power differentials will constrain confrontations between states." He is less sanguine about the long term.

This apparent lack of consensus among the contributors, however, is not total. They allow that the ethnocentric character of Western political thought has created a body of International Relations Theory that is either not relevant to the Third World, or in need of significant revision. They further agree that an unqualified systemic approach is unable to adequately explain interstate relations in the post–Cold War world. Regional, domestic, and cultural factors, in their view, are necessary to understand not only the foreign policies of Third World states but the presence of conflict and order in interstate relations. They also believe, however, that in spite of the need to consider internal factors, the impact of the international system, its norms and structure, as well as the policies of other states on Third World countries, cannot be ignored. My reading of the majority opinion, is that it is not in favor of granting theoretical priority to the nature of the states. Rather, most of the contributors want domestic factors to be at least considered by and at best integrated into system theories. Thus, some blend of reductionist and holistic approaches is called for. As Ayoob observes, problems of international order cannot be understood in isolation from problems of domestic order. They are inextricably intertwined.

Tentative accord is also reached on the question of the state. Although most contributors acknowledge that the state as we know it in the West is not evident in many Third World regions, they believe that some variant of it is slowly evolving in these countries. The process of evolution may be difficult, and the final version may not resemble the Western form but, in the end, they consider a strong state to be the most likely political organization to provide security and welfare to individuals, and stability in international relations.

I think I am not misstating another tacit area of agreement among the contributors. Although they find the claim for universalism by mainstream IR theorists annoying, as do many scholars who study the Third World, most would, I believe, agree that the goal of good theory is to achieve as much universalism as the evidence will permit.[73] Clearly, more empirical and creative work needs to be done to test the relevance of IR concepts, the boundaries of their applicability, and the extent to which they are truly universal. Ironically, as David observes, it is no longer clear that Western models accurately depict what is happening in the North. Today he remarks, "instead of the Third World 'developing' to where Eurocentric theories become applicable, many 'developed' states are reaching the point in which the Third World experience has become applicable to them." Shifting our gaze from the few powerful actors in world affairs to the many who are less powerful may help us to revise and strengthen the conceptual foundations upon which IR Theory is built, so that it better reflects what is happening globally today. The study of small states may answer big questions.

The contributors would also not disagree, I am sure, that maintaining IR Theory's aspiration to objective, scientific knowledge is critical to its future. The criticism leveled here is not meant to imply that the whole body of IR Theory is irredeemably flawed. Rather it holds that the question of relevance itself needs to be empirically tested. What is required is the construction of a paradigm, as free as possible of ethnocentric bias, based on a set of observational hypotheses that can be applied and tested in many global environments. Colin Gray's complaint about strategic studies 15 years ago applies just as well to the field of International Relations today. The United States and the West represent only one group of related cultures, and for a field of inquiry "to be rooted in so narrow and unique a set of predispositions" can only diminish its capacity to accommodate the diversity of national political styles that exists worldwide.[74] The contributors to this volume and I concur.

Notes

1. Some analysts consider the term *Third World* inaccurate. Donald Puchala for example, maintains that by "using descriptors such as 'weak,' 'developing,' 'South,' etc., or even conventional regional designations like Asia, Africa, Latin America, etc. you are indicating either that the Third World is a PLACE or an ECONOMIC CONDITION. This is a western perspective. In the thinking of people who identify as 'third worlders,' the third world is neither a place, nor an economic condition, but rather a STATE OF MIND. It's a perspective, an attitude, a world view. Therefore, the third world exists as surely in New York City, Paris, London, etc. as it does in Lagos or Mexico City because there are 'third worlders' in all of these places. Unless we can shake loose from western conceptualizations, we are never going to understand the third world in the way that the third world understands itself." (Correspondence with the editor, March 26, 1997.) Others find the term offensive, but lacking another satisfactory nomenclature retain it in their work nevertheless. See Asoka Bandarage, "Global Peace and Security in the Post–Cold War Era: A 'Third World' Perspective," in *Peace and World Security Studies: A Curriculum Guide,* ed., Michael T. Klare (Boulder, CO and London: Lynne Rienner Publishers, 1994), pps. 29–42. Since the end of the Cold War and the disappearance of the so-called Second World, the term Third World seems increasingly inapt. Unfortunately, none other has gained general recognition or acceptance. In this work, absent an alternative satisfactory referent, various terms such as weak, developing, South, non-Western, LDCs, industrializing or nonindustrializing countries, peripheral states and Third World are used interchangeably to refer to countries in Africa, Asia (except Japan), the Middle East, Latin America, and the newly independent states of the former Soviet Union (other than Russia).

2. James E. Dougherty and Robert L. Pfaltzgraff, Jr., eds., *Contending Theories of International Relations* (NY: HarperCollins Publishers, 1990), p. xii.

3. The concepts examined in this chapter are by no means exhaustive. They were selected as examples largely because they were questioned most frequently in classroom discussions and by some of the assigned course readings. The ethnocentric bias noted here, however, is not limited to International Relations Theory. Scholars in other disciplines are also beginning to challenge their own fields' basic assumptions on similar grounds. In a discussion about how one defines the concept of "Europe," for example, one geographer observes that the standard definition—that the Ural mountains are the Eastern limits of Europe—is ethnocentric in origin. The tradition invoked is, of course, European tradition; or rather, geographers in London, Paris, Berlin, Rome, and Madrid, found it convenient to state that Europe ended at the Urals for the simple reason that in the early nineteenth century, further inland was very much a *terra incognita.* Remember, further inland was the land of the Tatars, the Cossacks, the Mongols, and then China . . . populations viewed with the highest suspicion. Europe extended to where the maps ended. . . . This tradition evolved into convenience of reference. We are talking of course of convenience for

Western Europeans, and the West at large. It might be an idea to ask the Ukranians, or the Republics to the North of the Caspian where they think Europe starts and why. (E-mail message to int-boundaries@mailbase.ac.uk, November 19, 1996 from Michael Davie, Department of Geography, Universite Francois-Rabelais, Tours, France.)

4. See Steve Smith, Ken Book, and Marysia Zalewski, eds., *International Theory: Positivism and Beyond* (Cambridge: Cambridge University Press, 1996) for the "critical theorists" or "post-positivist" attack on the assumptions and methods of the dominant IR theories.

5. Kenneth N. Waltz, *Theory of International Politics* (Reading, MA: Addison-Wesley, 1979), pps. 102–4. For variations on this definition, see Helen Milner, "Anarchy in International Relations," in *Neorealism and Neoliberalism,* ed., David Baldwin (NY: Columbia University Press, 1993), pps. 143–69.

6. Waltz, ibid., p. 88. Keohane confirms the agreement between neorealists and neoliberals (whom he terms *institutionalists*): "Institutionalism accepts the assumptions of realism about state motivation and lack of common enforcement power in world politics, but argues that *where common interests exist,* realism is too pessimistic about the prospects for cooperation and the role of institutions . . ." Robert O. Keohane, "Institutional Theory and the Realist Challenge after the Cold War," in *Neorealism and Neoliberalism,* ed., David Baldwin, pps. 269–300, p. 277.

7. Alexander Wendt and Michael N. Barnett, "Dependent State Formation and Third World Militarization," *Review of International Studies,* vol. 19 (1993), pps. 321–47, p. 335. Wendt and Barnett define three "informal empires" in the contemporary states system: the United States in the Caribbean, and to a lesser extent South America, parts of the Middle East, and assorted Asian states, France in West Africa and, until 1989, the USSR in Eastern Europe (p. 334). See also Nicholas Onuf and Frank F. Klink, "Anarchy, Authority, Rule," *International Studies Quarterly,* vol. 33 (1989), pps. 149–73; particularly the section on heteronomy, pps. 168–69.

8. Waltz, *Theory of International Politics,* p. 61.

9. J. David Singer, "The Global System and Its Subsystems: A Developmental View," in *Linkage Politics: Essays on the Convergence of National and International Systems,* ed., James N. Rosenau (NY: Free Press, 1969), p. 30.

10. See, for example, James M. Goldgeier and Michael McFaul, "A Tale of Two Worlds: Core and Periphery in the Post–Cold War Era," *International Organization,* vol. 46, no. 2 (Spring 1992), pps. 467–91. Goldgeier and McFaul argue that the neorealist model is applicable to the periphery, where armed conflict will continue, but not within the core, which will resolve its competing interests through bargaining and adjudication. For a different theoretical formulation, see the large dependency literature published during the 1970s, for example, Johan Galtung, "A Structural Theory of Imperialism," *Journal of Peace Research,* vol. 8 (1971), pps. 81–117; André Gunder Frank, *Dependent Accumulation and Underdevelopment* (London: Macmillan, 1978); Fernando Cardoso and Enzo Faletto, *Dependency and Development in Latin America*

(Berkeley, CA: University of California Press, 1979); and Peter Evans, *Dependent Development* (Princeton, NJ: Princeton University Press, 1979.)

11. According to Robert Jervis: "A system exists when elements or units are interconnected so that the system has emergent properties—i.e., its characteristics and behavior cannot be inferred from the characteristics and behavior of the units taken individually—and when changes in one unit or the relationship between any two of them produce ramifying alterations in other units or relationships." Robert Jervis, "Counterfactuals, Causation, and Complexity," in *Counterfactual Thought Experiments in World Politics,* eds., Philip E. Tetlock and Aaron Belkin (Princeton, NJ: Princeton University Press, 1996), p. 309.

12. Waltz declares that in "international politics, as in any self-help system, the units of greatest capability set the scene of action for others as well as for themselves. . . . The fates of all the states . . . in a system are affected much more by the acts and interactions of the major ones than of the minor ones." Waltz, *Theory of International Politics,* p. 72.

13. Goldgeier and McFaul, "A Tale of Two Worlds"; see also Max Singer and Aaron Wildavsky, *The Real World Order: Zones of Peace Zones of Turmoil* (Chatham, NJ: Chatham House Publishers, 1993).

14. Yezid Sayigh, "Confronting the 1990s: Security in Developing Countries," Adelphi Paper no. 251 (Summer 1990), (London: International Institute for Strategic Studies), p. 14.

15. Singer and Wildavsky, *The Real World Order,* pps. xi, 3.

16. W. Seth Carus, "Military Technology and the Arms Trade: Changes and their Impact," ANNALS (The Arms Trade: Problems and Prospects in the Post–Cold War World), September 1994, pps. 163–74.

17. Stanley Lieberson, "Einstein, Renoir, and Greeley: Some Thoughts about Evidence in Sociology," *American Sociological Review,* vol. 56 (February 1992), pps. 1–15, p. 4 quoted in Gary King, Robert O. Keohane, and Sidney Verba, *Designing Social Inquiry: Scientific Inference in Qualitative Research* (Princeton, NJ: Princeton University Press, 1994), p. 19.

18. Robert P. Abelson, "The Secret Existence of Expressive Behavior," *Critical Review,* vol. 9, nos. 1–2 (Winter-Spring 1995), pps. 25–36. Abelson challenges "the unrealistic, excessive reliance on instrumental motives" of the rational choice model, citing empirical findings to indicate the importance of noninstrumental motives in human behavior (p. 27).

19. Joel Larus, *Culture and Politico-Military Behavior: The Hindus in Pre-Modern India* (Calcutta: Minerva Associates, 1979).

20. Robert H. Jackson and Carl G. Rosberg, "Why Africa's Weak States Persist: The Empirical and the Juridical in Statehood," *World Politics,* vol. 35, no. 1 (October 1982), pps. 1–24. Jackson and Rosberg find that most of black Africa's 40-odd states do not conform to the classic Weberian empirical definition of the state: "a corporate group that has compulsory jurisdiction, exercises continuous organization, and claims a monopoly of force over a territory and its population, including 'all action taking place in the area of its jurisdiction'"(p. 2). Jackson and Rosberg also find that juridical definitions that incorporate empirical indicators, such as a permanent population,

and an effective government are equally limited in their applicability to Africa. Few African states, they point out, qualify as stable communities nor are many African governments effective governments in the Western sense of the word: "Constitutional and institutional offices that are independent of the personal authority of rulers have not taken root in most Black African countries" (p. 7). Clifford Geertz writes that postindependence rulers in Africa and Asia: "are autocrats, and it is as autocrats and not as preludes to liberalism (or, for that matter, to totalitarianism), that they, and the governments they dominate, must be judged and understood." Clifford Geertz, "The Judging of Nations: Some Comments on the Assessment of Regimes in the New States," *European Journal of Sociology,* vol. XVIII, no. 2 (1977), p. 252, quoted in Jackson and Rosberg, "Why Africa's Weak States Persist," p. 7.

21. Jackson and Rosberg, "Why Weak African States Persist," pps. 2–3.

22. Elie Kedourie, *Nationalism,* fourth expanded edition (Oxford: Blackwell Publishers, 1993), p. 134; see especially chapter 7.

23. Sayigh, "Confronting the 1990s," p. 6, see also, p. 10.

24. Barry Buzan, *People, States, and Fear: The National Security Problem in International Relations* (Chapel Hill, NC: University of North Carolina Press, 1983), pps. 65–69. In these states, he claims, there is no political or social consensus regarding the institutional and ideological character of the state. For much of the population the state itself represents a threat to their security and the state is preoccupied with domestic threats to its existence.

25. Jackson and Rosberg argue, however, that juridical statehood—the rights of sovereignty and legitimacy conferred upon new states by international society—is more important than empirical statehood. African states, in their view, persist as states because the international community recognizes them as such and supports their legitimacy and independence. Explaining why states and their boundaries created by departing colonial powers have proven so durable, Jackson and Rosberg write: "International organizations have served as 'postimperial ordering devices' for the new African states, in effect freezing them in their inherited colonial jurisdictions and blocking any post-independence movements toward self-determination" (p. 21).

26. Krasner claims that "sovereignty" has been used in four different and distinct ways: by theorists: (1) international law sovereignty—the recognition and acceptance by other states of a state's juridical equality; (2) Westphalian sovereignty—based on territory and the exclusion of external authority; (3) domestic sovereignty—the ability of public authorities to exercise effective control within the borders of their polity; (4) interdependence sovereignty—the ability of public authorities to control the flow of information, ideas, goods, people, pollutants, or capital across the borders of their state. Stephen D. Krasner, "Sovereignty and Its Discontents," unpublished paper, October 18, 1996. The discussion in this chapter centers on what Krasner refers to as Westphalian sovereignty, namely, the recognized right of domestic political authorities to be the only arbiters of legitimate behavior within the territorial boundaries of their state, free from external interference.

27. See Krasner "Sovereignty and Its Discontents"; Caroline Thomas, *New States, Sovereignty and Intervention* (Aldershot, UK: Gower Publishing Co., 1985), p. 4; and Robert H. Jackson, *Quasi-States: Sovereignty, International Relations and the Third World,* (Cambridge: Cambridge University Press, 1990). Jackson distinguishes between what he calls "negative" and "positive" sovereignty. "Negative sovereignty can . . . be defined as freedom from outside interference: a formal-legal condition. [It] is the legal foundation upon which a society of independent and formally equal states fundamentally rests." Positive sovereignty, on the other hand, exists when a government "not only enjoys the rights of nonintervention and other international immunities but also possesses the wherewithal to provide political goods for its citizens." Jackson claims that today new states have been legally accorded negative sovereignty, but they do not have positive sovereignty. See pps. 27, 29, 48.

28. Janice E. Thomson, "State Sovereignty in International Relations: Bridging the Gap Between Theory and Empirical Research," *International Studies Quarterly,* vol. 39 (1995), pps. 213–33, provides a critical review and analysis of recent research on sovereignty and the state.

29. The British school of theorists treats sovereignty as an empirical reality—as an accurate description of the autonomous power held by units that compose the international system. Sovereignty is a function of the agreed-upon rules of the game among the players in the international society. In this view, "the rules of sovereignty give full autonomy over activities within their own borders and prohibit intervention in the internal affairs of other states" (Krasner, "Sovereignty and Its Discontents," pps. 15–16). For examples of this school of thought, see Jackson and Rosberg, "Why Africa's Weak States Persist," and John W. Burton, *Systems, States, Diplomacy and Rules* (Cambridge: Cambridge University Press, 1968). He writes: "In contemporary world society, states of greatly different power are tending toward an actual as well as legal egalitarianism" (p. 241).

30. Thomas, *New States, Sovereignty and Interventions,* pps. vii, 4.

31. Combatants generally view international peacekeeping missions as a form of military assistance either to themselves or their enemy. See Stephanie G. Neuman, "Peacekeeping or Military Assistance?" *The Washington Times,* July 10, 1995, p. A19. The UN peacekeeping efforts in Rwanda are a case in point. French troops, acting under the UN mandate on a mission that was "strictly humanitarian," were viewed by the Tutsis as a source of military support to their enemies, the Hutus. The Tutsis feared that intervention by the French, who were former supporters of the Hutus, would rob them of their certain victory in the civil war. "We have no doubt whatsoever that their (French) intentions are far from humanitarian," said one of the Rwandan Patriotic Front leaders. See Keith B. Richburg, "French Troops Cross Border into Rwanda," *International Herald Tribune,* June 24, 1994, pps. 1 and 4. See also, the SIPRI YEARBOOK that describes how the UN Assistance Mission for Rwanda (UNAMIR) lost credibility with both the government forces and the rebels who questioned its impartiality. Jaana Karhilo, "Case Study on Peacekeeping:

Rwanda," SIPRI YEARBOOK, 1995 : Armaments, Disarment and International Security (Stockholm: Stockholm International Peace Research Institute; NY and London: Oxford University Press, 1995), pps. 106–10.

32. Howard W. French, "Congo Aid at Risk in Defiance of U.N. Over War Refugees," *The New York Times,* September 15, 1997, pps. A1 and A3.

33. James N. Rosenau defines a penetrated political system as one in which "non members of a national society participate directly and authoritatively, through actions taken jointly with the society's members, in either the allocation of its values or the mobilization of support on behalf of its goals." James N. Rosenau, "Pre-theories and Theories of Foreign Policy," in *Approaches to Comparative and International Politics,* ed., R. Barry Farrell (Evanston, IL: Northwestern University Press, 1966), p. 65.

34. Xavier Alcalde Cardoza, *Development, Decay, and Social Conflict: An International and Peruvian Perspective* (Lanham, MD: University of Virginia, 1991), p. 40. For a poststructuralist analysis that argues that development is a Western derived, historically constructed discourse that created the "Third World," see Arturo Escobar, *Encountering Development: The Making and Unmaking of the Third World* (Princeton, NJ: Princeton University Press, 1995).

35. Alexander Wendt and Michael Barnett, focusing on military development in the Third World, argue that external influences have predominated in this sector as well. They state: "Like dependency theorists of Third World economic development, then, we argue that the hierarchical structure of the world system conditions the form of Third World military development via is impact on state formation." Wendt and Barnett, "Dependent State Formation and Third World Militarization," p. 323.

36. For a description of attempts by the CIA and other United States organizations to influence the domestic political politics of states around the world, see John M. Broder, "Dollars and Foreign Policy: Practice vs. Preaching," *International Herald Tribune,* April 1, 1997, pps. 1, 6.

37. Sayigh, "Confronting the 1990s," p. 12.

38. Robert Keohane and Joseph S. Nye, *Transnational Relations and World Politics* (Cambridge, MA: Harvard University Press, 1972), p. 393.

39. Krasner, "Society and Its Discontents," pps. 5, 12, 19–20.

40. John W. Burton, *World Society* (Cambridge: Cambridge University Press, 1972).

41. United States military assistance regulations provide an interesting example. A letter to several military contractors in 1988 announced the new rules that a foreign government buying arms with the help of United States loans is required to agree in advance to make available all of its records and files relating to the use of such aid. In addition, the government must guarantee that its officials and other citizens will be made available for questioning by either the Pentagon, the Justice Department, or a federal grand jury investigating the use of United States military aid. (At issue were foreign military sales programs particularly in the Philippines, El Salvador, and Egypt.) These regulations prompted one lawyer to declare: "It's appalling that they would ask sovereign

nations to sign these documents." Robert Pear, "U.S. Plans New Rules for Foreign Arms Aid," *International Herald Tribune*, November 11, 1988, pps. 1, 4.

42. Theodore Couloumbis, "Traditional Concepts and the 'Greek Reality,'" in *Theory of International Relations: The Crisis of Relevance*, ed., Abdul Said (Englewood Cliffs, NJ: Prentice-Hall, 1968), pps. 160–75, p. 163. Couloumbis concludes: "Greece, in sum, does not fit by far the theoretical model which pictures national units as sovereign, independent, and engaging in atomistic irresponsibility in International Relations. . . . To the culture-bound Greek theorist of international relations, the temptation will be great to consider international dependence, intervention, and manipulation as the key characteristics of international intercourse, rather than sovereignty, independence, and equibalanced coexistence" (p. 174).

43. There is no universal agreement on the meaning of the term alliance. Most IR theorists define it in terms of military cooperation, but differ on whether informal agreements should be included. Walt, for example, states: "the defining feature of any alliance is a [formal or informal] commitment for mutual military support against some external actor(s) in some specified set of circumstances." Snyder, on the other hand, defines alliances as "formal associations of states for the use (or non-use) of military force, intended for either the security or the aggrandizement of their members, against specific other states, whether or not these others are explicitly identified." See Stephen M. Walt, "Why Alliances Endure or Collapse," *Survival*, vol. 39, no. 1 (Spring 1997), pps. 156–79, p. 158; and Glenn H. Snyder, "Alliance Theory: A Neorealist First Cut," in *The Evolution of Theory in International Relations: Essays in Honor of William T. R. Fox*, ed., Robert L. Rothstein (Columbia, SC: University of South Carolina Press, 1991), pps. 83–103, p. 84.

44. Exceptions include Robert L. Rothstein, *Alliances and Small Powers* (NY: Columbia University Press, 1968); Michael Handel, *Weak States in the International System* (London: Frank Cass, 1981); Yaacov Bar-Siman-Tov, "Alliance Strategy: U.S.-Small Allies Relationships," *The Journal of Strategic Studies*, vol. 3, no. 2 (September 1980), pps. 202–16; and David, "Explaining Third World Alignment," *World Politics*, vol. 43, no. 2 (January 1991), pps. 233–56.

45. Stephen M. Walt, "Why Alliances Endure or Collapse," p. 158.

46. Handel, *Weak States in the International System*, p. 153.

47. Few explanations are offered as to why alliances between Third World states are rare. Most address the question of why there are so few formal alliances between the former superpowers and Third World states. Even here, however, there is little agreement. Some analysts believe that the international system, and the major powers in it, determine the alliance behavior of weaker states; others find the answer at the state level in the policy preferences of Third World decision makers. Walt, for example, claims that on the one hand Third World states are so weak they can not affect the superpower balance anyway, but, on the other hand, during the Cold War both superpowers were willing to pay a relatively high price to keep Third World states from straying to the other side. Snyder maintains that the dearth of formal alliances in the Third World is due to Third World states' reluctance to accept outright alliance with a Great Power because

"it carries overtones of colonial domination." See Stephen M. Walt, *The Origins of Alliances* (Ithaca, NY: Cornell University Press, 1987), ch. 5, and Walt, "Why Alliances Endure or Collapse," pps. 164–65; Snyder, p. 103.

48. Steven David, "Explaining Third World Alignment," pps. 233–56.
49. George Liska, *Alliances and the Third World*, Washington Center of Foreign Policy Research, Studies in International Affairs, no. 5 (Baltimore, MD: Johns Hopkins Press, 1968), p. 50.
50. Larus, *Culture and Politico-Military Behavior.*
51. IR Theory predicts, for example, that alliance behavior will be substantially different in multipolar and bipolar systems. See Waltz, *Theory of International Politics,* pps. 168–70; Handel, *Weak States in the International System,* chapter IV.
52. Rothstein, *Alliances and Small Powers,* p. 263.
53. See Handel, *Weak States in the International System,* p. 191. He writes that the competition between the superpowers gives considerable leverage to the weak non-aligned states, and costs "the hegemonial powers a fortune in resources." Walt also observes that "alliances are more likely to persist when a strong power is both willing and able to pay the costs associated with leadership" ("Why alliances endure or collapse," p. 164 ff).
54. Waltz, *Theory of International Politics,* p. 171.
55. Steven David, "Explaining Third World Alignment"; Snyder, "Alliance Theory," p. 102; Walt, *The Origins of Alliances,* p. 162; and Yaacov Bar-Siman-Tov, p. 203.
56. Realists, neorealists, and neoliberals expect the alignment behavior of states to be sensitive to structural changes in the international system. They hold that because states operate in a self-help system, states that do not respond to these changes by seeking to strengthen themselves by balancing or bandwagoning will be disadvantaged by those that do. See, for example, Michael Mastanduno, "Do Relative Gains Matter? America's Response to Japanese Industrial Policy," in *Neorealism and Neoliberalism,* pps. 250–66, p. 255; and Robert O. Keohane, "Institutional Theory and the Realist Challenge after the Cold War," in *Neorealism and Neoliberalism,* pps. 288; Waltz, *Theory of International Politics,* p. 118.
57. Waltz, ibid., p. 125.
58. Waltz maintains that a general theory of international politics is necessarily based on the behavior of Great Powers but applies to lesser states as well "insofar as their interactions are insulated from the intervention of the great powers of a system, whether by the relative indifference of the latter or by difficulties of communication and transportation" (Waltz, ibid., p. 73).
59. Handel, *Weak States in the International System,* pps. 194–95. Handel maintains that "the greater the collaboration and cooperation between the superpowers, the lower the price the non-aligned weak states can expect for their cooperative behavior" (p. 195). Bar-Siman-Tov observes that "Small allies require . . . the existence of the other bloc in order to maintain their value as allies for their own bloc" (p. 203). Walt, argues, for similar reasons, that in the future it will become more difficult to convince U.S. citizens to bear the costs

of alliance, even with regard to NATO. Walt, "Why Alliances Endure or Collapse," pps. 170–73.
Michael Desch believes that the end of the Cold War has markedly reduced the strategic importance of some, but not all, regions in the Third World. Michael C. Desch, "Why Realists Disagree about the Third World (and Why They Shouldn't)," *Security Studies,* vol. 5, no. 3 (Spring 1996), pps. 375–77.

60. Perruci, Gamaliel Jr., "The North-South Security Dialogue in Brazil's Technology Policy," *Armed Forces and Society,* vol. 21, no. 3 (Spring 1995), p. 384.
61. Alcalde, *Development, Decay, and Social Conflict,* p. 39.
62. Ibid., p. 53. See also Adam Prezeworski and Fernando Limongi, "Modernization: Theories and Facts," *World Politics,* vol. 49, no. 2 (January 1997), pps. 155–83. Prezeworski and Limongi conclude that "the emergence of democracy is not a by-product of economic development. Democracy is or is not established by political actors pursuing their goals, and it can be initiated at any level of development" (p. 177).
63. Alcalde, *Development, Decay, and Social Conflict,* p. 57.
64. Examples include Escudé, chapter 3 in this volume; Alcalde, *Development, Decay, and Social Conflict;* and Sayigh, "Confronting the 1990s."
65. For opposing viewpoints see Stephen Van Evera, "Why Europe Matters, Why the Third World Doesn't: American Grand Strategy after the Cold War," *Journal of Strategic Studies,* vol. 13, no. 2 (June 1990), pps. 1–51; Steven R. David, "Why the Third World Matters," *International Security,* vol. 14, no. 1 (Summer 1989), pps. 50–85.
66. Desch, "Why Realist Disagree about the Third World," p. 359.
67. James Rosenau defines a puzzle as: "first, one needs to be puzzled by observable outcomes for which existing explanations seem insufficient or erroneous and, second, one needs to be puzzled by huge outcomes, by events or patterns that encompass most of humankind and that appear to spring from somewhere in the core of human affairs. If these two criteria are met when posing a problem, one has what I call a genuine puzzle." James N. Rosenau, "Probing Puzzles Persistently: A Desirable but Improbable Future for IR Theory," in *International Theory: Positivism and Beyond,* p. 311.
68. In 1995 alone there were 25 ongoing wars with annual deaths of 1,000 or more, 24 of them in the Third World (excluding Bosnia). Ruth Leger Sivard, *World Military and Social Expenditures,* 1996 (Washington, DC: World Priorities, Inc., 1996), p. 7.
69. According to Michael Desch's calculation, since 1945 approximately 20 million people have lost their lives in wars, more than 19,500,000 of these deaths (almost 98 percent) occurred as a result of wars in the Third World. He bases his calculation on Sivard, *World Military and Social Expenditures,* 1987–1988, pps. 28–31. Desch, "Why Realists Disagree about the Third World," p. 359, fn. 6.
70. Rosenau, "Probing Puzzles Persistently," p. 312.
71. David holds, however, that neorealism does not explain internal wars where anarchy is not present, nor does it explain how anarchy was created or how to restore central control.

72. Correspondence with editor, April 11, 1997.
73. I am grateful to Robert Jervis for this idea, which he offered at a Columbia University symposium: "Comments for the Rational Choice Symposium," November 6, 1996 (unpublished paper).
74. Colin Gray, *Strategic Studies and Public Policy* (Lexington, KY: University Press of Kentucky, 1982), p. 194, cited in Joseph S. Nye, Jr., and Sean M. Lynn-Jones, "International Security Studies: A Report of a Conference on the State of the Field," *International Security,* vol. 12, no. 4 (Spring 1988), pps. 5–27, p. 14.

Bibliography

Abelson, Robert P. "The Secret Existence of Expressive Behavior," *Critical Review.* vol. 9, nos. 1–2 (Winter-Spring 1995), pps. 25–36.

Alcalde, Cardoza Xavier *Development, Decay, and Social Conflict: An International and Peruvian Perspective.* Lanham, MD: University of Virginia, 1991.

Azar, Edward E. and Chung-in Moon, eds. *National Security in the Third World: The Management of Internal and External Threats.* Hampshire, UK: Edward Elgar, 1988.

Bandarage, Asoka. "Global Peace and Security in the Post–Cold War Era: A 'Third World' Perspective." In *Peace and World Security Studies: A Curriculum Guide.* Ed. Michael T. Klare. Boulder, CO: Lynne Rienner Publishers, 1994, pps. 29–42.

Bar-Siman-Tov, Yaacov. "Alliance Strategy: U.S.-Small Allies Relationships," *The Journal of Strategic Studies.* Vol. 3, no. 2 (September 1980), pps. 202–16.

Broder, John M. "Dollars and Foreign Policy: Practice vs. Preaching." *International Herald Tribune.* April 1, 1997, pps. 1, 6.

Buzan, Barry. *People, States, and Fear: The National Security Problem in International Relations.* Chapel Hill, NC: University of North Carolina Press, 1983.

Cardoso, E. Fernando and Enzo Faletto. *Dependency and Development in Latin America.* Princeton, NJ: Princeton University Press, 1979.

Carus, W. Seth. "Military Technology and the Arms Trade: Changes and their Impact." ANNALS (The Arms Trade: Problems and Prospects in the Post–Cold War World). September 1994, pps. 163–74.

Couloumbis, Theodore. "Traditional concepts and the 'Greek reality.'" In *Theory of International Relations: The Crisis of Relevance.* Ed. Abdul Said. Englewood Cliffs, NJ: Prentice-Hall, 1968, pps. 160–75.

David, Steven. "Explaining Third World Alignment." *World Politics.* Vol. 43, no. 2 (January 1991), pps. 233–56.

David, Steven R. "Why the Third World Matters." *International Security.* Vol. 14, no. 1 (Summer 1989), pps. 50–85.

Desch, Michael C. "Why Realists Disagree about the Third World (and Why They Shouldn't)." *Security Studies.* Vol. 5, no. 3 (Spring 1996), pps. 358–81.

Dougherty, James E. and Robert L. Pfaltzgraff, Jr., eds. *Contending Theories of International Relations.* New York: HarperCollins Publishers, 1990.

Escobar, Arturo. *Encountering Development: The Making and Unmaking of the Third World.* Princeton, NJ: Princeton University Press, 1995.

Evans, Peter. *Dependent Development.* Princeton, NJ: Princeton University Press, 1979.

Frank, André Gunder. *Dependent Accumulation and Underdevelopment.* London: Macmillan, 1978.

Galtung, Johan. "A Structural Theory of Imperialism." *Journal of Peace Research.* Vol. 8 (1971), pps. 81–117.

Goldgeier, James M. and Michael McFaul. "A Tale of Two Worlds: Core and Periphery in the Post–Cold War Era." *International Organization.* Vol. 46, no. 2 (Spring 1992), pps. 467–91.

Gray, Colin. *Strategic Studies and Public Policy.* Lexington, KY: University Press of Kentucky, 1982.

Handel, Michael. *Weak States in the International System.* London: Frank Cass, 1981.

Jackson, Robert H. *Quasi-States: Sovereignty, International Relations and the Third World.* Cambridge: Cambridge University Press, 1990.

Jervis, Robert. "Comments for the Rational Choice Symposium." Unpublished paper, November 6, 1996.

———. "Counterfactuals, Causation, and Complexity." In *Counterfactual Thought Experiments in World Politics.* Eds. Philip E. Tetlock and Aaron Belkin. Princeton, NJ: Princeton University Press, 1996, pps. 309–16.

Job, Brian L. "The Insecurity Dilemma: National, Regime, and State Securities in the Third World." In *The Insecurity Dilemma: National Security of Third World States.* Ed. Brian L. Job. Boulder, CO: Lynne Rienner Publishers, 1992.

Kedourie, Elie. *Nationalism,* fourth expanded edition. Oxford: Blackwell Publishers, 1993.

Keohane, Robert O. "Institutional Theory and the Realist Challenge after the Cold War." In *Neorealism and Neoliberalism.* Ed. David Baldwin. NY: Columbia University Press, 1993.

Keohane, Robert O. and Joseph S. Nye. *Power and Interdependence: World Politics in Transition.* Boston, MA: Little Brown, 1977.

Krasner, Stephen D. "Sovereignty and its Discontents." Unpublished paper, October 18, 1996.

Larus, Joel. *Culture and Politico-Military Behavior: The Hindus in Pre-Modern India.* Calcutta: Minerva Associates, 1979.

King, Gary, Robert O. Keohane, and Sidney Verba. *Designing Social Inquiry: Scientific Inference in Qualitative Research.* Princeton, NJ: Princeton University Press, 1994.

Mastanduno, Michael. "Do Relative Gains Matter? America's Response to Japanese Industrial Policy." In *Neorealism and Neoliberalism.* Ed. David Baldwin. NY: Columbia University Press, 1993, pps. 250–66.

Milner, Helen. "Anarchy in International Relations." In *Neorealism and Neoliberalism.* Ed. David Baldwin. NY: Columbia University Press, 1993, pps. 143–69.

Neuman, Stephanie and Robert Harkavy, eds. *Arms Transfers in the Modern World.* NY: Praeger, 1979.

Neuman, Stephanie. "Defense Planning in Less Industrialized States: An Organizing Framework." In *Defense Planning in Less Industrialized States.* Lexington, KY: Lexington Books, 1984, pps. 1–28.

Onuf, Nicholas and Frank F. Klink. "Anarchy, Authority, Rule." *International Studies Quarterly*. Vol. 33 (1989), pps. 149–73.

Packenham, Robert. *Liberal America and the Third World*. Princeton, NJ: Princeton University Press, 1973.

Perruci, Gamaliel Jr., "The North-South Security Dialogue in Brazil's Technology Policy." *Armed Forces and Society*. Vol. 21, no. 3 (Spring 1995), pps. 371–94.

Przeworski, Adam and Fernando Limongi. "Modernization: Theories and Facts." *World Politics*. Vol. 49, no. 2 (January 1997), pps. 155–83.

Rosenau, James N. "Probing Puzzles Persistently: A Desirable but Improbable Future for IR Theory." In *International Theory: Positivism and Beyond*. Eds. Steve Smith, Ken Booth and Marysia Zalewski. Cambridge: Cambridge University Press, 1996.

————. "Pre-theories and Theories of Foreign Policy." In *Approaches to Comparative and International Politics*. Ed. R. Barry Farrell. Evanston, IL: Northwestern University Press, 1966, pps. 65–71.

Rothstein, Robert L. *Alliances and Small Powers*. NY: Columbia University Press, 1968.

Sayigh, Yezid. "Confronting the 1990s: Security in Developing Countries." Adelphi Paper no. 251 (summer 1990). London: International Institute for Strategic Studies.

Singer, J. David. "The Global System and its Subsystems: A Developmental View." In *Linkage Politics: Essays on the Convergence of National and International Systems*. Ed. James N. Rosenau. New York: Free Press, 1969.

Singer, Max and Aaron Wildavsky. *The Real World Order: Zones of Peace/Zones of Turmoil*. Chatham, NJ: Chatham House Publishers, 1993.

Sivard, Ruth Leger. *World Military and Social Expenditures* (series). Washington, D.C.: World Priorities, Inc.

Smith, Steve, Ken Booth, and Marysia Zalewski, eds. *International Theory: Positivism and Beyond*. Cambridge: Cambridge University Press, 1996.

Snyder, Glenn H. "Alliance Theory: A Neorealist First Cut." In *The Evolution of Theory in International Relations: Essays in Honor of William T. R. Fox*. Ed. Robert L. Rothstein. Columbia, SC: University of South Carolina Press, 1991, pps. 83–103, p. 83.

Thomas, Caroline. *New States, Sovereignty and Intervention*. Aldershot, UK: Gower Publishing Co., 1985.

Thomson, Janice E. "State Sovereignty in International Relations: Bridging the Gap between Theory and Empirical Research." *International Studies Quarterly*. Vol. 39 (1995), pps. 213–33.

Walt, Stephen M. "Why Alliances Endure or Collapse." *Survival*. Vol. 39, no. 1 (Spring 1997), pps. 156–79.

————. *The Origins of Alliances*. Ithaca, NY: Cornell University Press, 1987.

Waltz, Kenneth N. *Theory of International Politics*. Reading, MA: Addison-Wesley, 1979.

Wendt, Alexander and Michael N. Barnett. "Dependent State Formation and Third World Militarization." *Review of International Studies*. Vol. 19 (1993), pps. 321–47.

TWO

Subaltern Realism: International Relations Theory Meets the Third World

Mohammed Ayoob

The importance of theory in International Relations is now well recognized. Theories are lenses that one puts on to view, understand, structure, or construct reality (depending upon where one stands in the debate between positivists and post-positivists on this issue).[1] The central questions we ask about our subject are determined by our theoretical preferences. Theories, therefore, both explain and occlude, include and exclude. It is this process of inclusion and exclusion, in other words, of selection, that we refer to as parsimony. Parsimony is perceived to be a positive aspect of theorizing because it simplifies complex realities and makes their comprehension an intellectually manageable exercise. But in doing so, theorists are often tempted to oversimplify and may well end up constructing a reality that is not in accord with all the important dimensions of the "real" reality out there.[2]

This process of inclusion and exclusion is extremely important because it helps to reinforce, reproduce, and perpetuate images of reality on which analysts and policymakers base their prescriptions, decisions, and policies. Therefore, inadequate or faulty theories can lead to policies and practices that may be either irrelevant or, worse, turn out to be counterproductive because they grossly misrepresent "reality"—thus making empirical data subject to the requirements of wishful thinking.

It goes almost without saying that all theories of International Relations have a perspective, sometimes explicit but often implicit. Given the nature of the phenomena that scholars have to deal with in this field this is inevitable. These perspectives, as Robert Cox has pointed out, "derive from a position in time and space."[3] In other words, theories of International Relations, no matter how refined and complex they may be, derive their perspectives from their historical and geographic contexts. Most theorists tend to make claims of universal validity for their theories. However, almost all paradigms in International Relations are, in the final analysis, the products of theorists' perceptions of what they see around them. These perceptions are in turn shaped by the theorists' experiences, and theories, therefore, become prisoners of time and space.

However, all theories that claim to capture or closely approximate reality, even if they are modest enough to claim to do so within the parameters set by historical time (and many theories and theorists are not), must possess the power to *describe, explain,* and *predict* the behavior of their subjects to the uncommitted majority if not in all cases and circumstances then at least in a majority of cases and circumstances within the historical epoch in which, and about which, they claim to theorize. Additionally, in the case of International Relations, as political sociologist Michael Mann points out, "What . . . outsiders really want from IR is substantive theory on its most important issue of all: the question of war and peace."[4]

Therefore, at this juncture one of the major functions of any successful paradigm in International Relations should be to diagnose and predict the basic sources of present and future conflicts. Equally important, it must be able to explain the behavior of the large majority of the members of the international system especially in relation to issues of conflict and order. The expansion of the international system in the last half century to include the entire planet has resulted in an unprecedented proliferation in the membership of that system.[5] Most analysts' twin obsessions with the bipolar structure of the postwar system and with the issue of nuclear deterrence had led to a grave underestimation during the four decades of the Cold War of the long-term importance of this expansion in the system's membership. It had also led to a serious underrating of the potential impact of conflict and disorder in the global periphery, the Third World—where most of the new members of the international system are located—on the international security agenda, especially in an age of globalized travel, information, and communication.[6] This underestimation was primarily the result of the propensity among analysts to provide Cold War–centered explanations for the origins of almost all of the conflicts in the international system from the late 1940s to the late 1980s.

The undervaluing of the impact of the unparalleled enlargement of the membership of the international system on issues of international order has had a seriously limiting effect on the explanatory capacities of theories that purport to provide holistic explanations for the workings of the international system, especially as they relate to the paramount issues of war and peace, order and anarchy. Consequently, major theories of International Relations on offer today fail to pass the basic test of adequacy primarily because they do not concern themselves with the behavior of the large majority of members of the international system and, therefore, fail to provide adequate explanations for the causes of most manifestations of conflict and disorder in the system. As a corollary to this failure, such paradigms do not provide adequate theoretical bases for the exploration of avenues for the management and resolution of most conflicts witnessed in the international system.

It may be argued by some that given the near-total concentration of power—military, economic, and technological—in the hands of the industrialized countries of the global North and the consequent inability of the conflict-ridden periphery to have any major impact on the security concerns of the major powers, it is not imperative for the powerful states (and analysts residing within them) to be overly concerned with conflict and disorder in the periphery. There is, therefore, little need from a prescriptive perspective for a theory that focuses on issues of war and peace as they relate to the Third World because these issues are marginal, if not irrelevant, to the North's principal concern in this arena, namely, the prevention of conflict among the major powers.

I believe that such a perspective is shortsighted in the extreme. First, at least two of the major military powers in the international system—China and Russia—share many of the characteristics of prototypical Third World countries, especially in the political arena where their state boundaries, state institutions, and governing regimes are under challenge to significant degrees. They also possess economies that are gravely distorted, both sectorally and regionally, and are in a state of asymmetrical interdependence with the core countries of the global North. As a result, they are subject to many of the same internal and external pressures that operate upon much of the Third World and that create fertile ground for internal and interstate conflict within and among them. If the fragile political and economic balances within Russia and China shift to any substantial degree, the two polities are likely to become extremely vulnerable to internal disruption, even chaos, that may lead to major regional conflicts involving one or both of them.

Secondly, given the relative ease with which human beings and weapons can now be transported across great distances, it is wishful thinking on the part of the industrialized democracies to believe that they can insulate themselves from conflict and disorder in the Third World. Movements of refugees on a massive scale as a result of intrastate conflicts have so far largely been limited within regions and from one Third World country to another. However, this is a pattern that may be subject to change and movements of people from the South to the North on a major scale cannot be ruled out if the present trends relating to conflict and disorder continue in some parts of the

Third World. Such migrations are expected to accentuate racial and social tensions in the developed world and in some countries, such as France and Germany, have already begun to do so.[7]

Moreover, there are already expatriate communities from Third World countries that reside in substantial numbers in the countries of the global North. It will not be far-fetched to assume that they will inevitably begin to export some of the conflicts from their home to their host countries, especially if the latter are perceived as taking sides in the former's internal conflicts. This has already begun to happen in the case of North African expatriates in France, Turkish and Kurdish populations in Germany, and veterans of the Afghanistan war in the United States and elsewhere.

Furthermore, acts of terrorism and drug smuggling, both intimately linked, either as cause or as effect, to conditions of domestic disorder and conflict in parts of the Third World (for example, in Afghanistan, Burma, Pakistan, and Central America), can target, and have targeted, major powers in the global North, as well as countries in the global South. Finally, the growing economic interdependencies witnessed in the last few decades, even if asymmetrical in character, have intertwined the fortunes of the developed and developing countries to such a degree in terms of access to markets, raw materials, production facilities, investments, and so on, that large-scale disorder in the Third World is bound to affect the economies and lifestyles of the industrialized countries in a deleterious fashion. In short, the "zone of peace" cannot insulate itself completely, or even in large measure, from the "zone of conflict" as we reach the end of the twentieth century. A Lockean core can no longer exist engulfed as it might be by a Hobbesian periphery.

It is, therefore, essential for analysts of the international system, including those in the global North, to fashion tools of analysis that can explain and predict the nature and intensity of conflict in the large part of the international system that we term the South, especially as the Third World is likely to dominate the international security agenda in the twenty-first century.[8] "Subaltern realism," my alternative to the currently dominant paradigms in International Relations, attempts to do just that. It presents a coherent explanation for the large majority of conflicts in the international system by tracing their origins, both as beginnings and causes, to the premier ongoing political endeavor in the Third World, namely, that of state-making (and its obverse state breaking and state failure). Its explanatory capacity is further enhanced by its ability to demonstrate the linkage between this primarily domestic activity and issues of regional balances of power, and by laying bare the impact of global structures, international norms, and great power policies on the evolution and course of both the state-making enterprise and regional conflicts. As a consequence, I believe it possesses explanatory power relating to issues of war and peace, order and disorder, that is far superior to other paradigms that are currently available. It, therefore, possesses much greater predictive and prescriptive capacity than either neorealism or neoliberalism in the arena of conflict and conflict resolution.

However, before we move on to explicate the basic assumptions and predictive capacities of subaltern realism we need to make a case for the inadequacies of the major theories that dominate the International Relations literature. It is but appropriate that we begin with a discussion of structural or neorealism because it professes to be the dominant paradigm in International Relations and "in an important sense . . . continues to define the discipline."[9] Structural realism's preoccupation with the systemic level of analysis, and its fundamental premise that the anarchical nature of the system determines the behavior of units (or states), is based upon a clear and rigid distinction between anarchy outside the state and order within it—the former determining its search for relative advantage in terms of power and/or security, and the latter facilitating rational behavior on the state's part in search of those goals.

There are minor differences of emphasis within the neorealist school as to whether states balance against power or against threats.[10] Occasionally, a perceptive historian like Paul Schroeder may point out that the structural realists' reading of European history from the seventeenth to the nineteenth centuries is incorrect because frequently states, and more particularly major powers, balanced neither against power nor against threat but attempted to bandwagon or hide in the face of both power and threat.[11] Even Schroeder's corrective, however, does not significantly challenge the primacy of third-image determinants that neorealists have made the linchpin of their theories.[12]

As is the case with neorealism, its main challenger, neoliberalism (in its many variations), also provides a primarily system-based explanation for the behavior of states. Neoliberal ideas have been challenging the dominance of realism since the 1970s.[13] However, the end of the Cold War has given a great boost to this challenge by demonstrating the presumed failure of neorealist theory to account for the end of the Cold War.[14] The neoliberal challenge has been further augmented by the assumed irrelevance of neorealism to "the profoundly altered attributes of the post–Cold War setting."[15]

Unlike neorealism, neoliberalism is based on the premise that cooperation among states, especially among the major industrialized states, is not only possible but necessary. Scholars working within this paradigm emphasize not so much the distribution of power among the major powers as the economic and technological, and, therefore political, interdependence among the industrialized states. This interdependence is augmented by the transnational character of their economies and by the information revolution that have wiped out the distinction between issues of "high" and "low" politics and thus drastically reduced the salience of traditional security issues in the political calculations of these countries.[16]

Neoliberals argue that states—especially the major industrialized powers—are, or if they are not should be, more concerned with absolute gains that they can achieve in cooperation with one another than with relative gains that they can achieve at one another's expense or by competing with one another. Since the absolute gains they are likely to achieve by cooperation in an interdependent world are expected to be so much greater than the relative gains they may achieve by competition, it is no longer rational for them to indulge in adversarial modes of conduct toward one another. Therefore, war and conflict are (or must be) ruled out as instruments of policy by the industrialized states (including the Great Powers) at least in their relationship with one another.

What is most remarkable is that with the end of the Cold War one sees clear evidence of a convergence between neorealism and neoliberalism. The end of bipolarity has led some scholars to give an interesting twist to the structural realist paradigm. They have argued that, given the change in the nature of power at the end of the twentieth century and the lack of identifiable enemies after the Cold War, Great Powers in the international system are no longer engaged in primarily balancing against one another but have begun to bandwagon with one another and thus have created a concert of powers or an international security directorate that has assumed the prime responsibility for maintaining international order. Adopting a basically realist perspective, Barry Buzan has termed this new phase in the global balance "unipolarized multipolarity"—"multipolar in the sense that several independent great powers are in play, but unipolarized in the sense that there is a single dominant coalition governing international relations."[17] Arguing from a neoliberal position, John Gerard Ruggie has similarly concluded that "the most promising Institutional model from the past is that of a concert of powers—or perhaps overlapping concerts of powers—performed, at least in part, through the UN."[18]

It is in this convergence between neorealism and neoliberalism that one sees the maturation of, what Ole Waever has termed, a neo-neo synthesis whose beginnings can be traced to the 1980s. According to Waever, "no longer were realism and liberalism 'incommensurable'—on the contrary they shared a 'rationalist' research programme, a conception of science, a shared willingness to operate on the premise of anarchy (Waltz) and investigate the evolution of co-operation and whether institutions matter (Keohane) . . . Regime theory, co-operation under anarchy, hegemonic stability, alliance theory, trade negotiations, and Buzanian security analysis can all be seen as located in this field."[19]

However, to the discerning observer it becomes clear that the most significant thing that neorealism and neoliberalism share is their preoccupation with Great Power relations (or, to use the imagery preferred by neoliberals, the major industrialized democracies), whether manifested in terms of balance or concert, of competition or cooperation, to the near total exclusion from their selected universe of the large majority of members of the international system. Where the latter figure, they figure as objects of the policies of Great Powers (or of the industrialized democracies) with very little autonomy of their own in terms of their capacity to have an impact on the levels of order, stability, or welfare in the international system. In this sense both neorealism and neoliberalism share a neocolonial epistemology that privileges the global North over the global South, the powerful minority over the weak but numerous majority.

However, as a result of its epistemological limitations this neo-neo synthesis captures only a partial reality within the international system. Neither the clear-cut distinction between anarchy outside and order inside the state nor the postulate about increasing harmony of interests among states, correspond to the reality in much of the international system outside of North America, Western Europe, and Japan. However, it is in the global periphery outside the industrial heartland that three-quarters of the members of that system and 80 percent of the world's population are located. In many states in the Third World, elements of anarchy clearly coexist with those of order within the boundaries of the state. In several such cases elements of anarchy dominate the political landscape to such an extent that little semblance of political order is visible within their juridical boundaries. Moreover, the notion of harmony of interests among Third World countries (with the partial exception of certain subregions, and even there such harmony is more apparent than real) is conspicuous by its absence. The proliferation of intrastate and interstate conflicts (and the symbiotic relationship between them) attest to the existence of conditions in large parts of the Third World that are significantly different from those existing in Western Europe and North America—the primary points of reference for both neorealist and neoliberal theories.

In the context of this wide divergence in the conditions prevailing between the different categories of states, it is at best problematic and at worst absurd to accept the assumption about the sameness of states on which much of neorealist and neoliberal analysis is based. The image of the prototypical state as the successful version of the Westphalian model is contrary to the reality witnessed in much of the international system. The principal concern or preoccupation of most Third World states is not the conduct of interstate relations according to the Westphalian script, that is, balancing against other powers and/or against external threats (neorealism). Nor is it to move beyond Westphalia to construct economic and security communities based on the harmony of interests reflected in the term *interdependence* and encapsulated in the concept of regimes (neoliberalism).

Their principal concern is, in fact, to be able to move toward the ideal of the effective and legitimate state that can become the true repository of sovereign power as envisioned in the Westphalian discourse. The critical importance of approximating this ideal of the sovereign, territorial state results from the undisputed fact that there is no alternative form of political organization on the horizon that is able or willing to address, tackle, and manage the issue of political order within communities. This is why groups that desire to secede from existing states demand their own states and not a fundamental restructuring of the system of states. This lack of alternatives to the state in the performance of the quintessential political task of providing order and security has been aptly underlined by John Herz in the following words: "For the time being . . . it is not internationalism, universalism, or any other supranational model that constitutes the alternative to the territorial . . . system, but genuine, raw chaos."[20] This process of providing and maintaining political order is primarily domestic in character, albeit one that is crucially affected by external variables, including the operation of international norms and interventionary policies espoused by the major powers.[21]

Neorealist and neoliberal theories equally neglect domestic variables affecting conflict and order. This explains their inability to account for the origins—in both senses of that word, as beginnings and causes—and evolution of the large majority of conflicts currently prevalent in the international system. Computations made by scholars from a variety of backgrounds demonstrate that the overwhelming majority of conflicts in the international system since 1945 were, and continue to be, located in the Third World. While some of them have had participants from the industrialized world, their geographic locations and their target populations have been firmly situated in the Third World.

A few illustrations will suffice to demonstrate the validity of this assertion. Evan Luard concluded from his computations that the Third World was the scene of 98 percent of all international conflicts between 1945 and 1984.[22] Kalevi Holsti calculated that 97 percent of all major wars and armed interventions between 1945 and 1989 occurred in the Third World.[23] According to the latest set of figures compiled by Holsti, out of 164 armed conflicts worldwide between 1945 and 1995 all but five (three in Western Europe and two in Eastern Europe) were located in either the traditional Third World (Asia, Africa, and Latin America) or in the new Third World (the Balkans and the non-European parts of the former Soviet Union).[24]

Holsti, however, excludes anticolonial wars of national liberation from his data. If one includes those figures the concentration of conflicts in the Third World would appear to be even more dramatic.

What is equally important is that even a cursory analysis of conflicts in the Third World contradicts the fundamental neo-neo (but especially neo-realist) assumption regarding the primacy of systemic factors in explaining state behavior. Once again, figures from a variety of sources demonstrate that the large majority of conflicts are primarily intrastate in character (what are euphemistically termed "civil wars"). To give just one illustration, according to Holsti 77 percent of the conflicts between 1945 and 1995 were internal in character although 30 percent of such intrastate conflicts involved external armed intervention.[25] Once again, if one includes anticolonial wars (which Holsti excludes), which were in essence internal wars of regime change, the proportion of intrastate to interstate wars would be much higher.

Furthermore, if one looks behind many conflicts in the Third World that ostensibly appear to be interstate in character, one would find that the origins of many such conflicts are deeply rooted within the domestic polities of at least one of the participants. The Iran-Iraq War of 1980–88 is a good illustration of this point since the Iraqi regime was propelled into conflict with Iran primarily by its fear of the demonstration effect of the Iranian Revolution on the Iraqi populace and the consequent threat to the Ba'athist regime.[26]

These findings also challenge the validity of the neorealist (and, indeed, the neo-neo) assumption that there is order inside the state and anarchy in the sphere of interstate relations. They make it imperative, in R. B. J. Walker's words, that we "begin by examining the account of political life within autonomous communities which makes possible the claim to a realist tradition about relations between such communities." It is "the absence of any serious theory of the state" in neorealism that is the Achilles' heel of that theoretical tradition.[27] The proliferation of internal conflicts in the international system can only be explained in the context of a theory that makes the process of state-making and the building of political communities its centerpiece.

Such a theory—and I call it subaltern realism, a term that I shall explain later—would involve, among other things, a return to the most basic insights of political thinkers who, it is commonly accepted, have laid the foundations of realist thought in International Relations. Unlike structural or neorealists, the classical propounders of realism—Machiavelli and Hobbes foremost among them—were, as theorists, primarily interested in the formation and ordering of political communities and only secondarily in the analysis of international structures. As Walker points out, Machiavelli's principle concern in *The Prince* was to address issues of political community, political life, *virtu* (in essence issues of political order) within states at an early stage of state-making. Machiavelli is, therefore, "more usefully understood as a theorist of political practice, of the possibility of creating new forms of political community, rather than as the theorist of the unchanging realities of *realpolitik.*"[28] Michael Williams points out, much in the same vein, that "Hobbes's ideas lend support not to contemporary analyses that focus upon the structural determinations of anarchy but to those that focus upon the interrelationship between domestic political structures and global processes."[29]

The primary insights of both Machiavelli and Hobbes as they related to the international system were that issues of international order cannot be analyzed, leave alone tackled, in isolation from the problems of domestic political order, for the two are inextricably intertwined, and domestic order deserves analytical priority because it is an essential ingredient on which the foundations of international order are based. Sovereignty, according to Hobbes's formulation of social contract theory, is a combination of coercive power and consent, and it is this combination that provides legitimacy to political authority and resolves the problem of order within societies. A well-ordered international system is constituted by well-ordered states where sovereigns are both powerful and legitimate because this prevents the exportation of domestic anarchy to interstate relations and vice versa.

As Williams has pointed out, "The coercive powers of the sovereign will alone, Hobbes argues, never be sufficient to maintain a political order. Only if the people understand why the polity must be ordered as it must, and only if they continue to view the sovereign as a legitimate authority and trust in its judgement, can a political order be secure."[30] Richard Peters succinctly summed up this symbiotic relationship between power and legitimacy, coercion and consent, in the construction and preservation of the Leviathan by stating that Hobbes "used the social contract theory to demonstrate the necessity of an absolute sovereign—by consent." At the same time, "Although he held that government was by the consent of the people . . . there could be no legitimacy, he argued, without power."[31] For Thomas Hobbes, power and consent, effectiveness and legitimacy, are two sides of the same state-building coin.

There is no abstraction of international structure in Machiavelli and Hobbes to the near-total neglect of the constituting units and their internal dynamics. This is why classical realism captures the security predicament of the majority of states in the international system that are currently at an early stage of the state-making process more clearly and honestly than either neorealism or neoliberalism does. The primary intellectual preoccupation of these leading progenitors of realism reflected the historical context in which they were operating and this is what makes them so relevant to the current predicaments faced by the majority of states today. Most of the latter are currently at the same stage of historical development in terms of consolidation and legitimation of state power as Florence was in the fifteenth century or England in the seventeenth century, respectively the historical and geographic settings within which Machiavelli and Hobbes lived and wrote. Classical realism's relevance to the Third World situation today lies in the fact that, unlike in neorealism, in the classical writings on realism "the state is no absolute; the state is historicized."[32]

It is this focus on historical time and their openness to possibilities of change that make Hobbes's and Machiavelli's concern about the right mix between power (effectiveness) and consent (legitimacy) so relevant to the central problem of political order facing Third World states today. In much of the Third World, the basic conundrum confronting state elites is that without power they suffer from a lack of legitimacy, and without consent they may possess coercive force but little political capacity. For, as Robert Jackman has argued, power without the exercise of force is the true measure of the political capacity of states.[33]

However, unlike their counterparts in early modern Europe, political entities in the Third World that emerged into independence have had no choice in terms of determining the organization of their polities according to their felt needs. They have been obliged to adopt the model of the sovereign, territorial state (with the corollary that every state must evolve into a nation-state) as the exclusive form of organization to order their political lives. The options that had been available to political entities in late medieval and early modern Europe included city-states and city-leagues, not to mention the revival and/or reassertion of feudal and imperial forms of political organization, in addition to the sovereign territorial state.[34] These other options were no longer available to colonial populations at the time of decolonization. The sovereign state, having triumphed over its competitors several centuries ago in Europe, had become the only legitimate form of political organization sanctioned by the international system and it was the benchmark of a political community's independent existence. Therefore, sovereign state-making—including both domestic authority and external recognition over clearly demarcated territorial domains—became absolutely imperative for the participation of Third World countries in the international system. Building states and controlling them became synonymous not only with political order but with political existence itself.[35]

A major reason why neorealism and neoliberalism fail to come to grips with the relationship between state-making and conflict is the *ahistorical* nature of both these scholarly traditions, which concentrate on the present (or at best on the immediate past) that is of direct concern to their intellectual and political constituencies. Had scholars belonging to these two schools delved deeper into the historical record of West Europe and North America and charted the course of state-building in England under the Tudors and the Stuarts, France under the Capetians and the Bourbons, and the United States in the eighteenth and nineteenth centuries (especially concentrating on the period of the Civil War, not to mention the conflicts involving European settlers and native Americans that led to the virtual decimation of the native population), they would have realized the validity of the proposition that state-making and what we now call "internal war" are two sides of the same coin. It needs to be pointed out that we currently characterize such conflicts as internal in character because we assume the territorial legitimacy of postcolonial states within their colonially crafted boundaries. In early modern Europe the distinction between internal and external wars was far more uncertain as territorial domains were continuously contested (and changed hands often) without the notion of legitimacy privileging any one party over the other until quite late in that historical process.

It is no wonder, therefore, that states caught in the early stages of state-making are more prone to conflict and that much of this conflict takes place within rather than between states. However, this does not mean that the external or interstate dimension is completely missing from conflicts in the Third World. All it means is that the external dimension is usually secondary in character and comes into play largely because of the existence of sources of disorder that inhere within states and either drag unwilling external actors into these conflicts or allow such actors to take advantage of domestic conflicts, thus turning them into interstate ones.

Neighboring states are likely to get involved in internal conflicts in the Third World primarily because colonially crafted boundaries of most Third World states paid little attention to the populations' precolonial affinities and shared myths and loyalties. As a result, these borders often divide populations that are tied to each other on the basis of kinship, tribe, religion, and so on. Domestic conflicts in postcolonial states can, therefore, easily spill across political boundaries into contiguous states whose populations may provide aid and succor to protagonists in such conflicts, thus involving neighboring populations and eventually neighboring states into these conflicts.

One cannot deny the fact that many such conflicts also involve regional dynamics usually relating to divergent conceptions of preferred local power balances. However, these regional balance of power considerations normally become salient because favorable regional balances are perceived by state elites as essential for the success of their state-building enterprise, especially since this is an activity usually undertaken concurrently by neighboring states that are at the same stage in the development of their polities. Construction of favorable balances, in such contexts, becomes a necessary component of state-building strategy because it facilitates state-making on the part of the stronger state at the expense of its weaker neighbors. This is especially the case, as in South Asia, the Middle East, the Horn of Africa, or the Balkans, where one or more of the latter may be engaged in contesting the former's control over demographic and territorial space over which, according to them, they also have legitimate claims.

Neorealism totally neglects the domestic dimensions of state-building, and their interaction with the dynamics of regional balances as well as with global power rivalries and international norms, as explanations for conflict in the international system. Since an overwhelming number of conflicts in the international system today have their origins in the state-making process (and the simultaneous operation of this process in contiguous and proximate states) and in its obverse phenomena, state-breaking and state failure, neorealism's inability to explain and predict these conflicts and, consequently, to prescribe strategies for their management should come as no surprise.[36] Neoliberalism is even less concerned with the dynamics of these conflicts than is neorealism. Its narrow, ethnocentric focus on the changing nature of interstate interaction in the interdependent world of industrial democracies renders it incapable even of conceptualizing the problem of disorder and conflict in much of the international system.

What is needed, therefore, is a paradigm that can combine the fundamental insights of classical realism with an appreciation of the dynamics of conflict currently clearly visible in large parts of the international system. It is only such a hybrid paradigm that can succeed in providing adequate explanations for the level and intensity of conflict and disorder in the system today. Hopefully, it will also prove capable of suggesting prescriptive strategies for the amelioration and management of the large majority of conflicts currently prevailing in the international system.

Such a paradigm can only be constructed by marrying the diagnoses for disorder and prescriptions for order provided by classical realists like Machiavelli and Hobbes with the perceived realities of political life within Third World states, including their struggle to balance the need for effectiveness with the requirements of legitimacy at the early stage of state-making at which they find themselves. As in the time of Hobbes, coercion and consent are both seen as essential to the success of the state-making project and the consequent provision of order and security within territorially demarcated political communities. Such domestic order is now, as it was then, an essential prerequisite for the construction and maintenance of a stable and legitimate international order.

However, certain very crucial new factors have emerged on the global scene that have made this task immeasurably difficult for the new entrants into the international system. These variables have materialized partially because of the existence of effective, responsive, and representative states in West Europe and North America that have had tremendous demonstration effect on the rest of the international system. Their existence has put enormous pressure on Third World states to emulate both their effectiveness and their representative and responsive character within a drastically shortened time frame. What European states had four or five centuries to achieve, Third World states are expected to achieve in four or five decades by telescoping different (usually sequential albeit overlapping) stages of state-making into one mammoth process.[37] This has created colossal overloads on their political systems and contributed directly and indirectly to the exacerbation of domestic disorder as states in the Third World alternate between repression and appeasement of different segments of their populations.

The workings of the international system, now more securely established than in the sixteenth or seventeenth century with a well-developed set of norms and with a much more sharply delineated hierarchy of power, have also made the task of Third World state-makers infinitely more difficult than was the case with their counterparts in early modern Europe. The contradictory demands placed on Third World states by international norms, which require them to be both effective as well as humane in their treatment of their populations (both individuals and groups), have left many of them in a perpetual state of schizophrenia.[38] Furthermore, the Third World states' lack of effective control over their economic resources in the context of an international division of labor that perpetuates dependency (a propensity accentuated by the globalization process) and detracts from their sovereignty has put the legitimacy of their political orders in grave jeopardy.[39] Again, the sustained policy of the major powers (witnessed very clearly during the Cold War) of exporting their conflicts to the periphery in order to preserve stability at the core of the system in the nuclear era, has had extremely deleterious effects on the state-building enterprise in the Third World. It has done so by virtually holding this process hostage in many instances to the requirements of global Great Power rivalry.[40]

In short, the operation of all these international factors has made the process of building and maintaining political order infinitely more difficult than was the case in Europe between the sixteenth and nineteenth centuries. The systematic incorporation of these experiences of the global South into International Relations Theory can only be done by fashioning a perspective on state-building and the construction of domestic order that looks at this enterprise from the inside and in its own right as a major variable that affects the level of order and conflict in the international system. At the same time, such a perspective must be extremely sensitive to external variables that impact upon such state-building activity and crucially influence its trajectory. It is this combination of perspectives that I have termed *subaltern realism* because it draws upon the experience of the subalterns in the international system that are largely ignored by the elitist historiography of the system popularized by both neorealists and neoliberals as a result of their concentration on the dynamics of interaction among the Great Powers and the industrialized states of the global North.

The dictionary definition of the term *subaltern* denotes those that are weak and of inferior rank. However, it is the common experience of all human societies that these are the elements that constitute the large majority of members in any social system. The term, Gramscian in its inspiration, is borrowed from the subaltern school of history, composed primarily of historians of India, that is engaged in studying the role of the less powerful elements—peasants, artisans, and so on—within societies, elements that form a majority within their societies but whose histories are ignored by elitist historiography of the traditional kind, which tends to focus on the activities of the powerful.[41] Third World states form the quintessential subaltern element within the society of states given their relative powerlessness and the fact that they constitute a large majority in the international system.

It is clear that the subaltern realist paradigm, even in the preliminary form in which it is presented here, is based on the following assumptions: first, issues of domestic order and those of international order are inextricably intertwined, especially in the arena of conflict and conflict resolution; second, issues of domestic order, which are primarily the by-products of the state-making enterprise within states, must receive analytical priority if one is to be able to explain most conflicts currently underway in the international system for the simple reason that they are the primary determinants of such conflicts; third, issues of domestic order/conflict are, however, not immune to external influences, either regional or global, especially given the permeability of the majority of states by external political and economic actors and, therefore, such external variables must be integrated into any explanation of the course and intensity of domestic conflicts and the behavior of states in the international system; and fourth, the linkage between domestic and external variables also explains the nexus between intrastate and interstate conflicts, and the intertwining of the state-making enterprise with regional balance of power issues.

When examined in the light of these assumptions, it becomes clear that subaltern realism will be able to predict the location and intensity of conflicts as well as map out strategies for their amelioration by looking at the following variables: first, the stage of state-making reached by a particular juridically sovereign state is an important factor. This can be determined by the level of political capacity (ascertained by combining the variables of effectiveness and legitimacy, or coercion and consent) attained by that state. The more primitive the stage of state-making and the more incomplete the state's capacity to control and/or gain the acquiescence of the large majority of its population, the greater the possibility of internal conflict and disorder.

Second, the ethnopolitical composition of a state's population, especially as measured by the popular acceptance of definitions of political community that differ radically from the one adopted by state elites must be considered. In other words, the balance of approval or attachment between the state-defined conception of nationalism and its (usually ethnically defined) alternatives must be analyzed. The greater and more coherent the challenges to the state-defined conception of nationalism, the greater the possibility of internal conflict and disorder.

Next, the existence or otherwise of contested territorial and demographic space between contiguous states undergoing state-building concurrently should be looked at. The more the contestation, the greater the possibility both of the intensification of internal conflicts (because of the provision of external encouragement and support to domestic dissidents and/or secessionists) and the likelihood of their transformation into interstate conflicts.

We also have to consider the impact of Great Power rivalries on, and the nature of great power policies toward, particular states/regions and the capacity of major powers to exacerbate or alleviate conflicts within those states/regions. The greater the proclivity of one or more of the Great Powers to intervene in domestic conflicts against those in control of the state and the greater the capacity of one or more of the Great Powers to carry out such intervention politically, economically, or militarily, the greater the likelihood of the exacerbation of domestic conflicts. Similarly, the greater the proclivity of Great Powers to support regional antagonists engaged in disputes over contested territorial and demographic space, the greater the resistance of such conflicts to strategies of conflict management and conflict resolution will be.

Finally, the existence and impact of international norms that promote or discourage intrastate and/or interstate conflicts relating to state-making, in particular the permissive or restrictive character of such norms in relation to the breakup of existing states needs to be examined. The more such norms are perceived to permit the breakup of existing states (as in the immediate aftermath of the end of the Cold War), the greater will be the possibility of the intensification of wars of state-breaking and the incidence of state failure in the international system as a whole.

The affinities of the subaltern realist perspective with that of classical realism, as witnessed in the writings of Machiavelli and Hobbes, is striking. However, there are also differences. Subaltern realism does not underestimate the influence of the anarchical, and especially the hierarchical, nature of the international system on state behavior. In fact, it is very sensitive to systemic influences not only of structure but of the policies of individual Great Powers that emanate out of Great Power rivalries but that have a crucial impact on the political lives of Third World states. It is also sensitive to the effect of the international division of labor, and the consequent dependence of Third World states on the centers of international economic power concentrated in the global North, on both the legitimacy and the effectiveness of Third World states vis-à-vis their populations.

These differences with classical realism emerge out of the fact that the classical theorists of realism were writing at a time when modern states and the states system were evolving simultaneously and the impact of the latter's dynamics on the former was minimal. Similarly, the evolution of the international capitalist economy was in its infancy and its long-term impact on the political project of state-making was not at all clear. With a well-developed structure, elaborate international norms, and a highly stratified global economic, military, and political hierarchy, this is no longer the case.

Therefore, subaltern realism acknowledges more than classical realism the influence of external variables emanating out of the hierarchical nature of the system on the behavior of states, especially of the majority of states that constitute the subaltern element in the system. However, it does not make the structure of the international system the sole or even the predominant independent variable determining such behavior. According to subaltern realism, the majority of states suffer from a security predicament that is much more complex and much more driven by domestic factors than the security dilemma that neorealism posits. Subaltern realism may not provide explanations for all that goes on in the international system. Insights from the neo-neo synthesis that explain the nature of Great Power relations, or of interactions within the industrialized core of the system that may be operating on the premise of complex interdependence and absolute gains, will still be necessary to supplement the explanations provided by subaltern realism. But its explanatory power in terms of unraveling the sources of the large majority of conflicts in the international system and illuminating the internal and external behavior of the large majority of states far surpasses that of any other theory available.

Paradigms in the social sciences in general, and in International Relations in particular, need not explain everything in every situation. In the absence of other paradigms with more comprehensive and more powerful explanations of issues of war and peace in the international system, subaltern realism fills a principal gap in the theoretical literature because it has the capacity to explain what, at the current juncture, is the most crucial dimension of International Relations—the origins and sources of the large majority of conflicts in the international system.

This explanatory power also provides it with the capacity at least potentially to help map strategies for the management and alleviation of such conflicts, if not their resolution. If policymakers in the major capitals of the world become conversant with this paradigm and use its lenses to view the majority of conflicts in the international system today, they will be better able to understand the fundamental nature of these conflicts. Such comprehension may well act as the beginning of wisdom for the fashioning of international strategies to contain and manage conflicts.

By using the insights of the subaltern realist paradigm, world statesmen and political analysts will begin to realize that such conflicts are neither the reflection of ancient hatreds nor are they primarily the result of external machinations. They are part and parcel of the state-making odyssey of the new entrants into the system of states, an exercise that is made almost impossibly difficult by the operation of international norms and the policies of major powers. Furthermore, they will begin to understand that moving beyond Westphalia and creating regional confederations based on weak states will not provide the remedy for such conflicts.

Such a paradigm will also help policymakers and analysts comprehend the fact that historically states have preceded the creation of nations. Nationalism, as Ernest Gellner has argued, "emerges only in milieux in which the existence of the state is already very much taken for granted. The existence of politically centralized units, and of a moral-political climate in which such centralized units are taken for granted and are treated as normative, is a necessary though not sufficient condition of nationalism."[42] The fact that the civic nationalism of countries such as Britain, France, and the United States today is the linear and direct descendant of a state-defined nationalism that triumphed over more particularistic definitions of political identity (invariably by the force of arms as the American Civil War demonstrated very clearly) confirms the dependent relationship of the nation on the state. Where this order has been reversed it has been a recipe for grave disorder (for example, the Balkans).

Once having understood this historical process, policymakers are also likely to recognize that relaxing international norms regarding the inviolability of the boundaries of existing states and sanctioning the creation of ethnic states (as happened in the case of the former Yugoslavia) will not solve the problem of disorder in the international system. It will not do so for the simple reason, as William Pfaff has pointed out, that "The ethnic state is a product of the political imagination; it does not exist in reality. . . . The idea of the ethnic nation thus is a permanent provocation to war."[43] As the Balkan experience demonstrates, ethnically defined ministates will only provide the incentive for the creation of even more ethnically pure microstates since there are hardly any unadulterated ethnic homelands left anymore.

The comprehension of this fact is likely to make policymakers understand that the notion of self-determination needs to be delinked from the idea of secession and linked to the concept of political empowerment. This, they will discern, is also the surest way of making states both legitimate and effective. At the same time, they will realize that there are fundamental tensions between the imperatives of state-making and the consolidation of state power on the one hand, and the demands for political participation and empowerment on the other. They may, therefore, conclude that a delicate balance needs to be maintained between the requirements of effectiveness and those of legitimacy of states because they are two sides of the same state-making coin. Democratization by itself is unlikely to solve the problem of conflicts within states unless it is accompanied by a concentration of the instruments of violence in the hands of the state.

It will also lead them to conclude that the strengthening and not the weakening of the Westphalian order, especially at the level of the unit (state), is essential for the effective management of most conflicts in the international system. In turn, this is likely to lead the Great Powers to be more circumspect in intervening in the internal affairs of states, especially if such intervention involves a serious derogation of the sovereignty of the target state (for example, Iraq).

Neorealism and neoliberalism (theories in which policymakers in the major capitals of the West are often, and frequently subconsciously, socialized) do not possess adequate explanatory and predictive capacity, especially in the arena of managing and alleviating the majority of conflicts in the international system. Their inability to do so emerges out of the fact that these conflicts are inextricably enmeshed with the process of state-building and the formation of political communities that both the above-mentioned theories either do not address or do so very inadequately. The subaltern realist paradigm, on the other hand, makes this process its centerpiece, thus equipping itself at the present juncture with explanatory and predictive power in matters of conflict and order that is far superior to that possessed by the traditionally dominant paradigms.

Notes

1. For an interesting dialogue between positivists and post-positivists on the relative merits of their approaches, see Steve Smith, Ken Booth, and Marysia Zalewski, eds., *International Theory: Positivism and Beyond* (NY: Cambridge University Press, 1996).

2. Despite all the postmodernist and social constructivist critiques of the assumption that there is a "real" reality out there independent of our constructions and perceptions, one has to posit such an object if one is to theorize

meaningfully within any of the social sciences. Otherwise, one will be constantly engaged in deconstruction for its own sake thus turning it into a truly nihilist exercise. This does not deny that one's construction of reality is affected by one's perceptions and that the latter, in turn, are to a substantial degree products of one's experiences and are dependent upon where one is situated in terms of time, space, social class, political predilections, and so on. However, even the concept of perceptions makes sense only in the context of an object that the perceiver is trying to perceive. In the absence of such an identifiable object (even if the meaning of that object is contested), the concept of perception will make no sense at all. The same applies to the concept of construction. One cannot construct meaningful phenomena (for example, state, sovereignty) that are totally out of sync with the requirements of time and space. Devoid of meaning and utility such constructions will die a very quick death. Therefore, while it is essential to explore who perceives and who constructs reality, taking such exploration to the absurd limit of denying the very existence of all objects that are perceived and constructed becomes a meaningless exercise.

3. Robert Cox, *Approaches to World Order* (NY: Cambridge University Press, 1996), p. 87.

4. Michael Mann, "Authoritarianism and Liberal Militarism: A Contribution from Comparative and Historical Sociology," in *International Theory: Positivism and Beyond*, eds., Steve Smith, Ken Booth, and Marysia Zalewski (NY: Cambridge University Press, 1996), p. 221.

5. Mohammed Ayoob, "The Third World in the System of States: Acute Schizophrenia or Growing Pains?" *International Studies Quarterly*, vol. 33, no. 1 (1989), pps. 67–79; Hedley Bull and Adam Watson, eds., *The Expansion of International Society* (Oxford: Clarendon Press, 1984).

6. Mohammed Ayoob, "The New-Old Disorder in the Third World," *Global Governance*, vol. 1, no. 1, (1995b), pps. 59–77.

7. Myron Wiener, "Security, Stability, and International Migration," in *Global Dangers: Changing Dimensions of International Security*, eds., Sean M. Lynn-Jones and Steven E. Miller (Cambridge, MA: MIT Press, 1995), pps. 183–218.

8. For a convincing statement of this argument, see Amitav Acharya, "The Periphery as the Core: The Third World and Security Studies," in Keith Krause and Michael Williams, eds., *Critical Security Studies*, (Minneapolis, MN: University of Minnesota Press, 1997), pps. 299–327.

9. Ethan B. Kapstein, "Is Realism Dead? The Domestic Sources of International Politics," *International Organization*, vol. 49, no. 4 (1995), p. 751.

10. Kenneth Waltz, *Theory of International Politics* (Reading, MA: Addison-Wesley, 1979); Stephen Walt, *The Origins of Alliances* (Ithaca, NY: Cornell University Press, 1987).

11. Paul Schroeder, "Historical Reality vs. Neo-realist Theory," *International Security*, vol. 19, no. 1 (1994), pps. 108–48.

12. For first, second and third image assumptions, see Kenneth Waltz, *Man, the State and War* (NY: Columbia University Press, 1954).

13. Robert O. Keohane and Joseph S. Nye, Jr., eds., *Transnational Relations and World Politics* (Cambridge, MA: Harvard University Press, 1972).

14. Richard Ned Lebow, "The Long Peace, the End of the War, and the Failure of Realism," in *International Relations Theory and the End of the Cold War*, eds., Richard Ned Lebow and Thomas Risse-Kappen (NY: Columbia University Press, 1995), pps. 23–56.

15. Charles W. Kegley, Jr., "The Neoliberal Challenge to Realist Theories of World Politics: An Introduction," in *Controversies in International Relations Theory*, ed., Charles W. Kegley, Jr. (NY: St. Martin's Press, 1995), p. 9.

16. Joseph S. Nye, Jr., "What New World Order?" *Foreign Affairs*, vol. 71 (1992), pps. 83–96.

17. Barry Buzan, "New Patterns of Global Security in the Twenty-first Century," *International Affairs*, vol. 67, no. 3 (1991), p. 437.

18. John Gerard Ruggie, "Peacekeeping and U.S. Interests," in *Order and Disorder After the Cold War*, ed., Brad Roberts (Cambridge, MA: MIT Press, 1995), p. 212.

19. Ole Waever, "The Rise and Fall of the Inter-Paradigm Debate," in *International Theory: Positivism and Beyond*, eds., Steve Smith, Ken Booth, and Marysia Zalewski (NY: Cambridge University Press, 1996), pps. 163–64.

20. John H. Herz, "The Territorial State Revisited," in *Classic Readings of International Relations*, eds., Phil Williams, Donald M. Goldstein, and Jay M. Sharitz (Belmont, MA: Wadsworth, 1994), p. 105.

21. For a detailed analysis of the interaction between the internal process of state-making in the Third World and external variables, see Mohammed Ayoob, *The Third World Security Predicament: State-Making, Regional Conflict, and the International System* (Boulder, CO: Lynne Rienner Publishers, 1995).

22. Evan Luard, *War in International Society* (London: I.B. Tauris, 1986), pps. 442–46.

23. Kalevi J. Holsti, *Peace and War: Armed Conflicts and International Order, 1648–1989* (NY: Cambridge University Press, 1991), pps. 274–78.

24. Kalevi J. Holsti, *The State, War, and the State of War* (NY: Cambridge University Press, 1996), pps. 22, 210–24.

25. Ibid.

26. Mohammed Ayoob, "The Iran-Iraq War and Regional Security in the Persian Gulf," *Alternatives*, vol. 10, no. 4 (1985), pps. 581–90.

27. R. B. J. Walker, *Inside/Outside: International Relations as Political Theory* (NY: Cambridge University Press, 1996), pps. 48, 117.

28. Ibid., p. 45.

29. Michael Williams, "Hobbes and International Relations: A Reconsideration," *International Organization*, vol. 50, no. 2 (1996), p. 215.

30. Ibid., p. 220.

31. Richard S. Peters, "Introduction to Collier Books Edition," in *The Leviathan* by Thomas Hobbes, eds., Michael Oakeshott and Richard S. Peters (NY: Collier Books, 1962), pps. 11–12.

32. Robert W. Cox, *Approaches to World Order*, p. 502.

33. Robert Jackman, *Power Without Force: The Political Capacity of Nation-States* (Ann Arbor, MI: University of Michigan Press, 1993).

34. Hendrik Spruyt, *The Sovereign State and Its Competitors* (Princeton, NJ: Princeton University Press, 1994).

35. Mohammed Ayoob, "The Third World in the System of States," p. 67–79.

36. For a detailed analysis of state-making, state-breaking, and state failure as structural sources of conflict in the international system and the close interconnection between the three phenomena, see Mohammed Ayoob, "State-making, State Breaking, and State Failure," in Chester A. Crocker and Fen Osler Hampson, *Managing Global Chaos: Sources of and Responses to International Conflict* (Washington, DC: United States Institute of Peace Press, 1996), pps. 37–51.

37. For a discussion of the sequential stages of state-making that draws upon the European experience, see Stein Rokkan, "Dimensions of State Formation and Nation-Building: A Possible Paradigm for Research on Variations Within Europe," in Charles Tilly ed., *The Formation of National States in Western Europe*, (Princeton: Princeton University Press, 1975), pps. 562–600.

38. Mohammed Ayoob, "The Security Predicament of the Third World State: Reflections on State Making in a Comparative Perspective," in *The Insecurity Dilemma: National Security of Third World States*, ed., Brian L. Job (Boulder, CO: Lynne Rienner Publishers, 1992), pps. 63–80.

39. Naeem Inayatullah, "Beyond the Sovereignty Dilemma: Quasi-States as Social Construct," in *State Sovereignty as Social Construct*, eds., Thomas J. Biersteker and Cynthia Weber (NY: Cambridge University Press, 1996).

40. Mohammed Ayoob, *The Third World Security Predicament*, ch. 5.

41. For a collection of seminal writings in the field of subaltern history, see Ranajit Guha and Gayatri Chakravorty Spivak, eds., *Selected Subaltern Studies*, (NY: Oxford University Press, 1988).

42. Ernest Gellner, *Nations and Nationalism* (Ithaca, NY: Cornell University Press, 1983), p. 4.

43. William Pfaff, "Invitation to War," *Foreign Affairs*, vol. 72, no. 3 (1993), pps. 99, 101.

Bibliography

Acharya, Amitav. "The Periphery as the Core: The Third World and Security Studies." In *Critical Security Studies*. Eds. Keith Krause and Michael Williams. Minneapolis, MN: University of Minnesota Press, 1997, pps. 299–327.

Ayoob, Mohammed. "State-making, State Breaking, and State Failure." *Managing Global Chaos: Sources of and Responses to International Conflict*. Eds. Chester A. Crocker and Fen O. Hampson. Washington, DC: United States Institute of Peace Press, 1996, pps. 37–51.

———. *The Third World Security Predicament: State Making, Regional Conflict, and the International System*. Boulder, CO: Lynne Rienner Publishers, 1995.

———. "The New-Old Disorder in the Third World." *Global Governance*. Vol. 1, no. 1, (1995), pps. 59–77.

———. "The Security Predicament of the Third World State: Reflections on State-making in a Comparative Perspective." In *The Insecurity Dilemma: National Security of Third World States*. Ed. Brian L. Job. Boulder, CO: Lynne Rienner Publishers, 1992, pps. 63–80.

———. "The Third World in the System of States: Acute Schizophrenia or Growing Pains?" *International Studies Quarterly*. Vol. 33, no. 1, (1989), pps. 67–79.

———. "The Iran-Iraq War and Regional Security in the Persian Gulf." *Alternatives*. Vol. 10, no. 4 (1985), pps. 581–90.

Bull, Hedley and Adam Watson, eds. *The Expansion of International Society*. Oxford: Clarendon Press, 1984.

Buzan, Barry. "New Patterns of Global Security in the Twenty-first Century." *International Affairs*. Vol. 67, no. 3, (1991), pps. 431–51.

Cox, Robert W. *Approaches to World Order*. NY: Cambridge University Press, 1996.

Gellner, Ernest. *Nations and Nationalism*. Ithaca, NY: Cornell University Press, 1983.

Guha, Ranjit and Gayatri Chakravorty Spivak, eds. *Selected Subaltern Studies*. NY: Oxford University Press, 1988.

Herz, John H. "The Territorial State Revisited." In *Classic Readings of International Relations*. Eds. Phil Williams, Donald M. Goldstein, and Jay M. Sharitz. Belmont, MA: Wadsworth, 1994, pps. 97–107.

Holsti, Kalevi J. *The State, War, and the State of War*. NY: Cambridge University Press, 1996.

———. *Peace and War: Armed Conflicts and International Order, 1648–1989*. NY: Cambridge University Press, 1991.

Inayatullah, Naeem. "Beyond the Sovereignty Dilemma: Quasi-States as Social Construct." In *State Sovereignty as Social Construct*. Eds. Thomas J. Biersteker and Cynthia Weber. NY: Cambridge University Press, 1996.

Jackman, Robert. *Power Without Force: The Political Capacity of Nation-States*. Ann Arbor, MI: University of Michigan Press, 1993.

Kapstein, Ethan B. "Is Realism Dead? The Domestic sources of International Politics." *International Organization*. Vol. 49, no. 4, (1995), pps. 751–74.

Kegley, Jr., Charles W. "The Neoliberal Challenge to Realist Theories of World Politics: An Introduction." In *Controversies in International Relations Theory*. Ed. Charles W. Kegley, Jr. NY: St. Martin's Press, 1995, pps. 1–24.

Keohane, Robert O. and Joseph S. Nye, Jr., eds. *Transnational Relations and World Politics*. Cambridge, MA: Harvard University Press, 1972.

Keohane, Robert O. and Joseph S. Nye, Jr. *Power and Interdependence*. Boston: Little, Brown, 1977.

Lebow, Richard Ned. "The Long Peace, the End of the Cold War, and the Failure of Realism." In *International Relations Theory and the End of the Cold War*. Eds. Richard Ned Lebow and Thomas Risse-Kappen. NY: Columbia University Press, 1995, pps. 23–56.

Luard, Evan. *War in International Society*. London: I.B. Tauris, 1986.

Mann, Michael. "Authoritarianism and Liberal Militarism: A Contribution from Comparative and Historical Sociology." In *International Theory: Positivism and*

Beyond. Eds. Steve Smith, Ken Booth, and Marysia Zalewski. NY: Cambridge University Press, 1996.

Nye, Jr., Joseph S. "What New World Order?" *Foreign Affairs.* Vol. 71, (1992), pps. 83–96.

Peters, Richard S. "Introduction to the Collier Books Edition." In *The Leviathan* by Thomas Hobbes. Eds. Michael Oakeshott and Richard S. Peters. NY: Colliers Books, 1962, pp. 7–16.

Pfaff, William. "Invitation to War." *Foreign Affairs.* Vol. 72, no. 3, (1993), pps. 97–109.

Rokkan, Stein. "Dimensions of State Formation and Nation- Building: A Possible Paradigm for Research on Variations Within Europe." In *Formation of National States in Western Europe.* Ed. Charles Tilly. Princeton, NJ: Princeton University Press, 1975, pps. 562–600.

Ruggie, John Gerard. "Peacekeeping and U.S. Interests." In *Order and Disorder After the Cold War.* Ed. Brad Roberts. Cambridge, MA: MIT Press, 1995.

Schroeder, Paul. "Historical Reality vs. Neorealist Theory." *International Security.* Vol. 19, no. 1, (1994), pps. 108–48.

Smith, Steve, Ken Booth, Marysia Zalewski. eds. *International Theory: Positivism and Beyond.* NY: Cambridge University Press, 1996.

Spruyt, Hendrik. *The Sovereign State and Its Competitors.* Princeton, NJ: Princeton University Press, 1994.

Waever, Ole. "The Rise and Fall of the Inter-Paradigm Debate." In *International Theory: Positivism and Beyond.* Eds. Steve Smith, Ken Booth, and Marysia Zalewski. NY: Cambridge University Press, 1996.

Walker, R. B. J. *Inside/Outside: International Relations as Political Theory.* NY: Cambridge University Press, 1993.

Walt, Stephen. *The Origins of Alliances.* Ithaca, NY: Cornell University Press, 1987.

Waltz, Kenneth. *Theory of International Politics.* Reading, MA: Addison-Wesley, 1979.

———. *Man, the State and War.* NY: Columbia University Press, 1954.

Weiner, Myron. "Security, Stability, and International Migration." In *Global Dangers: Changing Dimensions of International Security.* Eds. Sean M. Lynn-Jones and Steven E. Miller. Cambridge, MA: MIT Press, 1995, pps. 183–218.

Williams, Michael. "Hobbes and International Relations: A Reconsideration." *International Organization.* Vol. 50, no. 2, (1996), pps. 213–36.

THREE

An Introduction to Peripheral Realism and Its Implications for the Interstate System: Argentina and the Cóndor II Missile Project

Carlos Escudé

Because Third World states often pose threats to the interstate order, their behavior cannot be ignored when constructing an International Relations Theory. When these states are included in a theoretical analysis of world order, the "structure" of the international system (for issues related to peace and security) is characterized more by imperfect and incipient hierarchy than anarchy. I will argue that the "real" structure of the interstate system includes three types of functionally differentiated states: States that command (for example, Great Powers among whom there is anarchy but that preside over the rest), states that obey, the majority of the interstate community, including the Third World and advanced but militarily weak industrialized states, and rebel states (a small number of Third World states that choose to be part of the anarchical system of the Great Powers by challenging the right of the Great Powers to dominate). I will also argue that a Third World state can only be part of an anarchical system by sacrificing the interests of its citizens. Third World states have to accept the hierarchical character of the international system led by the Great Powers, just as the great majority of the advanced but militarily weak industrialized states do, if they want to develop their own political and economic systems.

Introduction

Argentina's past and present foreign policies provide many interesting insights for International Relations Theory and throw light on the age-old question of how interstate order is generated. Is this order best understood as a complex process of mutual adjustment among various states and types of domestic and international demand, as neoliberal institutionalists would suggest? Or is it imposed under conditions of anarchy as most realists would argue? Or is it created by an interstate hierarchy, as I will argue here? In this chapter I will demonstrate how the Argentine case can help us identify logical flaws in mainstream International Relations (IR) Theory, irrespective of whether we opt for a realist or a neoliberal perspective.

One reason why the Argentine case can help us identify fallacies and give answers to major theoretical questions is that Argentina is not a leading state but a distinctly peripheral one. Introducing the behavior of peripheral states into systemic analysis puts the above questions in an altogether different perspective: the perspective of weak vis-à-vis strong states, that is, the perspective of the relative absence of power.[1] It means looking at the same issues from a quite different angle: from the point of view of Melos, rather than Athens.

Another reason for looking at Argentina is that it is a peripheral state that has, in the past, challenged the interstate order. Like India, Pakistan, North Korea, Iraq, Libya and Iran, which have also challenged the international order, the Argentine case shows that the analysis of the role of peripheral states in the interstate system is not irrelevant.

Mainstream International Relations Theory looks at international order and disorder exclusively from the perspective of the "leading states," thereby ignoring many essential factors. Peripheral states must be included in theory-building efforts that focus on the world order. This will not only strengthen general theory but it will also lead to the formulation of subsets of concepts, explanatory hypotheses, and normative judgments specifically applicable to peripheral states, that is, states relatively devoid of power resources. I call these subsets "peripheral theory," although it should be noted that I see them as falling under the "umbrella" of general theory.[2]

The Story of the Cóndor II: A Case Study

Argentina is a country that has not faced credible external threats for many decades, but none the less has engaged in arms races, proliferation projects, and other activities that, from the perspective of the Great Powers, challenged the international order, until the Menem administration (mid-1989 to the present) bandwagoned with the United States and disarmed unilaterally. Let's look at the case of Argentina's deactivated ballistic missile project in order to demonstrate that changing societal conditions and governmental structures can generate important changes in a state's foreign policy position. In this case Argentina dropped its posture of defiance of the international order and adopted the foreign policy profile of a trading state.

In January 1984, President Raúl Alfonsín, head of state of the then recently redemocratized Argentina, signed a secret agreement with Egypt and Iraq for the development and production of an intermediate-range ballistic missile, the Cóndor II. According to the media the missile was to be slightly superior to the U.S. Pershing II, capable of carrying a payload of more than 1,000 pounds across a distance of more than 1,000 km, and to have a state-of-the-art guidance system. In other words, it would be capable of carrying an average-size nuclear warhead from Patagonia to the Falklands/Malvinas or from Baghdad to Tel Aviv. Libya was also to assist in the financing of the project. The technology was basically contraband from Germany, France, and the United States, in some cases with the complicity of important and prestigious Western firms. A very advanced technical plant was built in Falda del Carmen, Province of Córdoba, Argentina, almost entirely with smuggled technology.

The project continued until, toward the end of the Alfonsín administration, it began to stagnate because of lack of funds. Although the funds came mainly from Iraq and Libya, the Argentine government did contribute a few hundred million dollars. When President Carlos Menem took office in mid-1989, it was decided to totally deactivate and, moreover, destroy the Cóndor II, despite intense domestic opposition. The decision was mainly a response to U.S. pressure. Argentina's desire to be admitted to the Brady Plan, and to restructure its foreign debt[3] made that pressure all the more compelling. Argentina had earlier exported some preliminary, untested and ill-calibrated specimens of the Cóndor II to Iraq. U.S. intelligence services later found pieces of destroyed Cóndors in Iraqi territory after the Gulf War. Indeed, almost all of the information that is available on the Cóndor II comes either directly or indirectly from U.S. intelligence sources.[4] Even the information put out by the Argentine government about Argentina's "best-kept secret" was only revealed because of U.S. pressures and the fact that there was little secrecy left after the U.S. intelligence "leaks" were revealed.

The Menem administration's decision to destroy the Cóndor II did not take immediate effect, however. Opposition by the Radical party, the military, and factions within the ruling Justicialist party, and the fact that the government had invested money and effort in the project, generated resistance within the government itself to the decision.

One alternative was for Argentina to cooperate with Spain, a member of the Missile Technology Control Regime (MTCR),[5] in converting the two-stage missile into a three-stage satellite-launching vehicle. Spain had a green light from the MTCR to develop and produce such vehicles, but Argentina had more experience with missile technology than Spain and possessed territories in the extreme south that are well-located for satellite launching. The Spaniards were interested and agreement was reached on the proposal. But it was discovered that while Spanish entry into the satellite-launching business, either alone or with an MTCR-approved partner, was approved by the United States and the MTCR, there was an unequivocal veto on cooperation with Argentina. The Spanish government therefore had to inform the Argentine government confidentially that it could only cooperate in the development of satellites, not satellite-launching vehicles.

Given the country's economic vulnerability and the prohibitive costs of going on with the ill-fated project, the Argentine government resigned itself to destroying the missile. However, because there had been an agreement with Spain to "recycle" the Cóndor, an attempt was made to disguise its actual destruction. The 14 unfinished missiles in Argentina were sent to Spain in the first stage of an operation that would later bring them to the United States. This was thought preferable to destroying them in Córdoba under U.S. supervision. Rejecting Argentina's proposal that cement be injected into the missiles, the U.S. government had demanded that they be blown up. Each blast would have been heard clearly in the city of Córdoba, giving a clear indication of who rules and who obeys in the interstate system. The political blow to the government could have been irreparable. To make things worse, the explosions would have had to have been at 24- or 48-hour intervals to minimize damage to the environment. The *cordobeses* would have heard a strong blast every day for two weeks, news of which would be propagated via the newspapers, television, and radio to the entire population, something the government wished to avoid.

It was therefore deemed preferable to ship the missiles to the United States via Spain. The press saw this as farcical and, despite the attempt to save face, the operation become a symbol of Argentina's subordination to the United States. Nevertheless, the political damage was much smaller than if the missiles had been destroyed in Argentina under direct U.S. supervision.

On the other hand, the government had little choice. To continue with the project as originally conceived by the Alfonsín administration and the Argentine Air Force would have been very costly, with negative commercial and economic consequences for the population. Both the government in particular and Argentine society in general were against such costs, and this was probably also true of the Radical party (during whose administration the project was launched). Alfonsín had signed the original agreement to produce the Cóndor II partly because of Air Force pressures and partly because of his own convictions regarding the meaning of national independence and sovereignty, but probably without a realistic appraisal of what the eventual costs stemming from great power opposition and the drain on Argentina's resources would be. Although Radical party leaders opposed the deactivation of the Cóndor II as part of their opposition politics, none is likely to even consider its rebirth in the event of regaining power.

The Theoretical Relevance of the Cóndor II Episode

In my opinion, this episode has a great relevance for theory-building for several reasons: First, the destruction of the Cóndor II was an imposed solution, not the result of an agreement stemming from the free will of both states. While there was no direct application of force, the public or covert sanctions that would have been imposed on Argentina had the project continued were, given the country's economic vulnerability, a forceful argument against continuation. The episode appears to be most convincingly explained through realist rather than any other arguments.

But nonetheless, the mere fact that the Cóndor II project existed and became an issue in the United States and in the MTCR shows that any middle-class state can significantly challenge the interstate order and become a source of instability, provided that it is willing to accept the very high costs involved. By this I mean, for example, a willingness to endure significant commercial and economic *discrimination,* with negative consequences for the welfare of the population and with destabilizing economic and political effects.

On the other hand, a government's willingness to spend heavily for a strong foreign or defense policy does not depend solely on the will of its officials and their individual preferences, but is rather the result of very complex domestic processes as put forward in Robert Cox's concept, the "state/society complex."[6] Thus domestic sources of stability or instability play an important role in the foreign policy stance of many middle-class and Third World states.

Next, as Stephen D. Krasner has suggested from a completely different perspective,[7] a theory based only upon the study of the role of the so-called leading states in the interstate system will exclude other potential sources of instability from the analysis, such as the middle-class states. This is to the detriment of theoretical efforts to understand the working of the international system, because in the post–Cold War era these states will probably be one of the main sources of insecurity for the entire world.[8]

Finally, the most promising theory-building strategy is that which emphasizes comparative empirical research on the state/society complex, a bottom-up approach to analyzing interstate relations at the systemic level. It is a mistake to emphasize the systemic level and ignore the state/societal level of analysis. If any middle-class state able to pay the high costs of a policy of proliferation, for example, is a potential source of instability, then the most promising theory-building strategy is that which focuses on the state/society complex, which makes it possible to evaluate the level of tolerable costs for a specific society and its structure of preferences. In other words, the best theory-building strategy will be that which leads to the study of specific states and their structures of preferences, without which the very concept of rational choice is devoid of meaning. Without such a research strategy, events such as the Islamic revolution, the invasion of the Falklands/Malvinas Islands, the birth of the Cóndor II and the Persian Gulf Crisis will continue to take International Relations theorists by surprise and completely off-guard.[9]

Indeed, the very concept of "systemic limitations" has a fallacy or ethnocentric bias according to where the theory has been developed. When we think in terms of the systemic limitations on the foreign or defense policies of a middle-class state, we do so from the perspective of a certain unspecified level of tolerable costs, and hence from the perspective of a similarly unspecified structure of preferences, while in reality these tolerable costs and structures of preferences vary from one state/society complex to another. Therefore, except in its most general traits—which are mere platitudes—systemic analysis can only be carried out from the perspective of a certain structure of preferences, that is, on a case-by-case basis that explicitly incorporates certain specific characteristics of the state/society complexes involved.

Hence (and contrary to Waltz's claims), if we want to understand world politics, systemic analysis is but a secondary complement to the analysis of specific societies and the domestic factors that condition their foreign policies. It is essential to study these factors in order to understand the interstate order and its potential sources of instability, and it is not necessary to abandon realism to identify major flaws in Waltzian realism. By incorporating state/society factors, peripheral realism is a corrective to, rather than an abandonment of, the realist paradigm.

Hierarchy versus Anarchy: A First Approximation

However, the above conclusions about the state/society level of analysis do not mean that peripheral realism ignores the systemic level of analysis that might allow us to better understand not only the position of middle-class states in the international system but the policy options open to them as well. One relevant question that could be posed as a result of the Cóndor II episode is: what implications does this example have in terms of the alleged "anarchy" that neorealists have attributed to the interstate system? As in most of the relevant IR literature, interstate "anarchy" is defined here as the absence of government or of an oligopolic governance principle in interstate relations.[10] It is not synonymous with chaos or disorder (the dictionary meaning of the term).

I think this is an imperative and obvious question. Earlier I stated that my historical example gives a vivid illustration of who rules and who obeys in the international order. This may seem trivial at first glance, since most IR Theory acknowledges that there are states that command and states that obey (while in blatant contradiction clinging to the concept of "anarchy"). But both realists and neorealists have tended to limit their analysis to "leading states." This, in turn, has led many theorists to claim that weak states (and I consider these to include middle-class states) have no foreign policy unless they interact in an interstate system isolated from the main one, in which case they tend to reproduce the patterns of the Great Powers.

Peripheral realism holds that this argument is not valid. Middle-class and Third World states do have foreign policies, some of which are profoundly disturbing to the stability of the international system. To use my historical example, the Cóndor II did indeed exist before it was deactivated and destroyed by the Menem government (as did Argentina's unsafeguarded nuclear program, or its invasion of the Falklands/Malvinas), and it was a source of significant and legitimate concern for those devoted to nonproliferation and international stability. To complicate matters still further, the Cóndor II was born under the auspices of an unquestionably democratic government, and the Radical party strongly criticized and opposed its deactivation and destruction.

Therefore, it is not true to say that middle-class states lack foreign policy. Theories that focus solely on the interstate system are weakened by their exclusion of such relevant phenomena as Saddam's Iraq, the Iran of the Islamic Revolution, Khadaffi's Libya, the Argentine Cóndor II, and General Leopoldo Galtieri's 1982 invasion of the Falklands/Malvinas.

If we agree that weaker states do have foreign policies and that for analytical purposes any theoretical construct of the international system needs to include them, then in what way are these states similar to or different from the dominant powers in the international system? Peripheral realism would argue that contrary to the neorealist model, the interstate system is not characterized by "anarchy," but by an incipient and imperfect "hierarchy" in which we find states that command, states that obey, and states, without the power to command, that refuse to obey. The foreign policy options of those that "obey" are, therefore, constrained by that hierarchy in ways that do not apply to the Great Powers. The fact that a state can choose to "obey" or "not to obey" does not contradict peripheral realism's concept of an "incipient and imperfect hierarchy" nor does it contradict the Thucydidean logic on which it is based. In his classic *History of the Peloponesian War,* the Greek historian wrote that the strong do what they can while the weak "suffer" what they must. Notwithstanding, weak states have options regarding the type of suffering that they will endure. For example, in the famous Melian dialogue, it is clear that Melos had the option of obeying Athens or suffering the costs of losing a ruinous war. Likewise, Argentina could have opted to continue the Cóndor II project at the cost of not being admitted into the Brady Plan, of not regaining the confidence of Western bankers, and of continuing to suffer a ruinous monetary crisis with a massive capital flight. Melos opted for not obeying Athens and suffered total destruction. Menem's Argentina opted for obeying the United States (thus "suffering" subordination), and consequently was able to benefit from the stability generated by a well-engineered economic plan, which would not have been forthcoming had Argentina insisted on continuing its challenge of the United States in the strategic sphere. The case of the Cóndor II clearly points in the direction of hierarchy rather than anarchy, and the presence of an oligopolic governance principle in interstate relations that realists tend not to acknowledge.

The Fallacy of the Autonomy of the Political Sphere

It is interesting to examine the origin of the IR myth of interstate anarchy. It is, I would argue, closely related to the fallacy of the autonomous political sphere. The legal equality of states was a juridical fiction until the signature and ratification of the UN charter. After that, it was no longer even a fiction, insofar as the charter, with five permanent members of a Security Council endowed with veto power, establishes the principle of the juridical *in*equality of states in matters of security. Furthermore, Chapter 7 of the UN charter *formally* awards intervention powers to the oligopolic Security Council. The same principle is seen in such international regimes as the Nuclear Non-Proliferation Treaty, whereby it is *juridically* established that some states have the right to possess nuclear weapons, whereas others do not. The issues ruled by such regimes are few in number but extremely relevant in substance. States are not formally equal; admittedly, informally they are even less equal.[11] The provisions of chapter 7 of the charter were mostly not applied during the Cold War, but *formally* they have been there since 1945, and they have acquired practical relevance in the post–Cold War era.[12]

Where does this misconception, which flies straight into the face of the world we know, come from? How did it become so powerful a myth, that as prominent a theoretician as Kenneth A. Oye began his introductory essay to a special issue of *World Politics* dedicated to the theme of "cooperation under anarchy," with the phrase "states live in *perpetual* anarchy"?[13]

In the first place, I think it is relatively clear that the myth of anarchy is part of the ideology of sovereignty. My central argument is that a fallacy is built into the central nucleus of the realist and neorealist theories, whose flawed logic leads to the exclusion from systemic analysis of *the sources* of events such as the Gulf War, the Islamic Revolution, the Falklands/ Malvinas War, or the Cóndor II incident itself. This logic ultimately stems from Hans J. Morgenthau and is clearly projected into the alleged anarchy that Waltz and other neorealists claim characterizes the structure of the interstate system.

A serious fallacy is introduced into the logical matrix of realist thought when Morgenthau tells us that power is an autonomous sphere of interest, as compared to other allegedly autonomous spheres, such as interest defined as wealth.[14] This is an oversimplification even for the Great Powers. However, at the periphery the link between political power and wealth is much more immediate. Had a peripheral viewpoint been contemplated in IR Theory, this error probably would never have been made (and the concept of anarchy would never have taken root). We can paraphrase Morgenthau and say that, from a peripheral perspective, the "main signpost that helps political realism to find its way through the landscape of international politics" is the concept of interest defined in terms of economic development, without which there is neither real power in the long term nor welfare for the population in the short or long term. If the main principle of political realism is so redefined, the sacrifice of the Cóndor II was the obvious normative consequence of a realist analysis of the situation by the Argentine government.

Ultimately, this shortcoming of Morgenthau's conceptual framework seems to spring from a certain ahistoricity: time and the long term, which link wealth to political power, are not included as variables, and this lends a static quality to his work.

From the perspective of peripheral realism, Morgenthau's definition of politics, which ignores the link between economic factors and politico-military power, leads not only to unsatisfactory explanations but also to misguided normative judgments and conclusions. If one were to take its ultimate logical consequences seriously, it would give Third World leaders only two foreign policy options—either to dedicate themselves to a conflictual form of power politics in the traditional, politico-military sense of the concept, or to abdicate from the quest for power altogether, fatalistically accepting a permanent subordinate status.[15]

With such a conceptual starting point as Morgenthau's, the post–World War II West German or Japanese experiences are simply incomprehensible. Indeed, most Third World leaders proceed as if these experiences simply did not exist, while in actual fact the postwar strategy of these countries (that is, a low interstate political profile, with a concentration on development and trade) is the only way in which a vulnerable country can eventually be in a position to compete for world power. Moreover, International Relations Theory does not help Third World leaders to reach this healthy conclusion, but rather tends to encourage the search for other avenues to power, with greater costs and risks to the world and themselves, and are likely to be painfully unsuccessful.

It is not that political realism does not work, it is not that the world (or certain crucial dimensions of the interstate order) cannot be understood from the perspective of the pursuit of power, but that the pursuit of power includes the pursuit of wealth (and the avoidance of excessive costs). From this point of view, Japan's post–World War II policy has always been "power politics," whereas the development of the Cóndor II and the invasion of the Falklands/Malvinas, which carried more costs than benefits for a peripheral state, were nothing of the sort.

Thus, the traditional distinction between "high politics" and "low politics" is inverted when a time axis is introduced and the analysis becomes dynamic. For the periphery, there is a hierarchy of policy preferences in which the economy takes precedence above politico-military resources. Ultimately, this is the *realist* logic that underlies not only the deactivation and destruction of the Cóndor II missile project, but most of the Menem administration's foreign policy shift away from Argentina's long-standing tradition of political confrontation with the so-called First World.

Delving Deeper into the Issue of "Anarchy" versus "Hierarchy"

The principle stated earlier—if a time axis is included in the realist construct then the economy takes precedence over politico-military resources—is of course universally valid. However, the weaker a country is, the shorter the term for which the sacrifice of the economy becomes intolerable. In other words, although survival is a quest common to states of both the center and the periphery, in the periphery economic factors become a more immediate determinant of survival and of the relative place that the state occupies within the system. As noted ealier, it is my contention that this essential difference leads to a categorization of states that acknowledges *functional* differences between "Great Powers" and "weaker states"; although the difference is one of degree and empirically there exists a continuum, for analytic purposes this dichotomy can be useful.

In their relations with weaker states Great Powers are in a position to link crucial economic issues to desirable political behavior by weaker states and demand political concessions from peripheral governments whose structure of preferences and/or state/society complexes cannot tolerate a high level of costs. For example, the United States was able to link Argentina's admission to the Brady Plan to the deactivation of the Cóndor II missile project.

As suggested before, this difference is sufficiently important to imply that Great Powers and weaker states are not "like units." Contradicting Waltz once again, both formally and informally, each unit is *not* the equal of all the others in interstate political systems. Indeed, on this score Thucydides understood the world better than contemporary neorealists. The strong do what they can; the weak suffer what they must. This implies functional differentiation. This difference between the Great Powers and weaker states implies that the "structure" of the interstate system is not as Waltz describes it, and that there is an incipient hierarchy in the said system. A different operating principle is involved than that of a simple anarchy (as defined by Waltz), or a (somewhat more consolidated and overarching) domestic hierarchy.

My contention (accepting Waltzian semantics), is that for issues related to peace and security (and for them alone) "hierarchy" is a concept that better describes the structure of the interstate system than "anarchy." This is, of course, seen more easily from the periphery than from the center. The role of sanction-linkages as an instrument of enforcement of the hierarchy is also seen more clearly from the periphery than from the center.

Indeed, I find U.S. literature on sanction-linkages ethnocentric to the point of theoretical insufficiency. A case in point is a 1993 article on the effectiveness of sanction-linkages, in which it is stated that although the mechanisms of linkage politics have often been studied, the effectiveness of linkage politics has rarely been explored appropriately.[16] But the author does not even mention another dimension of linkage politics that is even more unexplored—the costs, for the weak, of making the sanction-linkages of the strong *in*effective. In *Power and Interdependence,* Robert O. Keohane and Joseph S. Nye make a similar ethnocentrically derived point. They claim that, with complex interdependence, the effectiveness of the issue-linkages implemented by central states vis-à-vis the Third World is decreasing, hence there is a greater margin for maneuvering by Third World states.[17] This argument fails to consider two facts that, seen from the periphery, would be obvious: first, that the ineffectiveness of sanction-linkages does not mean that sanction-linkages will not be applied by the strong countries, and second, that the costs, for the weak country, of making the sanction-linkages of a strong country ineffective can at times be exceedingly high, to the point that despite the ineffectiveness of the linkage (that is, the strong state does not get what it wanted), the weak state often loses more, at least in relative terms, than the strong state.[18]

Sanction-linkages are therefore an important instrument for the enforcement of hierarchy. And hierarchy goes with functional differentiation. In issues related to peace and security, sanction-linkages will tend to be unidirectional, from the strong to the weak. Strong states tend to be the "initiator states" of sanction-linkages, whereas weak states will tend to be the "target states" of such linkages.

Thus, for issues of peace and security the Waltzian concept of interstate "structure" is better described by the concept of "hierarchy," as Waltz defines it, than by the concept of "anarchy." It is not necessary to study the case of peripheral states to reach this conclusion, but it is certainly easier to perceive from the perspective of the weak rather than that of the strong.

On the other hand, this hierarchy is far less perfect and developed than a domestic hierarchy. There is hierarchy between the Great Powers and the rest of the world, but among the Great Powers there is anarchy. No one will butt in too intrusively to make sure that Japan is not violating the Nuclear Non-Proliferation Treaty (though we often encounter this sort of double standard even in domestic societies, as anyone who lives in Cali, Colombia, and observes the operations of the drug cartel in broad daylight, knows full well).

Thus, states are not "like units": there are rather three types of state in the interstate system: (a) Great Powers and (b) weaker states, which are divided into those that tend to abide by a citizen-centric rationality—that is, avoiding high-cost or high-risk foreign and defense policies in favor of the welfare of its citizens—and those that clearly abandon citizen-centric rationality and play a high-risk game in interstate politics, whereby the level of tolerable costs to its citizenry is very high. In turn, these different types of state are functionally differentiated according to whether they rule, obey, or rebel.

Although a structure of anarchy prevails among them, the Great Powers tend to "rule" over the weaker states on issues related to international peace and security, imposing order on their interrelationships, while the weaker states that do not abide by a citizen-centric rationality and rebel against this "rule" tend to play a destabilizing role in world affairs and contribute to international anarchy. The latter states are the equivalent of outlaws or mafias in domestic societies. The "obedient states," however, are not necessarily renouncing their pursuit of power, but simply adopting a tactic whereby the economic bases of power and welfare take priority and the costs of politico-military rebellion are intentionally avoided. It should be reemphasized that Japan's cooperative postwar policies in the politico-military front—combined with Japanese economic successes—were in essence more clever power-generating policies than anything Saddam, Khadaffi, or Galtieri ever did. This assertion is very much the product of a realist logic.

Thus, Waltz is wrong in assuming that there is no functional differentiation of states. The differences in capabilities—which he acknowledges—are so great that they are translated into functional differentiation. But to understand this it is necessary to overcome Waltz's and Morgenthau's static analysis.[19]

The arguments discussed earlier help to explain why there is less chaos and more order in the real world than one would suppose if anarchy really prevailed in the interstate system. In this respect, the Cóndor II episode illustrates the mechanisms through which the Great Powers usually succeed in imposing their will over weaker states with respect to vital issues related to peace and security. In Europe, Latin America, Africa, and most of the world, the number of middle-class states that have accepted their subordination to the Great Powers in fields such as nuclear and missile development by far outnumber the small group of rebel states.

We can conjecture that the Cóndor II was originally conceived in Argentina as an assertion of sovereignty with a commercial potential, with no clear appraisal of the costs of Great Power reaction. We can further conjecture that important segments of Argentina's political elites (who emphasize the right of a sovereign state to undertake such a project and the impropriety of Great Power interference) would favor the project. However, when both the costs and Argentina's vulnerability to hyperinflation, which ravaged the country in 1989 and 1990, became clearer, and when a new administration that did not need to justify the project's authorship came to power, the tables turned, and cost-sensitivity replaced sovereignty-sensitivity as the main consideration regarding the project.

This change of policy was possible and even predictable because the societal structure of preferences in Argentina hovers somewhere in between that of other middle-class states such as, for example, Canada, Mexico, Australia, or Spain on the one hand, and rebel states such as Iraq or Iran, on the other.[20] The Argentine state has proved more than once that the level of costs it can tolerate is higher than in most of the Western world. It did so when it refused to sign the Nuclear Non-Proliferation Treaty, when it refused to ratify the Tlatelolco Treaty, when it invaded the Falklands/Malvinas, and when it opted for the development of the Cóndor II in complicity with Middle Eastern states and Western smugglers. But it has also demonstrated more than once that the level of costs that it can tolerate—which is limited by the characteristics of its state/society complex—is much lower than those of Iran, Iraq, or Vietnam.

In this sense, we can say that unlike Spain vis-à-vis Gibraltar, the Argentine state invaded the Falklands/Malvinas and accepted a small-scale war with Britain in 1982, but unlike Vietnam or Iraq, it never really contemplated raising the stakes by placing, say, 50,000 or 100,000 Argentine conscripts in the islands to attempt to prevent the British recapture. Such costs, which would be acceptable for the Iraqi or Vietnamese state/society complexes, would be clearly unacceptable to the Argentine complex, no matter what the government. The same cost limitations were again visible in the case of the successive launching and deactivation of the Cóndor II missile project.

In-depth comparative studies of Argentina's culture, political dynamics, and social structure vis-à-vis those of, for example, Canada at one extreme and Iraq at the other, would probably show that these countries differ enormously in terms of the likelihood of high-cost foreign and defense policies. Indeed, the different behaviors of these middle-class states vis-à-vis the interstate system will probably be better explained by domestic factors than by systemic ones.

Conclusions

In my opinion, the arguments developed here suggest that: First, overall, for issues related to peace and security, the interstate order can be better understood in terms of power than through the concepts developed by neoliberal institutionalism. The realist mode of thought appears to have more explanatory potential than the available alternatives. The Menem administration destroyed the Cóndor II not because it wanted to, nor because of a process of mutual adjustment whereby this policy came naturally, but because it decided to avoid the costs of the sanction-linkages that would follow if it persisted with this project. If carried far enough these issue-linkages could have easily ruined the Argentine government's economic program and political prospects, given the fact that the key to the success of a well-drafted economic program in posthyperinflationary Argentina was both external and internal confidence. Putting it bluntly, what destroyed the Cóndor II was U.S. power (coupled with Western support) and the Menem administration's legitimate fears of domestic conflict and instability.

Second, destroying the Cóndor II was a choice, just like launching the project was a choice. Continuing the project was an option open to the Menem government, if it was ready to pay the price. The Menem administration perceived that its success, in the context of the hyperinflationary crisis that it inherited, depended largely on domestic confidence, and that domestic confidence depended in turn on external confidence, mainly from the Western powers. What the Argentine public really cared for was its pocketbook—that is, monetary stability. This is confirmed by the many polls that have attempted to measure the priorities of Argentine public opinion.[21] Therefore, given Argentina's societal structure of preferences, persisting with the Cóndor II project would have been a bad deal for the government. This was clear to the new government, which, not responsible for the launching of the project, could destroy it without losing face. In posthyperinflationary Argentina, public opinion clearly subordinates nationalism to monetary stability and economic well-being, so despite the appeals to nationalism and the cries of outrage of the opposition and of significant segments of the press, in this cultural-political battle the government was clearly the winner, as the 1995 reelection of Menem shows.

Third, despite the fact that the destruction of the Cóndor II was the product of U.S. pressure, it ended as it did because of Argentina's structure of social preferences (and the government's perception of this structure). If Argentina had not previously undergone a hyperinflationary experience, the structure might have been perceived differently (and might indeed have been quite different), and the government might have opted for a continued challenge to the United States and the MTCR. Similarly, if Argentina had been under a regime that was not dependent on suffrage, and the corporate interests of the military had ruled, the government might have continued with this proliferation project. Therefore, while realist analysis is stronger than other theoretical alternatives, domestic factors explain more than systemic ones. Under an authoritarian regime with a different *state* structure of preferences, the decision would have gone the other way. In this specific case, hyperinflation probably made an important difference, because it generated anger in the population and fear in the government, thus subordinating (though not eliminating) nationalism and changing both the societal and the state structure of preferences.

Fourth, despite the fact that the realist approach to world politics appears more useful for understanding this type of phenomena than the alternative theoretical approaches, the versions of realism and neorealism that have been developed have serious flaws. The Waltzian version of neorealism ignores the actual hierarchy that prevails in the interstate security order. The attribution of an anarchic structure to that order is an important conceptual error that peripheral realism tries to correct.

Fifth, although a middle-class state can break away from the hierarchy if it can tolerate high costs, this does not prove that the rule of hierarchy does not hold. In the present world order, drastic sanction-linkages can even be legal, with UN Security Council support. Regimes related to peace and security with hierarchical arrangements are not "simply once removed" from the power capabilities of the states that conform them, as Waltz has claimed. Wealth and economic development lie at the heart of the generative sources of power, and the link between the economic and the politico-military realms (which are not autonomous) is more immediate for the periphery than for the center. Hence, potential sanction-linkages are an effective mechanism for the enforcement of the hierarchy in the case of most peripheral states (though not of all), and they generate functional differentiation among states. The costs of making sanction-linkages ineffective in issues related to peace and security are so high that most peripheral states will not risk sanction-linkages. The ineffectiveness of sanction-linkages vis-à-vis rebel states does not prove that the hierarchy does not operate in the interstate system, just as in domestic society a hierarchy can be said to be in operation despite the ineffectiveness of criminal law in deterring criminals: Criminal law deters most (though not all) people from committing crimes.

Sixth, the hierarchy that characterizes the distribution of power at a global level when issues related to interstate peace and security are at stake is, however, an incipient and imperfect hierarchy, since among the Great Powers themselves there is anarchy, not hierarchy. As soon as we bring the middle-class state into the picture, we discover an interstate structure of hierarchy and order. We also find that societal structures of preference are a more relevant determinant of foreign policy behavior than systemic variables. These facts are more difficult to perceive when we limit our analysis to central states.

And finally, the inclusion of peripheral states in systemic analysis adds explanatory power to theory because it provides a different prism through which to observe the same phenomena. As I said at the beginning of this chapter, the perspective given by the analysis of interstate phenomena from the periphery, that is, from the perspective of a relative absence of power, helps to redress the narrowness and ethnocentricity of a body of IR Theory that has traditionally been limited to an analysis of "leading states."

Notes

1. "Peripheral" is used here to describe all states that are neither permanent members of the UN Security Council nor economic superpowers such as Germany and Japan. The "periphery" includes both developed and underdeveloped countries. "Third World" is used for the underdeveloped periphery.

2. See Carlos Escudé, *Foreign Policy Theory in Menem's Argentina* (Gainesville, FL: University Press of Florida, 1997).

3. A portion of Argentina's foreign debt was, in fact, later forgiven.

4. U.S. intelligence sources apparently also intercepted an Egyptian smuggling operation related to the Cóndor II. See Leonard S. Spector, *Nuclear Ambitions* (Cambridge, MA: Ballinger/Carnegie Endowment, 1990).

5. After the Cóndor II project was scrapped, Argentina joined the MTCR.

6. Robert W. Cox, "Social Forces, States and World Orders: Beyond International Relations Theory," in *Neorealism and its Critics,* Robert O. Keohane ed. (NY: Columbia University Press, 1986).

7. Stephen D. Krasner, *Structural Conflict: The Third World Against Global Liberalism* (NY: The Regents of the University of California, 1985).

8. This is a major limitation of the realist and neorealist theories coined by such major figures as Hans Morgenthau and Kenneth Waltz, both of whom say explicitly that their theories do not concern themselves with the foreign policies

of weaker states, but only of major powers. Waltz, for example, asserts that it would be ridiculous to build a theory of International Relations based on the cases of Malaysia and Costa Rica. See Kenneth N. Waltz, *Theory of International Politics* (Buenos Aires: GEL [Spanish-language edition], 1988), p. 109.

9. No systemic analysis can explain the Gulf War, and it is much more important to understand why Iraq attacked Kuwait (a phenomenon more related to Iraq's state/society complex than to systemic factors) than to understand why Saudi Arabia does not attack Kuwait (a phenomenon easily explained away by systemic analysis). See Waltz, *Theory of International Politics,* p. 96. On this point, my criticism of Waltz is similar to John Ruggie's: "Waltz reacts strongly against what he calls the reductionist tendencies in International Relations Theory. In the conventional usage . . . he finds that the system is all product and not at all productive. He takes pains to rectify this imbalance. He goes too far, however. In his conception of systemic theory, unit level processes become all product and not at all productive." See John G. Ruggie, "Continuity and Transformation in the World Polity: Toward a Neorealist Synthesis," in *Neorealism and its Critics,* ed. Robert O. Keohane (NY: Columbia University Press, 1986), p. 151.

10. According to Waltz, for the concept of anarchy to apply, the states of the world must be functionally similar sovereign units ("like units" in Waltz's terminology). Despite huge power differentials among them, none must be entitled to command and none must be required to obey.

11. Waltz has said that "formally, each (state) is the equal of all others. None is entitled to command; none is required to obey." Kenneth N. Waltz, *Theory of International Politics* (Reading, MA: Addison-Wesley, 1979), p. 114.

12. There may be good diplomatic reasons for not emphasizing this formal inequality that for many in the Third World is an unfortunate and "disgraceful" fact, but then we should not even pretend that International Relations is a science, but rather a scholarly extension of diplomacy. This omission by Anglo-American International Relations theorists is only one of several other omissions and logical flaws. There is also a clear reluctance by diplomats and theoreticians to acknowledge the inequality of states (including the unequal measure of their respective "sovereignties"). Contrariwise, there has been a generalized complacency with the myth of anarchy and with the ideology of sovereignty (a magical quality that all states supposedly share in equal measure, and which makes it possible for Waltz to make his far-fetched claims about the functional similarity of *all* states).

13. Kenneth A. Oye, "Explaining Cooperation Under Anarchy: Hypotheses and Strategy," *World Politics,* (October 1985), p. 1. Emphasis added.

14. Hans J. Morgenthau, *Politics Among Nations: The Struggle for Power and Peace* (NY: A. A. Knopf, 1948), p. 5.

15. Krasner tells us that Third World leaders seek power in the interstate system because their states are domestically weak and need to promote more advantageous interstate regimes, without even stopping to consider the costs of confronting the industrialized world, and thereby limiting the issue of costs to the

costs of acquiescing with the existing order. For Third World leaders, the normative implication of Krasner's analysis is to rebel against the existing order. This implication, if followed up, makes Waltz's anarchy a self-fulfilling prophesy insofar as it encourages confrontation (indeed, even if we leave Krasner out and limit ourselves to the normative implications for Third World leaders, in Morgenthau's analysis, the implicit advice is still to engage in traditional power politics, instead of developing the state's power base through an emphasis on economic growth). However, this criticism of Krasner cannot go too far because the regimes he uses as examples when he speaks of a "structural conflict" between the industrialized countries and the Third World, are always economic ones. Nonetheless, he never makes the distinction between economic regimes and regimes linked to peace and security. He seems to include the confrontations of countries like Iraq and Iran with the West as a part of the so-called structural conflict. His generalization that Third World states seek not only wealth but power, which is his starting point, leads us in that direction, and has perverse normative implications.

16. Chien-pin Li, "The Effectiveness of Sanction-Linkages," *International Studies Quarterly* (September 1993), pps. 349–70.

17. Robert O. Keohane and Joseph S. Nye, *Power and Interdependence,* second editon (Boston: HarperCollins, 1989). See especially the table on p. 37.

18. This was clearly the case with the relations between Argentina and the United States during World War II, when the latter applied devastating economic and political sanctions in order to force the former to break relations with the Axis powers and to side unambiguously with the democracies. The history of those years can be summarized in a long list of ineffective sanction-linkages implemented by the United States. This failure, however, had little or no costs for the United States, while the Argentine "success" at making U.S. sanction-linkages *in*effective meant the ruin of Argentina's economy and the destruction of its political system. See Carlos Escudé, *Gran Bretaña, Estados Unidos y la Declinación Argentina, 1942–1949* (Buenos Aires: Belgrano, 1983). There is a version in English, *The Argentine Eclipse: The International Factor in Argentina's Post World War II Decline,* Ph.D. dissertation, Yale University, 1981.

19. A similar argument is made by Helen V. Milner: "For Waltz, domestically force is less important as a means of control and is used to serve justice; internationally, force is widespread and serves no higher goal than to serve the state using it. But is the importance of force so different in the two realms? . . . It may be that norms and institutions are more prevalent forms of control domestically than internationally. But this depends on the state in question. . . . Since at times the frequency of violence domestically is acknowledged, perhaps the point is that force is legitimate and serves justice domestically and not internationally. Again, this depends upon the perceived legitimacy of the government and the particular instance of use. Have the majority of people in the Soviet Union, Poland, Ethiopia, South Africa, Iran, or the Philippines . . . felt that the state's use of force serves justice (all the time? some of the time?)? . . . On the other hand, does force never serve justice internationally?" Helen V.

Milner, "A Critique of Anarchy," in *International Politics,* eds., Robert J. Art and Robert Jervis (NY: HarperCollins, 1992), p. 32.

20. As understood here, a "societal structure of preferences" is the average of individual structures of preference, pondered by the degree of inequity of the specific political system and social structure.

21. This has come out throughout the 1990s in probabilistic surveys conducted by the Gallup Institute of Argentina, by Mora y Araujo, Noguera y Asociados, and by other major Argentine pollsters.

Bibliography

Books and Articles on International Relations Theory Relevant for this Discussion

Brown, Chris. *International Relations Theory: New Normative Approaches.* NY: Columbia University Press, 1992.

Bull, Hedley. *The Anarchical Society: A Study of Order in World Politics.* NY: Columbia University Press, 1977.

Carr, Edward H. *The Twenty Years' Crisis.* London: Macmillan, 1969.

Connor, Walker. "Nation-Building or Nation-Destroying?" *World Politics.* Vol. 24 (April 1972), pps. 319–55.

Cox, Robert W. *Production, Power and World Order: Social Forces in the Making of History.* NY: Columbia University Press, 1987.

———. "Social Forces, States and World Orders: Beyond International Relations Theory." In *Neorealism and its Critics.* Ed. Robert O. Keohane. NY: Columbia University Press, 1986.

Escudé, Carlos. *Foreign Policy Theory in Menem's Argentina.* Gainesville, FL: University Press of Florida, 1997.

Gilpin, Robert. *War and Change in World Politics.* Cambridge, U.K.: Cambridge University Press, 1981.

Grieco, Joseph. *Cooperation Among Nations.* Ithaca, NY: Cornell University Press, 1990.

Haggard, Stephen. *Pathways from the Periphery: The Politics of Growth in the Newly Industrializing Countries.* Ithaca, NY: Cornell University Press, 1990.

Hoffmann, Stanley. "International Relations: An American Social Science." In *Janus and Minerva.* Boulder, CO: Westview, 1987, chap. 1.

Katzenstein Peter, ed. *The Culture of National Security: Norms and Identity in World Politics.* NY: Columbia University Pres, 1996.

Keohane, Robert O. and Joseph S. Nye. *Power and Interdependence: World Politics in Transition.* Boston: Little, Brown and Co., 1989.

Krasner, Stephen D. *Structural Conflict: The Third World Against Global Liberalism.* Berkeley: The University of California Press, 1985.

———, ed. *International Regimes.* Ithaca, NY; Cornell University Press, 1983.

Midlarsky, Minus L. *The Onset of World War.* Boston: Unwin Hyman, 1988.

Milner, Helen V. "A Critique of Anarchy." In *International Politics*. Eds. Robert J. Art and Robert Jervis. NY: HarperCollins, 1992.

Morgenthau, Hans J. *Politics Among Nations: The Struggle for Power and Peace*. NY: Alfred P. Knopf, 1948.

Rosecrance, Richard. *The Rise of the Trading State: Commerce and Conquest in the Modern World*. NY: Basic Books, 1986.

Rosenau, John N. *The Study of Global Interdependence: Essays on the Transnationalization of World Affairs*. London: Frances Pinter Publishers, 1980.

Ruggie, John G. *The Antinomies of Interdependence*. NY: Columbia University Press, 1983.

Snyder, Jack. *Myths of Empire: Domestic Politics and International Ambition*. Ithaca, NY: Cornell University Press, 1991.

Stein, Arthur A. *Why Nations Cooperate*. Ithaca, NY: Cornell University Press, 1990.

Tilly, Charles. "War Making and State Making as Organized Crime," In *Bringing the State Back In*. Eds. Peter B. Evans, Dietrich Rueschemeyer and Theda Skocpol. Cambridge, U.K.: Cambridge University Press, 1985.

Viner, Jacob. "Power versus Plenty as Objectives of Foreign Policy in the Seventeenth and Eighteenth Centuries," *World Politics*. Vol. 1, no. 1 (October 1948), pps. 1–29.

Kenneth N. Waltz, *Theory of International Politics*. Reading, MA: Addison-Wesley, 1979.

———. *Man, the State and War: A Theoretical Analysis*. NY: Columbia University Press, 1954.

Wendt, Alexander. "Anarchy is What States Make of It: The Social Construction of Power Politics." *International Organization*. Vol. 46, no. 2 (Spring 1992), pps. 391–425.

Special October 1985 issue of *World Politics*, dedicated to the theme "Cooperation under Anarchy," with articles by Kenneth A. Oye, Duncan Snidal, Robert Jervis, Robert Axelrod, and Robert O. Keohane, among others.

Books and Articles on Argentina's Foreign Relations Relevant for this Discussion

Bouzas, Roberto and Roberto Russell, eds. *Estados Unidos y la Transición Argentina*. Buenos Aires: Legasa, 1989.

Domínguez, Jorge I., ed. *International Security and Democracy in Latin America and the Caribbean*. Pittsburgh, PA: University of Pittsburgh Press, 1998.

Escudé, Carlos. *La Rinconquista Argentina: Scuola e Nazionalismo*. Fiesole, Italy: Edizione Cultura della Pace, 1992a.

———. *Realismo Periférico: Fundamentos Para la Nueva Política Exterior Argentina*. Buenos Aires: Planeta, 1992b.

———. "Education, Political Culture and Foreign Policy: The Case of Argentina." Working Paper No. 4. Duke/UNC Chapel Hill Program on Latin American Studies. Durham, NC, 1992c.

————. "Argentina: The Costs of Contradiction." In *Exporting Democracy: The United States and Latin America.* Ed. Abraham F. Lowenthal. Baltimore, MD: Johns Hopkins University Press, 1991.

————. "U.S. Political Destabilization and Economic Boycott of Argentina During the '40s." In *Argentina Between the Great Powers, 1939–46.* Eds. Guido di Tella and D. Cameron Watt. London: Macmillan, 1989.

————. *Gran Bretaña, Estados Unidos y la Declinación Argentina, 1942–1949.* Buenos Aires: Belgrano, 1983.

Garzón Valdés, Ernesto, Manfred Mols, and Arnold Spitta, eds. *La Nueva Democracia Argentina.* Buenos Aires: Sudamericana, 1988.

Lanús, Juan A. *De Chapultepec al Beagle: Política Exterior Argentina, 1945–1980.* Buenos Aires: Emecé, 1984.

Russell, Roberto, ed. *La Política Exterior Argentina en el Nuevo Orden Mundial.* Buenos Aires: GEL, 1992.

Spector, Leonard S. *Nuclear Ambitions.* Cambridge, MA: Ballinger, 1990.

————. *Going Nuclear.* Cambridge, MA: Ballinger, 1987.

————. *The New Nuclear Nations.* NY: Vintage Books, 1985.

Tulchin, Joseph S. *Argentina and the United States: A Conflicted Relationship.* Boston: Twayne Publishers, 1990.

FOUR

The Primacy of Internal War

Steven R. David

Internal war needs to be of central concern to students of International Relations. War has always been a principal area of study for International Relations scholars and internal war is the wave of the future. For those concerned with global security, world order is threatened more by wars occurring within countries than among them. Nevertheless, our old tools are not fully adequate to understanding the causes and consequences of internal war. We remain focused on the study of interstate war, despite its diminishing importance. This chapter seeks to correct this imbalance by contributing to the effort to make internal wars understandable.

Internal war (defined as armed conflict occurring principally in one state causing at least 1,000 battlefield deaths per year) plays a pivotal role in world politics for several reasons. First, internal wars are commonplace. Of the more than 150 wars occurring after World War II (resulting in the deaths of some 23 million people), the great majority have been internal wars of one type or another.[1] Unlike wars between states, no one suggests that internal wars are becoming obsolete, cannot take place in democracies, or will diminish in the post–Cold War era. Internal war threatens key countries of the international system such as the People's Republic of China and Russia. Vital interests including access to imported oil and protection from nuclear attack are threatened by the prospect of internal war. Internal conflict is often at the root of humanitarian disasters including the killing of large numbers of innocents, massive migration, famine, and environmental degradation. For all of these concerns, the threat posed by internal war is almost always greater than that posed by outside states. Even for those who insist on focusing on interstate conflict there is no escaping the importance of internal war, which often is a principal cause of why states go to war with one another. Finally, internal war is a critical determinant of the behavior of states that it afflicts. Ignoring its impact means overlooking a principal cause of why states act as they do.

Despite its significance, internal war was given relatively little attention during the Cold War.[2] With the state seen as the primary actor in international affairs, and the Soviet threat looming, internal wars were consigned to those interested in country studies or the analysis of tactics in "low intensity" conflicts. Recently, however, there has been a new emphasis on internal war. Issues related to internal war such as the emergence of ethnic nationalism and the demands of peacekeeping have received a great deal of attention.[3] Moreover, a spate of articles and books have appeared that look at internal conflict as a nihilistic response to the breakdown of society.[4] Despite this work, our understanding of internal war remains very limited.

Given the primacy of internal war, it is imperative to understand its causes and cures. The literature on the causes of internal war and, more generally domestic violence, provides some useful insights, but it points in all directions. Internal war is seen as stemming from individual calculation by some, group calculation by others. It is rational and purposeful or emotional and nihilistic. It can be suppressed only through the application of superior power or the inculcation of values. What's worse, the empirical record supports (and contradicts) each of these approaches.[5]

A more promising avenue is the use of realism, and particularly its modern variant of neorealism, to make internal war understandable. Three of realism's fundamental insights are relevant to understanding internal war. Realism's emphasis on human nature as being fixed and flawed explains much about the brutality and persistence of civil conflict. Because people are forever trying to take advantage of one another, because (as Thucydides noted some 2500 years ago) they are driven by "fear, honor, and greed," in the pursuit of "security, glory and gain," peace can never be guaranteed.[6] Realism, and especially neorealism, emphasizes the centrality of anarchy in conflict. That some wars occur because there is nothing to stop them is as true for conflict within states as it is among them. Finally, neorealism focuses on balances of power. Discouraging a potential adversary from taking a certain action because the costs of doing so will be greater than the gains is as relevant for internal war as it is for interstate conflict.

Many neorealists are wrong, however, to assume that anarchy exists among states while order predominates within them. It is more accurate to assume a world of international order and domestic anarchy where the greatest threat to most states, including some of the principal powers of the international system, stems from developments within states rather than external to them.[7] Viewing the state as a microcosm of the international system seemingly makes neorealism as relevant for intrastate conflict as it is for interstate war. In fact, since violent conflict is far more common within states than among them, neorealism may be even more important for explaining domestic war than interstate war. For neorealists, internal wars happen for much the same reasons that wars between states happen. People or groups seeking to maximize their interests unchecked by any coercive power will conflict with one another. Internal wars are stopped when one group becomes powerful enough to impose its will on all challengers. Key neorealist concepts such as balance of power and the security dilemma are therefore as applicable to internal wars as they are for interstate conflicts.

Even with this fundamental revision, however, neorealism is unable to explain many internal wars fully. The emphasis of many neorealists on parsimony, generalizable propositions, and material interests leaves it ill-equipped to deal with the messy phenomenon of internal war. Understanding the motivations for why subnational groups go to war requires examination of such factors as religion, ideology, and the idiosyncratic interests of individual leaders. Values that inhibit or encourage rebellion irrespective of prospects of success are also critical in making internal war understandable. Generalizing about such diverse factors, and basing such generalizations upon considerations of power alone, misunderstands or ignores much of what is central to internal war. Moreover, because anarchy on the domestic level is not quite the same as anarchy on the international level, many of the implications of neorealism simply do not apply to what happens within states.

Repairing the defects in neorealism requires studying states that have fought internal wars or been threatened by them, especially in recent times. The experience of the Third World is particularly useful in this regard. An examination of the history of the Third World confirms that it is necessary to broaden neorealism to include the impact of internal war not only to understand domestic conflict itself, but also to explain why states act as they do. The experience of the Third World also demonstrates that the likelihood of internal war depends on more than simply the power of the state to compel obedience. By drawing our attention to how power is created and the motivations for obeying or defying governmental rule, developments in the Third World highlight factors critical for explaining internal war that are largely absent from a neorealist analysis. While a broadened neorealist approach is a useful way to begin to explain internal war, the experience of the Third World cautions us that it will rarely be sufficient.

My argument is in three parts. First, I consider various approaches for understanding internal war with a special emphasis on neorealism. Second, I explain how the experience of the Third World demonstrates the inadequacy of even a broadened version of neorealism. Finally, I propose some areas for future research on the causes and cures of internal war.

Explaining Internal War

The central importance of internal war makes it crucial to understand its causes.[8] There are a vast number of theories that purport to explain internal war including those that focus on individual calculation of self-interest, groups seeking collective gains, frustration, loss of respect for the government, and the sheer joy of killing. Although these approaches come to differing conclusions regarding the sources of domestic conflict, each contains insights that help explain the origins of internal war.

The belief that internal war stems from the rational calculation of individual self-interest was most persuasively expressed by Thomas Hobbes. Hobbes argued that people naturally seek to gain at the expense of others. Where there is no power to ensure order, people live in a constant state of fear that they will be attacked by their neighbors. In such an environment, there are no opportunities for individuals to better themselves and instead they are condemned to a miserable life. The solution to this unhappy state of affairs is for people to agree to obey the orders of a sovereign to whom they bestow absolute authority. The sovereign, in return, exercises its coercive power to ensure an environment under which people are safe from one another and free to pursue their self-interests. Internal war results when enough people believe that the sovereign can no longer provide them with the safety they require. The key to preventing internal war, therefore, is for a government to retain enough coercive power to discourage any would-be challengers to the existing order.[9]

Another set of theories, best exemplified by Charles Tilly, argues that it is not the individual but the group that serves as the source of internal war. Internal war is seen as a normal form of behavior by groups seeking to maximize their long-term interests. In this view, groups in power seek to maximize their collective interests by attempting to remain in power while groups out of power seek to maximize their collective interests by seizing power. Internal wars are most likely to begin when the incumbents' hold on power is weakened, thus creating an opportunity for their replacement. Because efforts to gain power are seen as purposeful and rational, a government can forestall internal war by convincing potential challengers they will not be successful. The key distinction with Hobbes is that for Tilly, it is necessary to convince *groups* that it is not in their *collective* interest to challenge the government as opposed to convincing individuals that it is not in their individual interest to do so. While violence is seen by Tilly as one of many tactics groups use to advance their goals, it is also one of the most effective. That violence works explains a good deal of its popularity.[10]

A third set of theories purporting to explain internal war are those that see frustration or relative deprivation as the key cause. Ted Gurr, one of the principal authors of this approach, argues that when an individual gets less than he or she believes they are rightfully entitled to, the result is frustration leading to violence. The prospects for violence increase when individuals believe they have a right to engage in violence and when they believe that violence will be effective in meeting their ends. The effectiveness of violence, in turn, will depend greatly on the balance of power between the insurgents and the regime. Weak challenges that do not threaten the government will produce few benefits, while serious threats are likely to achieve their goals.[11] In a similar vein, James Davies argues that revolutions occur after a long period of rising expectations that are met, followed by a sharp reversal in which expectations are not fulfilled. Davies argues his theory explains (among other events) the Russian Revolution of 1917, the Egyptian revolution of 1952, and the U.S. Civil War.[12] Samuel Huntington sees frustration deriving from inadequate institutionalization. Modernization mobilizes people to make political demands that, if not channeled appropriately by institutions, leads to violence and internal war. The high levels of violence in many developing societies such as Iran, Iraq, and China lends credence to this approach.[13]

Gurr's argument that a belief in the right to rebel enhances the prospects for internal war highlights the role of values in explaining civil conflict. From this perspective, internal war results not so much from people believing they can gain from toppling the government as it does from the belief that they are justified in seeking its overthrow. The belief in the justifiability of revolt can come from many sources. As the French sociologist Emile Durkheim argued, increased specialization in advanced societies destroys the moral compass that is necessary to check the selfish pursuit of private interest. If society cannot enforce the sense of values that promote a sense of self-restraint, the likely result is internal war.[14] Relatedly, people are less likely to revolt against governments they perceive as legitimate. The source of that legitimacy will be different in different societies as Max Weber's famous typology of charismatic, traditional, and bureaucratic forms of authority attests. Whatever the basis of legitimacy may be, what is critical in explaining the outbreak of internal war is not the raw power of the government to impose its wishes, but the belief of the people in the government's right to act as it does.[15]

Not all the theories of internal war explain it in rational, utilitarian terms. There is a long tradition that sees the motivation for internal war and domestic violence more generally, as emotional and nihilistic. One of the first to consider the nonrational motivations for domestic violence was the turn-of-the-century thinker Gustave LeBon, whose work *The Crowd* discussed how people in mobs could be swept away by emotion to act in ways they would not do so individually.[16] More recently, the seemingly senseless conflicts in Lebanon and western Africa have placed renewed attention on the irrationality of internal war. For the German theorist, Hans Enzensberger, much of internal war is about, "nothing at all" except violence as an end in itself.[17] This view is echoed by Martin Van Creveld who sees internal wars stemming from people fighting for the sheer joy of killing.[18] With governments increasingly unable to deal with problems of environmental degradation and population growth, Robert Kaplan argues, the distinction between widespread crime and internal war will disappear, and both will spread from the Third World to the West.[19]

The psychology of conflict, particularly conflict among similar groups, also purports to explain internal war. While there has been a great deal of contemporary work on why groups go to war with each other,[20] it is useful to go back to Sigmund Freud's "narcissism of minor differences" to understand why people who seemingly have so much in common, hate each other with unrestrained passion. According to Freud, "it is precisely the minor differences in people who are otherwise alike that form the basis of feelings of strangeness and hostility between them."[21] Freud seems to explain civil conflict stemming from this characteristic when he states, "It is always possible to bind together a considerable number of people in love so long as there are other people left over to receive the manifestations of their aggressiveness. I once discussed the phenomenon that it is precisely communities with adjoining territories, and related to each other in other ways as well, who are engaged in constant feuds and in ridiculing each other—like the Spaniards and Portuguese, for instance, the North Germans and South Germans, the English and Scotch. . . . We can now see that [it is through the] inclination to aggression, by means of which cohesion between the members of the community is made easier."[22]

In more contemporary times, Michael Ignatieff has invoked the "narcissism of small differences," to explain the ferocity of conflict in the Balkans between peoples who have much more in common with each other than they do with anyone else.[23] It may be that it is the similarities among us that threaten peoples' sense of identity and distinctiveness that is a greater source of conflict than our differences.

As persuasive as they may be, there are several problems with these approaches. First, they contradict one another. Is internal war the result of individual or group calculation? Is it rational and purposeful or emotional and nihilistic? Do people rebel because they believe the government's coercive power is on the wane or because they no longer view its exercise of power as legitimate? Second, the theories are so general that it is unclear how much they really explain. Any internal war can be explained after the fact by asserting that people were frustrated, or lost confidence in their government, or were driven by emotion. These feelings or beliefs are always present and the approaches tell us little why they sometimes produce internal war and sometimes do not. Finally, cases can be found to disprove each of these approaches. Changes in coercive abilities of governments often do not produce internal war (for example, witness Germany after World War I and Italy after World War II), many societies undergoing rapid modernization did not experience internal war (Taiwan, South Korea, Brazil), some internal conflicts are indeed purposeful (Iran) while others defy logic (Lebanon, Liberia), people very much alike often do not go to war with one another (for example, the Scandinavians) while people who are very different do (the United States and Japan during World War II). These approaches seemingly tell us little about how to think about internal war.

There is, however, a theme that underlies most of these efforts to explain internal war. Simply put, internal war is most likely when people believe they will benefit by its outcome and have a right to engage in it.[24] This formulation incorporates theories that focus on the group and the individual as well as those emphasizing power and values. Only the theories emphasizing the irrational and emotional bases of internal war are not covered, but that is no great loss since such domestic conflicts tend to have the least international effect. It remains to be seen how focusing on this utilitarian and normative view of domestic conflict can generate insights that explain the causes and consequences of internal war better than other approaches.

Neorealism

Although a theory usually associated with interstate behavior, realism has much to offer in making internal war understandable. In particular, realism explains much of why internal wars occur and provides useful prescriptions for how to stop them. Realism is an especially powerful tool in understanding the utilitarian side of internal war—why people feel they are likely to gain or lose in attacking the government. Realism is, inadequate, however, for dealing with the normative aspects of internal war—why people feel they are or are not justified in fighting.

Realism is a view of the way the world works. The modern versions that grew out of European history following the 1648 Treaty of Westphalia assume that states are the principal actors in the international system, that they are responsible for preserving their own security, and that they will seek to expand their power and/or combine with other states to prevent the preponderance of potentially threatening adversaries. Because human nature is imperfect and because there is no overarching authority to adjudicate conflicts that will inevitably arise, the threat of war or its actual occurrence is an ever present feature of international politics. Neorealism in particular emphasizes the importance of the international system in constraining the behavior of states as opposed to factors within the states themselves. Because neorealism has emerged as the dominant theory of International Relations, my efforts to repair realism's standing will focus on this approach.[25]

Although neorealism focuses on interactions among states, there is no reason that it cannot be modified to apply to domestic affairs, particularly internal war. Doing so requires a fundamentally different understanding of anarchy. Neorealists are correct to see anarchy not as chaos, but as the absence of a central authority capable of enforcing rules. Most neorealists are wrong, however, to assume that anarchy exists among states while order predominates within them. It is more accurate to assume a world of international order and domestic anarchy where the greatest threat to most states, including some of the principal powers of the international system, stems from internal challenges. The notion of applying neorealism to the domestic arena is not as far fetched as it may appear. "Classical" realists such as Thucydides, Machiavelli, and Thomas Hobbes focused as much on struggles for power and survival within states as among them.[26]

More contemporary realists recognize that the international dimension of politics—especially where the use of force is concerned—is not all that different from the domestic arena. As Hans Morgenthau writes, "The essence of international politics is identical with its domestic counterpart. Both domestic and international politics are a struggle for power, modified only by the different conditions under which this struggle takes place in the domestic and international spheres." For Morgenthau the "different conditions" are that the state is characterized by a "strong consensus and the normally unchangeable power of a central government."[27] Clearly, for cases where internal war breaks out, those different conditions no longer obtain. Kenneth Waltz recognizes that violence is more likely within some states than between them. This makes it impossible to draw a "distinction between the two realms [of domestic and international] . . . in terms of the use or the nonuse of force." For Waltz nonetheless, the focus on the state is justified because the central government can command the obedience of different groups under its authority. Presumably, this would no longer hold in the event of internal war. In fact, Waltz acknowledges that neorealist theory applies to political *units,* whether states or other groupings.[28]

These insights are directly relevant to understanding the causes and cures of internal war. Like Alexander the Great cutting the Gordian knot, neorealism slices through the muddled complexities of the causes and cures of internal war to produce insights of startling simplicity. For neorealists, the absence of any overriding authority to impose order means that conflicts will occur. Wars happen because there is nothing to stop them. As Barry Posen argues, under conditions of anarchy, groups and states behave in ways that are more alike than different: "In areas such as the former Soviet Union and Yugoslavia, 'sovereigns' have disappeared. They leave in their wake a host of groups—ethnic, religious, cultural—of greater or lesser cohesion. These groups must pay attention to the first thing that states have historically addressed—the problem of security—even though many of these groups still lack many of the attributes of statehood."[29]

Posen goes on to assert that a key concept of realism—the security dilemma—comes into play when states disintegrate. The security dilemma, that is, efforts to improve one's security heightens concerns among others ultimately lessening one's security, is likely to be especially acute in the wake of imperial collapse. Whether one considers this warfare between newly emerging states or internal warfare is largely a semantical question. Just as anarchy leads states to protect themselves with consequences that may inadvertently lead to interstate warfare, so too does the collapse of authority lead groups within states to take measures to defend themselves with consequences that may lead to internal warfare, regardless of whether that was their original intention.[30]

Neorealism is not only useful in explaining why internal war breaks out, it also provides useful insights into how to stop internal wars. Since internal war stems from imperfect human nature and anarchy, and since it is impossible to change human nature, the neorealist response to internal war is to eliminate anarchy. While this has been impossible on the level of the international system, it is quite feasible on the level of the state. Following from Hobbes, the neorealist answer to internal war is the emergence of a central government strong enough to take on all challengers. If the existing regime lacks the coercive capability to remain in power, it will be replaced by one that can. When potential rebels recognize they cannot achieve their interests by violence, there will be no violence (or, at the very least, it will be short-lived). The beauty of the response generated by the neorealist approach is that it should provide effective solutions regardless of the source of the challenge to the government. It does not matter if individuals feel insecure, if groups lack access to governmental rule, if people are frustrated or simply hate their neighbors. Whatever their grievance, people will not violently challenge the government if they recognize that they will not gain—and indeed may be severely punished—if they do so.

Neorealism offers two broad approaches for outside states seeking to establish strong governments in countries wracked by internal war. Since anarchy lies at the root of internal war, an outside power that is willing to pay the price to assert control and restore a centralized government can end the domestic strife. Syria terminated more than a decade of civil war in Lebanon by occupying much of the country and forcing the belligerents to obey its dictates—a policy that the United States ultimately did not follow in Somalia. In addition, an outside state can act to tilt the local balance of power in such a way as to allow one side to impose a settlement. Richard Betts argues this path is often far better for outside states to follow than to allow a conflict (such as the one in the former Yugoslavia) to go on indefinitely.[31]

Neorealism thus provides useful insights into the causes and cures of internal war. Removing the artificial constraints of a state-centered approach enables scholars and policymakers to draw upon neorealism's strengths to help make internal war understandable. As impressive as a broadened realist approach is to deciphering the complexities of internal war, however, it is far from sufficient. It is necessary to examine the experience of countries afflicted with internal war to determine what neorealism can—and cannot—explain.

Advantages and Limitations of Neorealism

The Third World is a good place to look to demonstrate the value and limitations of transposing neorealism to the domestic arena in unstable states.[32] While internal wars are just now emerging as the dominant form of conflict in the developed world, they have been by far the most frequent form of conflict in the Third World for the past 40 years. Virtually every Third World state has experienced internal war or been threatened by it. Internal wars have toppled far more Third World regimes than have fallen due to outside invasion. The origins and consequences of internal wars that have occurred in the Third World bear a strong resemblance to conflicts being fought in the Balkans and the former states of the Soviet Union. Instead of the Third World "developing" to where Eurocentric theories become applicable, many "developed" states are reaching the point in which the Third World experience has become applicable to them. This is not to deny the profound differences among many Third World states and those of East Asia and Central Europe. Clearly, the latter have higher levels of per capita income, education, and industrialization than is the case with most Third World states. But once threatened by internal war, the differences between these states become less important than the shared vulnerability of their regimes to domestic strife. Any effort to explain internal war, therefore, ought to draw upon the record of the Third World.

The Third World provides several fundamental lessons that show why it is necessary to broaden neorealism to include internal threats. First, the experience of the Third World demonstrates how the threat of internal war drives the behavior of states in ways not predicted or explained by contemporary realist theory. If internal war continues to threaten so many states, including major powers, ignoring its impact on state behavior will seriously undermine our understanding of International Relations.

In particular, the record of the Third World shows the central role played by domestic threats in causing *leaders* to act as they do. This focus on leaders is critical because once a state undergoes or is threatened by internal war, it ceases to act as a coherent unit. The appropriate level of analysis is no longer the state, but the leadership. Heads of state confronting an internal war will do what they can to remain in power. Understanding why leaders make the decisions they do, therefore, requires asking what the interests of the leaders are not what the interests of the state are. This is especially true when internal war threatens the survival of the leadership. Very few leaders need to worry about losing their country—the mortality rate for states is very low. It is reasonable to assume, however, that leaders do worry about the much more common prospect of being removed from power by domestic challenges. By focusing on the state as opposed to the leadership, and by emphasizing external threats while ignoring domestic ones, neorealism misses what drives leaders confronting internal war to make the decisions they do. This is seen by examining the central role played by internal threats in explaining why leaders align as they do, go to war, foster nationalism, and resist free trade. States whose leaders are threatened by internal war call into question one of the core assumptions of neorealist theory, namely that countries balance against their most powerful or most threatening *external* adversary.[33] Neorealism cannot explain why many developing states aligned with countries that threatened their security. Prominent examples of what is called "bandwagoning" behavior include Sadat's Egypt turning to the United States following the 1973 October War, and Ethiopia under Mengistu aligning with the Soviet Union in the mid-1970s. What does explain this seeming violation of balance of power logic is that it makes sense for leaders facing internal threats to align with threatening states, if by doing so they can undermine more pressing domestic challenges. In the case of Ethiopia, for example, the belief by Mengistu that Moscow could halt a revolt in the secessionist province of Eritrea that threatened his hold on power—a rebellion that the Soviet Union did much to create—played a major role in his decision to turn to the Soviet Union.[34] As both David Kaiser and Michael Doyle show, European leaders before the formation of strong states also aligned in ways to give priority to preserving their *personal* security from internal threats over protecting their state from external challenges.[35] Ignoring internal threats, therefore, will often mean ignoring the most powerful determinant of a leader's alignment decision.[36]

The concern for leadership survival in the face of domestic threats also explains much of why countries afflicted by internal conflict go to war with other states for reasons that are often ignored by neorealists. Neorealism asserts that a major reason (though not the only one) that states go to war is to guarantee their independence and security. The greatest concern of states is to ensure that no other state or group of states becomes so powerful as to threaten their existence. The Third World experience, however, demonstrates that concerns for leadership security are at least as powerful an explanation for going to war with other countries as are concerns for state security. If a leadership decides that making war will enhance its prospects of remaining in power by, for example, deterring internal conflict, the prospects for war will be high.[37] Saddam Hussein's 1990 invasion of Kuwait stemmed far more from his need for financial resources to deal with domestic challenges than it did from any Kuwaiti threat to Iraqi security.[38] Egypt's Anwar Sadat attacked Israel in 1973 not because Jerusalem posed any external threat, but because a continued stalemate threatened to provoke internal conflict in Egypt that endangered Sadat's rule.[39] Understanding when a state will go to war, therefore, requires more than simply looking at the balance of power among states. It is also necessary to look at the balance of power *within* states, as well as any ethnic, religious, or economic tensions that may drive a leadership to war.[40]

Why leaders seek to foster nationalism—a major source of conflict—is another area where neorealism's ignoring of the threat posed by internal war prevents it from explaining why states behave as they do. Some neorealists argue that leaders engender nationalism for reasons of national security. Barry Posen, for example, asserts that leaders incite nationalism because they recognize that mass armies are a potent weapon and that their best protection from other states with mass armies is to develop mass armies themselves. Since the development of mass armies requires nationalism and since the principal determinant of state behavior is protection from other states, leaders will have little choice but to cultivate nationalist fervor in order to create their own mass armies.[41] While this analysis may hold true for some European states, it fails to explain or predict the behavior of most Third World countries. The experience of Third World states demonstrates that by and large they do not develop mass armies. Most Third World leaders recognize they do not need mass armies because they do not face major threats from outside states. More important, Third World leaders recognize that because the principal threats they do face are internal, the development of a mass army will, in many cases, exacerbate those threats rather than undermine them. Neorealist predictions based on the European experience of state to state threats, therefore, will not hold for much of the Third World.[42]

If concerns over internal security call into question neorealist explanations for the behavior of Third World states in the fostering of nationalism, so too should it call into question neorealist explanations for the fostering of nationalism in non–Third World states threatened by internal strife. The conflict in the Balkans is a case in point. There is no doubt that leaders of the former Yugoslavia, particularly Serbian head Slobodan Milosevic, helped cause the Balkan wars by inflaming ethnic nationalism. Why did they do this? For many neorealists, the answer is simple. Rabid nationalist appeals were made to mobilize support in order to better protect the fledgling states from aggressive neighbors.[43] A more persuasive argument, however, looks at internal threats to understand why leaders fostered nationalism. This approach argues that Milosevic (and others) provoked ethnic conflict in order to remain in power. The chief threats to their staying in office lay not with other countries, but with non-Serbian groups within the state. Recognizing that it was impossible to hold onto power in a multiethnic Yugoslavia with a Serbian minority, they deliberately fostered a racist nationalism that resulted in the replacement of most of Yugoslavia with a state with a clear Serbian majority.[44]

Neorealists are correct that nationalism, in part, stems from concerns about security, but when the principal threats are internal, domestic considerations explain the fostering of nationalism far better than do threats from other states. By focusing on threats of external war over internal war, and state security over leadership security, neorealist analysis misses the essence of why explosive nationalism leading to war emerged in the former Yugoslavia and will miss much of what happens in other states where the threat of internal war looms large.

The threat of internal war also plays a major role in determining a state's economic policies. Neorealists are correct to assert that security—not efficiency—is the prime goal of states. As such, free trade that jeopardizes a state's key industries or allows potential adversaries to become *relatively* stronger may not be in a state's interests even if the economy of the state gains in an absolute sense. But a state's economic policies are not only driven by concerns of external threats. As some neorealists recognize, it often will make sense for a state to sacrifice efficiency to deal with the threat of internal war as well. Better to subsidize an inefficient group of producers than face the threat of a violent challenge to the regime. Protectionist policies, therefore, often make sense and indeed are practiced by many countries threatened by internal strife.[45]

Similarly, Stephen Krasner argues that the economic behavior of Third World governments can only be understood in terms of their political weakness. Third World leaders need resources to deal with domestic challenges, but they do not seek a free market regime that would maximize wealth for all. Instead, the leaders recognize that their position in power will best be secured by an authoritative system that gives control of resources to the leadership, which can then use them to stave off internal threats. Third World leaders (and presumably any weak leaders endangered by internal threats) resist free market regimes, therefore, because they recognize that while maximizing wealth may be in the interests of the state, it is not in their *personal* interests if it deprives the leaders of control over how the wealth is distributed. In international economics as well as politics, it is impossible to explain why states beset with internal threats act as they do unless the impact of those threats are taken into account.[46]

Another lesson from the Third World is that if neorealists are correct that the key to order is the existence of strong central governments, then we can expect internal war to persist in the Third World and elsewhere for a long time. The Third World experience demonstrates that the origins of internal war are intimately related to the development of the state—an area largely ignored by neorealists. As Charles Tilly has argued, the states of Western Europe emerged as strong, cohesive units only after a brutal evolutionary process of several centuries of conflict. Warfare not only weeded out the weak, it also enhanced the power of the strong. It did so by fostering a sense of identity and impelling the state to extend its control over the people in order to collect taxes and draft available manpower to meet external challenges. Although the great majority of states did not survive this ordeal, those that did emerged strong enough to deter or discourage serious internal threats. As Tilly observed, "War made the state, and the state made war."[47]

Unlike Western Europe, however, the newly emerging states of Central Europe and elsewhere are not likely to evolve into powerful entities free from the threat of internal conflict. It took Europe centuries to evolve to the point in which internal war ceased to be a danger. It is difficult to ask the newly emerging states to deal with domestic instability any more quickly, especially given the problems of poverty, ethnicity, and demands for mass participation that they must confront.[48] Moreover, as Robert Jackson points out, leaders no longer have to fear the loss of their state because the international community is committed to their existence. The incentive to strengthen the state in order to deal with external threats is consequently absent.[49] Even when efforts to increase the power of the state are attempted, they are not likely to be successful when undertaken by countries plagued with internal conflict. Unlike the strength enhancing effect of interstate warfare, internal conflict weakens the state over the long term by interfering with taxation and undermining attempts by the state to penetrate the society it seeks to control.[50] Only a major external shock can provide developing states with the impetus to centralize control, but the lack of interstate war to provide such a shock and the relatively low numbers of bureaucrats skillful enough to take advantage of one should it occur, make the prospects for establishing strong governments bleak.[51] Insofar as the experience of the Third World is a guide to the newly emerging states of Central Europe, the prognosis for peace and stability is bleak.

The role that power has played historically in the Third World calls into question central neorealist assumptions that limit the ability of this approach to make internal war understandable. Neorealists rely on superiority or at least a balance of power to discourage aggression. You do not go to war because it is likely you will lose. But as the pervasive instability in the Third World demonstrates, coercing internal peace over the long term is an expensive and often losing proposition. Literally hundreds of regimes armed with tools of repression have been forcibly removed in the Third World while others are subject to constant attack and threat. If lack of power were at the root of all these violent challenges then the neorealist response of somehow restoring central control would indeed be the correct one. But without minimizing the importance of coercion, the record of Third World instability indicates that other forces are at work in deterring internal war. If a government is legitimate—whether its power can be converted to authority—is clearly a central factor in explaining why internal war does or does not occur. The legitimacy of Costa Rica's regime allows it to be free from the threat of internal war despite maintaining weak suppressive capabilities. The illegitimacy of Saddam Hussein's regime makes it a constant target of domestic conflict, despite its wielding of a brutally effective internal security force. As Rousseau remarked, "the strongest is never strong enough to be always the master, unless he transforms strength into right and obedience into duty."[52] How states and societies can develop the values necessary to make civil conflict unthinkable is a key issue that is largely ignored by neorealists.[53]

Concerns over legitimacy reveal a broader problem with the neorealist approach to internal war. As the Third World experience demonstrates, the range of motivations for subnational groups to fight with one another or to challenge the government are virtually limitless. No doubt, many internal wars are driven by concerns for security and power and neorealism has much to say about their causes and cures. But a great number of internal wars are also driven by religious concerns (witness Islamic extremists in Algeria and Egypt), by ideology (for example, the struggles to remove or place in power Communist regimes during the Cold War), by ethnic hatred (Rwanda, the Balkans), and by the joyful excitement of fighting (an important reason why the Liberian civil war lasted as long as it did). It is true that concerns over power, security, and territory are present in every internal war and neorealism speaks to that. But to argue that these material interests are all that is necessary to explain why internal wars begin and how to end them is to fly in the face of history and common sense.

The experience of the Third World calls into question the neorealist notion that anarchy is an underlying cause of internal war. According to neorealist reasoning, the collapse or weakening of central authority is what makes war possible both on the international and state levels. In many internal wars, however, neorealist logic is reversed. It is the *strengthening* of central authority—rather that its weakening or collapse—that is often the permissive cause of internal war. Domestic conflict begins more by governments seeking to destroy suspected insurgents than it does from insurgents challenging governments. Just as states do not embark on wars they believe they will lose, so it is with governments. They tolerate threats to their rule if they cannot eliminate them, but make war on those challengers when they believe themselves strong enough to do so. Thus, for example, Ethiopia's internal war against Eritrea in the 1970s became far more intense *after* the Mengistu regime was strengthened by Soviet arms and advisers.[54] Because neorealism emphasizes the absence of a central authority to impose order as a cause of war, it has little to contribute to explaining those internal conflicts that occur in the wake of the strengthening of the state.

Neorealism similarly fails to explain the vast majority of internal wars that take place where strong central governments continue to exist. As the record of the Third World illustrates, most internal wars do not take place in states where there is no central authority to impose order. Instead, the greatest number of internal wars occur where effective governments are present. Internal wars in places as diverse as Nicaragua, Cambodia, and Iraq where powerful regimes preside are far more common than internal wars in places such as Liberia and Somalia where the neorealist assumption of anarchy is largely met. Moreover, even where domestic anarchy does emerge as a trigger of war, neorealism tells us nothing about how the collapse of governmental authority came about in the first place. For International Relations theorists, anarchy can be taken as a given. For students of internal war, however, how anarchy arises is a central problem that neorealism does little to illuminate.

Lessons from the Third World provide guidance—not suggested by neorealism—for outside states seeking to bring about the negotiated end of internal conflicts. Ending internal wars by negotiation is particularly difficult.[55] Only one-third of internal wars are settled by negotiation as compared to two-thirds of interstate conflicts.[56] The principal reason for the lack of negotiated settlements is that the adversaries, who have to live with each other after the war ends, find it difficult to reach agreements with guarantees they can trust.[57] The experience of the Third World suggests that outside powers can overcome this lack of trust in two ways. First, they can reassure the belligerents by guaranteeing the terms of the settlement. International treaty commitments to protect minorities, the dispatch of international peacekeeping forces, and outside monitors to police elections can all help to overcome the suspicions of the parties of the conflict. Such efforts helped bring about settlements of domestic conflicts in Haiti, Cambodia, and Angola. This use of multilateral tools and institutions to facilitate a settlement is largely absent from neorealist analyses.[58] Second, rather than tilt the balance of power to allow one side to dictate a settlement, outside states can work to create a situation in which neither side is preponderant. This produces what I. William Zartman calls a "mutually hurting stalemate" that provides incentives for agreement. American assistance to the Nicaraguan Contras arguably created such a stalemate, with free elections and the settlement of the civil war as the outcome. This kind of approach is likely to take some time and result in a large degree of suffering. But it has the advantage of requiring less of a commitment from an outside state than would be the case with an imposition of a settlement and it forces the belligerents to come up with their own solutions for living together once the fighting stops.[59]

Finally, the Third World experience calls into question neorealist and other analyses that assume that internal war is an unwelcome development that must be halted at all costs. The greatest threat to most of the people in the Third World comes not from internal war, but from their own leaders. Violent resistance is frequently the only way that groups can free themselves from the murderous tyranny their governments inflict upon them. According to R. J. Rummel, more than 169 million people have been killed by their own governments this century. This dwarfs the figure of 38.5 million killed in international and civil wars during the same period.[60]

Rarely, however, is internal war seen as a positive development by neorealists and others, as a means of removing horrific regimes or providing autonomy for repressed peoples. Instead, works on internal war tend to focus on the need of states to centralize power to enable them to defeat domestic challenges. It is understandable why many in the international community seek to bring an end to internal wars given their proclivity to spread and the humanitarian disasters they often leave in their wake. This does not justify, however, the assumption that the creation of strong governments capable of ending internal conflict is a goal that the international community should always embrace.

The Third World experience does not invalidate the use of neorealist theory to explain internal war. Neorealism, modified to recognize the sometime anarchy of the domestic realm and the role of domestic threats in driving regime behavior, remains a parsimonious and powerful tool for making some internal wars understandable. Even with these modifications, however, the record of the Third World shows that neorealism is better at explaining the actions of groups after state collapse than it is at explaining why the collapse occurred at all. Nor is neorealism much help in explaining internal wars that occur following the strengthening of central governments rather than their weakening or in explaining internal wars that stem from nonmaterial factors. Just how useful the neorealist approach will be for internal wars will vary from situation to situation. It is best to begin with an expanded view of neorealism and then bring in other approaches (comparativist, historical, sociological) as specific cases warrant.

Suggestions for Future Research

The persistence of internal war as the dominant form of armed conflict combined with the inadequacy of existing approaches for explaining its causes and cures means that much work remains to be done. The experience of the Third World provides a rich empirical base that has gone largely untapped for making internal war understandable. The insights generated from the Third World experience should be applicable both for Third World states and for countries not usually associated with the Third World but that nevertheless find themselves wracked by internal conflict.

As a first step, less emphasis needs to be placed on developing broad generalizations that purport to explain all internal wars. Comprising revolutions, insurgencies, civil conflicts, and secessionist struggles, internal war is too diverse a phenomenon to lend itself to parsimonious theory. It is better to concentrate on differentiating internal wars by type and seeing what kinds of contingent generalizations emerge. Chaim Kaufmann's essay that differentiates internal wars based on ethnic strife (such as Rwanda and Burundi) from those fought over ideological issues (such as Cambodia and Nicaragua), which argues that outside military intervention can succeed in ending the former type of conflict but not the latter is a good example of this kind of effort.[61] Other categories for study can include internal wars whose origins are mass-based versus elite-driven, wars fought for territory as opposed to political control, and wars in which outsiders played a major role and those where they did not. Making these distinctions will be difficult and scholars will have to scrupulous in applying objective criteria over the range of cases. What is lost in parsimony will hopefully be made up in better explanations for the very different conflicts that make up internal war.

The impact of internal war on world stability also warrants additional study. The greatest threat to key members of the international system today comes less from other states than from domestic conflict. China and Russia, for example, are far more vulnerable to internal war than they are from outside invasion. The impact on other states of the unraveling of the Great Powers from civil war is a key area of inquiry that has gone largely unnoticed. More generally, we need to do more to understand the threats to global stability from unintended harm. Traditionally, states worried about being attacked by other states. Now, they need to worry about the consequences of internal wars spreading beyond the borders of the countries in which they take place. The threat of a Soviet nuclear strike becomes one of "loose nukes" in a chaotic Russia, fear of an oil embargo is replaced by destruction of oil facilities in Saudi Arabia consumed by internal conflict, concern for a Warsaw Pact invasion of Western Europe is transformed to concern for an invasion of refugees fleeing civil strife. Much thinking needs be done on the effect of these and other "nondeterrable" threats on global stability.

Finally, more thought needs to be given to devising solutions to internal wars that do not assume the primacy of the nation-state. As evidenced by the number of collapsed states in Africa and the persistence of ethnic and other conflicts throughout the world, it is not clear that a European-style state is the desired end result for all peoples. As discussed by Jeffrey Herbst, other forms of political control based on regional, local, or mixed authority need to be given further thought.[62] Experimentation with other types of political organization has risks, of course. But the state has already failed many in the Third World and is failing many of those outside the Third World as well. Far better to try new approaches not grounded in the experience of eighteenth-century Europe that at least have the possibility of responding to the very different problems posed by internal war today.

While the outbreak of internal war will always be unthinkable for some states, no country will ever be immune from its effects. Internal war will continue to drive the behavior of states it threatens while affecting the interests of other countries. Coping with the implications of internal war will never be easy. It will become impossible if academics and policymakers ignore the lessons of the Third World and continue to place the threat of interstate warfare at the center of their concerns.

Notes

1. Ruth Leger Sivard, *World Military and Social Expenditures 1993* (Washington, DC: World Priorities, 1993), p. 21.
2. There was an early spate of interest in the 1960s that produced some interesting volumes. See, for example, Harry Eckstein, ed., *Internal War: Problems and Approaches* (Glencoe, IL: The Free Press, 1964); and *International Aspects of Civil Strife* (Princeton, NJ: Princeton University Press, 1964). Two more recent works of note are James B. Rule, *Theories of Civil Violence* (Berkeley, CA: University of California Press, 1988); and Ted Robert Gurr, "On the Outcomes of Violent Conflict," in *Handbook of Political Conflict: Theory and Research,* ed., Ted Gurr (NY: The Free Press, 1988), pps. 238–94.
3. Recent works on nationalism include Anthony D. Smith, *National Identity* (Reno, NV: University of Nevada Press, 1993); Michael E. Brown, ed., *Ethnic Conflict and International Security* (Princeton, NJ: Princeton University Press, 1993); Liah Greenfeld, *Nationalism: Five Roads to Modernity* (Cambridge, MA: Harvard University Press, 1992); and Benedict Anderson, *Imagined*

Communities: Reflections on the Origin and Spread of Nationalism, revised ed. (London: Verso, 1991). Less recent but still valuable is Ernest Gellner, *Nations and Nationalism* (Oxford: Basil Blackwell, 1983). On peacekeeping, see William Durch, ed., *The Evolution of UN Peacekeeping* (NY: St. Martin's Press, 1993); and *Peacekeeping and the U.S. National Interest,* Report of the Working Group on Peacekeeping and the U.S. National Interest, co-chaired by Senator Nancy L. Kassenbaum and Representative Lee H. Hamilton. Stimson Center Report no. 11, (February 1994).

4. See, for example, Martin Van Creveld, *The Transformation of War* (NY: The Free Press, 1991); Hans Magnus Enzensberger, *Civil Wars: From L.A. to Bosnia* (NY: New Press, 1994); and Robert Kaplan, "The Coming Anarchy," *Atlantic Monthly,* 273 (February 1994), pps. 44–76.

5. Some principal approaches toward understanding internal war include Thomas Hobbes, *Behemoth, or the Long Parliament,* second edition, ed. Ferdinand Tonnies, (London: Frank Cass, 1969); Thomas Hobbes, *The Leviathan,* ed., C. B. McPherson (NY: Penguin, 1968); Charles Tilly, Louise Tilly, and Richard Tilly, *The Rebellious Century* (Cambridge, MA: Harvard University Press, 1975); and Ted Robert Gurr, *Why Men Rebel* (Princeton, NJ: Princeton University Press, 1970). For an excellent overview of different theories of internal war with an emphasis on sociological explanations, see James B. Rule, *Theories of Civil Violence.*

6. The sheer rottenness of human nature is a theme of the two classics of realism, Thucydides, *The Peloponnesian War* (Baltimore, MD: Penguin, 1975), and Hans Morgenthau and Kenneth Thompson, *Politics Among Nations,* sixth edition (NY: Knopf, 1985).

7. The reversal of second and third images is found in the work of several scholars focusing on unstable states. See, for example, Robert Jackson, "Why Africa's Weak States Persist: The Empirical and Juridical in Statehood," *World Politics,* vol. 35, no. 1 (1982), pps. 1–24; Barry Buzan, *People, States and Fear: The National Security Problem in International Relations* (Chapel Hill, NC: University of North Carolina Press, 1983); and Mohammed Ayoob, "Security in the Third World: The Worm About to Turn," *International Affairs,* vol. 60, no. 1 (1983/84), pps. 41–51.

8. One of the best discussions of the various causes of internal war (along with their shortcomings) is found in James Rule, *Theories of Civil Violence,* upon which much of the following section is based.

9. Hobbes's arguments on internal war are put forth best in *Behemoth or The Long Parliament* and *The Leviathan.*

10. Some important works by Charles Tilly include, "The Changing Place of Collective Violence," in *Essays in Theory and History: An Approach to the Social Sciences,* ed., Melvin Richter (Cambridge, MA: Harvard University Press, 1970); "Does Modernization Breed Revolution," *Comparative Politics,* vol. 5 (April 1973), pps. 425–47; and *From Mobilization to Revolution* (Reading, MA: Addison-Wesley, 1979).

11. Ted Robert Gurr, *Why Men Rebel.*

12. James Davies, "Toward a Theory of Revolution," *American Sociological Review,* vol. 27 (February 1962), pps. 5–19; and James Davies, "The J-Curve of Rising and Declining Satisfaction as a Cause of Revolution and Rebellion," in *Violence in America: Historical and Comparative Perspectives,* eds., Ted Gurr and Hugh Davis (Beverly Hills, CA: Sage, 1979).

13. Samuel Huntington, *Political Order in Changing Societies* (New Haven, CT: Yale University Press, 1968).

14. Emile Durkheim, *The Division of Labor in Society* (Glencoe, IL: The Free Press, 1960 [orig. 1893]).

15. Max Weber, *From Max Weber: Essays in Sociology,* trans. and intro. by Hans Gerth and C. Wright Mills (NY: Oxford University Press, 1946).

16. Gustave LeBon, *The Crowd: A Study of the Popular Mind* (NY: The Viking Press, 1960).

17. Enzensberger, *Civil Wars,* pps. 28, 30.

18. Martin Van Creveld, *The Transformation of War,* (NY: The Free Press, 1991) pps. 225–26.

19. This gloomy forecast is one of the central arguments of Kaplan, "The Coming Anarchy," pps. 44–76.

20. Lewis Coser and Ted Gurr are best at explaining the psychological roots of civil conflict. See, for example, Lewis Coser, *The Functions of Group Conflict* (NY: The Free Press, 1964); Ted Gurr, *Why Men Rebel;* and Ted Gurr, ed., *Handbook of Political Conflict: Theory and Research* (NY: The Free Press, 1988).

21. Sigmund Freud, *The Five Lectures on Psycho-Analysis* [1909] in *The Standard Edition of the Complete Psychological Works of Sigmund Freud,* vol. 11, (London: Hogarth Press, 1971), p. 199.

22. Sigmund Freud, *The Future of an Illusion* [1927], in *Standard Edition,* vol. 21, p. 114.

23. Michael Ignatieff, *Blood and Belonging: Journeys into the New Nationalism* (NY: Farrar, Straus, and Giroux, 1993), pps. 21–28.

24. For a similar conclusion, see Edward N. Muller, "The Psychology of Political Protest and Violence," in *Handbook of Political Conflict,* ed., Ted Gurr, p. 97.

25. The founding view of neorealism comes from Kenneth Waltz, *Theory of International Politics* (Reading, MA: Addison-Wesley, 1979). Modern realism also stems from the classic work by Hans Morgenthau and Kenneth Thompson, *Politics Among Nations,* sixth edition (NY: Knopf, 1985). In general, Morgenthau emphasizes human nature as the root cause of conflict while Waltz emphasizes international anarchy.

26. Thucydides, *The Peloponnesian War* (NY: Penguin Classics, 1985); Niccolo Machiavelli, *The Prince* and *The Discourses* (NY: Modern Library, 1950); Thomas Hobbes, *Leviathan.* See also E. H. Carr, *The Twenty Years Crisis, 1919–1939: An Introduction to the Study of International Relations* (London: Macmillan 1939).

27. Morgenthau and Thompson, *Politics Among Nations,* pps. 39, 190.

28. Kenneth Waltz, *Theory of International Politics,* pps. 103, 89.

29. Barry R. Posen, "The Security Dilemma and Ethnic Conflict," in *Ethnic Conflict and International Security,* ed., Michael E. Brown (Princeton, NJ: Princeton University Press, 1993), p. 104.

30. Posen, "The Security Dilemma and Ethnic Conflict," pps. 104–5. The notion of the security dilemma comes from Robert Jervis, "Cooperation Under the Security Dilemma," *World Politics,* vol. 30, no. 2 (January 1978), pps. 167–213.

31. Richard Betts, "The Delusion of Impartial Intervention," *Foreign Affairs,* vol. 72, no. 6 (November-December 1994), pps. 20–33.

32. With the demise of the "Second World," the term, *Third World,* is especially problematic. For the purposes of this essay, I include in the Third World all countries *except* the United States, the European republics of the former Soviet Union, Canada, Japan, Australia, New Zealand, the European states, and the People's Republic of China. Despite the vast differences among Third World states, I maintain that states traditionally characterized as "Third World" maintain enough similarities (for example, they are relatively young states, have a colonial past and immature political institutions, and are peripheral to world politics) to justify considering them together. On this issue, see Christopher Clapham, *Third World Politics* (Madison, WI: University of Wisconsin Press, 1985).

33. For balancing based on the capabilities of other states, see Hans Morgenthau and Kenneth Thompson, *Politics Among Nations,* esp. ch. 11. For balancing based on the threat posed by other states, see Stephen M. Walt, *The Origins of Alliances* (Ithaca, NY: Cornell University Press, 1987), esp. pps. 21–26.

34. For background on why Mengistu aligned with the Soviet Union, see Marina Ottaway, *Soviet and American Influence in the Horn of Africa* (NY: Praeger, 1983); David A. Korn, *Ethiopia, the United States and the Soviet Union* (Carbondale, IL: Southern Illinois University Press, 1986); and Colin Legum and Bill Lee, *The Horn of Africa in Continuing Crisis* (NY: Africana, 1979).

35. David Kaiser, *Politics and War: European Conflict from Philip II to Hitler* (Cambridge, MA: Harvard University Press, 1990), esp. ch. 1; Michael Doyle, "Politics and Grand Strategy," in *The Domestic Bases of Grand Strategy,* eds. Richard Rosecrance and Arthur A. Stein (Ithaca, NY: Cornell University Press, 1993), pps. 26–31.

36. The tendency of leaders to align so as to counter their most pressing threat, be it domestic or international, which may result in leaders aligning with hostile states to better deal with immediate internal dangers, is a phenomenon that I call, "omnibalancing." See Steven R. David, "Explaining Third World Alignment," *World Politics,* vol. 43 (January 1991), pps. 223–56.

37. For a persuasive argument that domestic threats (presumably including internal war) to a leadership can lead to interstate war, see Richard Ned Lebow, *Between Peace and War: The Nature of International Crisis* (Baltimore, MD: Johns Hopkins University Press, 1981), pps. 66–69. According to Lebow, two major incentives for leaders to provoke a confrontation are the weakness of the political system and one's own political vulnerability.

38. The view that Saddam Hussein invaded Kuwait to preserve his rule is best expressed by Lawrence Freedman and Efraim Karsh in *The Gulf Conflict 1990–1991* (London: Faber and Faber, 1993), esp. chapters. 2 and 3. For how Saddam has tailored his policies to ensure his personal survival, see Samir al-Khalil, *Republic of Fear* (Berkeley, CA: University of California Press, 1989).

39. On Sadat's concern for internal conflict leading to the 1973 war, see Anwar el-Sadat, *In Search of Identity: An Autobiography* (NY: Harper and Row, 1978); Alvin Z. Rubinstein, *Red Star on the Nile: The Soviet Egyptian Influence Relationship since the June War* (Princeton, NJ: Princeton University Press, 1977); Raymond William Baker, *Egypt's Uncertain Revolution under Nasser and Sadat* (Cambridge, MA: Harvard University Press, 1978); and Raymond A. Hinnesbusch, Jr., *Egyptian Politics under Sadat* (Cambridge: Cambridge University Press, 1985).

40. For a similar view, see K. J. Holsti, "International Theory and War in the Third World," in *The Insecurity Dilemma*, ed., Brian Job.

41. Barry R. Posen, "Nationalism, the Mass Army, and Military Power," *International Security*, vol. 18, no. 2 (Fall 1993), pps. 80–124. For another view that emphasizes the need to engender nationalism for national security purposes, see John Mearsheimer, "Back to the Future: Instability in Europe After the Cold War," *International Security*, vol. 15, no. 1 (Summer 1990), pps. 5–56.

42. Alexander Wendt and Michael Barnett argue that the absence of mass armies in the Third World stems from colonialism, which created weak states led by illegitimate regimes that could not afford to bear the risk posed by mass armies. See Wendt and Barnett, "Dependent State Formation and Third World Militarization," *Review of International Studies* (1993), pps. 321–47.

43. This view is consistent with both Barry Posen and John Mearsheimer's arguments. See Posen, "Nationalism, the Mass Army, and Military Power," and John Mearsheimer, ""Back to the Future."

44. The case for Serbian nationalism resulting from Milosevic's desire to remain in power is made by many. Some persuasive examples are V. P. Gangon, Jr., "Ethnic Nationalism and International Conflict: The Case of Serbia," *International Security*, vol. 19, no. 3 (Winter 1994/95), pps. 130–66; Aleks Djilas, "A Profile of Slobodan Milosevic," *Foreign Affairs*, vol. 72, no. 3 (Summer 1993) pps. 81–96; Misha Glenny, *The Fall of Yugoslavia: The Third Balkan War* (NY: Penguin, 1992).

45. Susan Strange makes this point in "Protectionism and World Politics," *International Organization*, vol. 39, no. 2 (Spring 1985), pps. 233–60. See also, Robert Gilpin, *The Political Economy of International Relations* (Princeton, NJ: Princeton University Press, 1987), esp. chs. 1, 2, 5.

46. Stephen Krasner, "Power vs Wealth in North-South Economic Relations," in *International Politics: Enduring Concepts and Contemporary Issues,* third edition, eds., Robert Art and Robert Jervis (NY: HarperCollins, 1992), pps. 267–86.

47. Charles Tilly, "Reflections on the History of European State Making," in *The Formation of National States in Western Europe,* ed., Charles Tilly (Princeton, NJ: Princeton University Press, 1975). The quotation is from p. 42.

48. One of the best accounts of the problems that are encountered when state building is telescoped into a short time can be found in Mohammed Ayoob, "The Security Problematic of the Third World," *World Politics,* vol. 43, no. 2, (January 1991), pps. 257–83. Ayoob focuses on the difficulties that Third World leaders have in trying to undertake state building and nation building simultaneously, but his pessimistic outlook holds for new states outside the Third World as well.

49. Robert Jackson, *Quasi-States: Sovereignty, International Relations and the Third World* (Cambridge, MA: Cambridge University Press, 1990).

50. Jeffrey Herbst makes these points with regard to Africa. See Jeffrey Herbst, "War and the State in Africa," *International Security,* vol. 14, no. 4 (Spring 1990), pps. 117–39.

51. Joel S. Migdal, *Strong Societies and Weak States: State-Society Relations and State Capabilities in the Third World* (Princeton, NJ: Princeton University Press, 1988), pps. 262–76.

52. Quoted in Huntington's *Political Order in Changing Societies,* p. 9.

53. Some principal works that address this issue are Talcott Parsons, *The Structure of Social Action* (NY: McGraw-Hill, 1937) and Max Weber, *The Theory of Social and Economic Organization,* ed., Talcott Parsons (Glencoe, IL: The Free Press, 1964). For an overview of problems of political development for the Third World, see Brian L. Job, ed., *The Insecurity Dilemma,* esp. chapters by Mohammed Ayoob and Robert Jackson.

54. The intensification of the Ethiopian war against Eritrea *after* the strengthening of the Mengistu regime is discussed in Paul B. Henze, *Russians and the Horn: Opportunism and the Long View,* European-American Institute for Security Research, The EAI Papers, no. 5 (Marina del Ray, CA: European-American Institute, 1983).

55. There is a large literature on how to end internal wars through negotiations. See, for example, Richard A. Falk, *The International Law of Civil War,* (Baltimore, MD: Johns Hopkins University Press, 1971); Roy Licklider, ed., *Stopping the Killing: How Civil Wars End* (NY: New York University Press, 1993); Paul R. Pillar, *Negotiating Peace: War Termination as a Bargaining Process* (Princeton, NJ: Princeton University Press, 1983); William Zartman, ed., *Negotiating Internal Conflicts* (Columbia, SC: University of South Carolina Press, 1993); I. William Zartman, ed., *Negotiating an End to Civil Wars* (Washington, DC: Brookings, 1995); and Barbara F. Walter, *The Resolution of Civil Wars: Why Incumbents and Insurgents Fail to Negotiate,* unpublished thesis, University of Chicago, 1994.

56. Paul R. Pillar, *Negotiating Peace,* p. 25; and Roy Licklider, "How Civil Wars End: Questions and Methods," in *Stopping the Killing,* ed., Roy Licklider, p. 8.

57. Barbara F. Walter, *The Resolution of Civil Wars,* pps. 3–4.

58. Ibid., p. 29.

59. I. William Zartman, "The Unfinished Agenda," in *Stopping the Killing,* ed., Roy Licklider, p. 24.

60. R. J. Rummel, *Death by Government* (New Brunswick, NJ: Transaction, 1994), chap. 1.

61. Chaim Kaufmann, "Possible and Impossible Solutions to Ethnic Civil Wars," *International Security,* vol. 20, no. 4 (Spring 1996), pps. 136–75.
62. Jeffrey Herbst, "Responding to State Failure in Africa," *International Security,* vol. 21, no. 3 (Winter 1996/97), pps. 120–44.

Bibliography

Ayoob, Mohammed. "The Security Problematic of the Third World." *World Politics.* Vol. 43 (January 1991), pps. 257–83.

Betts, Richard. "The Delusion of Impartial Intervention." *Foreign Affairs.* Vol. 72 (November-December 1994), pps. 20–33.

Buzan, Barry. *People, States and Fear: The National Security Problem in International Relations.* Chapel Hill, NC: University of North Carolina Press, 1983.

David, Steven R. "Explaining Third World Alignment." *World Politics.* Vol. 43 (January 1991), pps. 233–56.

Eckstein, Harry, ed. *Internal War: Problems and Approaches.* NY: The Free Press, 1964.

Enzensberger, Hans Magnus. *Civil War.* London: Granta Books, 1994.

Gurr, Ted, ed. *Handbook of Political Conflict: Theory and Research.* NY: The Free Press, 1988.

———. *Why Men Rebel.* Princeton, NJ: Princeton University Press, 1970.

Hobbes, Thomas. *Behemoth or the Long Parliament,* second edition. Ed. Ferdinand Tonnies. London: Frank Cass, 1969.

Hungtington, Samuel. *Political Order in Changing Societies.* New Haven, CT: Yale University Press, 1968.

Jackson, Robert. *Quasi-States: Sovereignty, International Relations and the Third World.* Cambridge: Cambridge University Press, 1990.

Job, Brian, ed. *The Security Dilemma.* Boulder, CO: Lynne Rienner, 1992.

Licklider, Roy, ed. *Stopping the Killing: How Civil Wars End.* NY: New York University Press, 1983.

Migdal, Joel. *Strong Societies and Weak States: State-Society Relations and State Capabilities in the Third World.* Princeton, NJ: Princeton University Press, 1988.

Morgenthau, Hans and Kenneth Thompson. *Politics Among Nations,* sixth edition. NY: Knopf, 1985.

Posen, Barry R. "The Security Dilemma and Ethnic Conflict." In *Ethnic Conflict and International Security.* Ed. Michael E. Brown. Princeton, NJ: Princeton University Press, 1993.

Rule, James B. *Theories of Civil Violence.* Berkeley, CA: University of California Press, 1988.

Tilly, Charles, ed. *The Formation of National States in Western Europe.* Princeton, NJ: Princeton University Press, 1975.

Waltz, Kenneth. *Theory of International Politics.* Reading, MA: Addison-Wesley, 1979.

FIVE

International Relations Theory and Domestic War in the Third World: The Limits of Relevance

K. J. Holsti

Theories of International Relations were developed primarily in the European context. While there are examples of non-European systematic thought about the relations between independent communities—the works of Kautilya and Thucydides come to mind—the large corpus of work that has focused on the causes of war and the conditions of peace, security, and order has predominately European roots.[1] The main texts of contemporary realist and neorealist thought find their intellectual sources in the analyses of Rousseau, Meinecke, von Gentz, E. H. Carr, and Hans Morgenthau. The precursors of contemporary liberal strands of thinking on International Relations include Jeremy Bentham, the Mills, John Cobden, and Woodrow Wilson.

The backdrop for the theoretical efforts of these analysts was the European states system and the chronic incidence of war that took place within it. If the purpose of the analysis was predominately diagnostic—locating the sources of war—then the place to look, argued Rousseau and the others, was primarily to the relations between the Great Powers of the era in which they wrote. Those whose purposes were not only diagnostic but also prescriptive, spoke of balances of power within Europe, concerts of the Great Powers within Europe, disarmament among the European Great Powers, or collective security organizations organized and run predominantly by Europeans. Wars and security problems in other areas of the world received scant attention and were seldom culled for examples, illustrations, or comparative materials until well after World War II.

The history of the academic discipline of International Relations reflected the Eurocentric character of theory. It developed as a distinct field of study first in the United States, and soon thereafter in the United Kingdom. Aside from international law, it found few homes in universities in the rest of Europe and in Japan until after World War II. In post-1945 countries, it has developed slowly and unevenly.

This situation raises a dilemma. Since 1945, the main arena of international armed conflict has been in what was conventionally termed the Third World, and in the post–Socialist states. Most wars in these domains have been internal, not between states.[2] Yet, International Relations Theory developed and proliferated primarily in Europe, and focused primarily on the problem of war between states. Immediately, then, we have to raise questions about the capacity of experts in International Relations Theory, whose intellectual roots are European and international, to guide us in understanding the etiology of contemporary armed conflicts that are located in areas outside of Europe and that involve problems of relations primarily within states rather than between states. Is it the case, however, that classical and contemporary International Relations theories have little to tell us about the new kinds of wars?

International Theory and the Peripheries

Until the rise of dependency theory in the 1970s, no Western analyst attempted to configure a theory of international politics that would incorporate the perspectives and actions of peripheral states, particularly those of what came to be known as the Third World.[3] There were notable analyses of imperialism by J. A. Hobson (1938), and Lenin (1939) and other Marxists, but their ideational structures followed the Eurocentric pattern. Imperial relations were relations of centers *to* peripheries, relations of actors *to* objects, and relations of sources and consequences. The colonized areas were simply the locales where the Europeans played out their rivalries, their searches for "gold, god, and glory," and much later during the Cold War, their ideological competition.

The main currents of contemporary International Relations Theory subsumed under the titles realism and liberalism have always been Euro- and Cold-War-centric. Contemporary neorealism starts with the assumption that all states are fundamentally similar, and that the *real* problem of International Relations is war between the Great Powers. Kenneth Waltz's declaration that a theory of international politics is a theory of the relations among the Great Powers is notable for its clarity of expression.[4] In the statement, he is merely summarizing the practice of all realist thinkers about International Relations. The peripheries are simply unimportant, indeed invisible. Neoliberal theories similarly seek to explain primarily the nature of relations between modern industrial countries of the North. The terminology used in these efforts reflects the world that is being explored: "complex interdependence," "international regimes," "liberal institutionalism," and the like. Liberals of whatever school may not deliberately exclude 80 percent of the world's population contained in about 140 states, but their studies effectively do so. There is thus little in either realism or liberalism that helps us understand the etiology of war in the peripheries.[5]

Despite ignoring international politics outside of the European/Cold War contexts, most International Relations theorists have presented their descriptive and explanatory structures as universal. Whether realists, liberals, or their neo-progenies, authors do not qualify their generalizations according to time or, in particular, to location. The defining hallmark of International Relations Theory is precisely that it seeks to establish generalizations that transcend time, location, and personality. No author has suggested that his or her explanatory apparatus is confined to a regional or distinct cultural domain, or that patterns of diplomatic behavior in other areas might differ significantly from those observed in the European and Cold War worlds. If states are the critical actors in a global system of anarchy, we would expect behavior to be similar within this single context. Kenneth Waltz's classic theory of international politics carries on a tradition of universalistic thought that started with Rousseau and continues to predominate today. That tradition seeks to describe and explain behavioral patterns that exist anywhere there are sovereign, territorially based states, interacting in an anarchic realm. One does not have to attach names or places to "actors." As long as the "actors" are functionally similar, and as long as they operate within a single domain characterized by anarchy, then their fundamental behaviors should be similar.

But the empirical evidence does not sustain this expectation. For example, the pattern of war since 1945 in the peripheries has been fundamentally different than the pattern of war in Europe between 1648 and 1945. The incidence of interstate war in the Third World has been substantially lower than the incidence of war in Europe.[6] The statistical difference is already notable when we lump together all countries in the Third World. But it becomes particularly startling when we remove the Middle East, a scene of chronic warfare somewhat reminiscent of eighteenth-century Europe. Elsewhere, there have been several regions of peace, if we mean by that term the absence of interstate war. There has been no interstate war involving 1,000 or more casualties in South America since 1941. A similar pattern is found in West Africa and the Caribbean. Yet, millions of women, men, and children have perished through armed violence, and more millions have been displaced as refugees. But they are predominantly the victims of wars within states, not wars between states. Neither neorealism nor neoliberalism has acknowledged these patterns as empirical facts that need explanation.

War figures are the most prominent indicator of the differences between European and Third World historical patterns. There are others as well. Arms races between states are not common in the Third World. Arming of governments is common, however. But the reasons are often different. In European history, competitive arms races were occasioned primarily by security dilemmas between states. Arming in the Third World is designed, in contrast, to protect regimes from civil disturbances, to prop up governments that lack legitimacy, and to coerce various sectors of the population. One only has to look at the deployment of military capabilities throughout most Third World countries to see that their potential targets are domestic rather than external. There are important exceptions, such as Taiwan, Israel, Pakistan, and, in part, India. But the levels of arms in many other countries bear little relationship to external threats. Alliances, such a common feature of the European diplomatic landscape since the seventeenth century, are notable by their absence in most areas of the Third World. So are balances of power, deterrence strategies, and enduring rivalries such as those conducted between France and Spain/Holland in the seventeenth century, France and England in the eighteenth and early nineteenth century, Germany and England in the late nineteenth century, and the United States and the Soviet Union between 1945 and 1989. The search for continental hegemony is rare in the Third World, but was a common feature of European diplomacy under the Habsburg, Louis XIV, Napoleon, Wilhelmine Germany, Hitler, and Soviet Union and, arguably, the United States.

The list of Third World exceptions to the European and Cold War diplomatic and war patterns is so vast that one has to raise the question whether today there really is a single domain of International Relations.[7] It will not do to focus solely on the events in the peripheries that conform to European patterns, for in the larger scheme of things they are exceptions and not typical behaviors. Even where we do find competitive arms racing, balancing, alliances, and other European-type patterns, often their sources are internal. For example, the tensions between India and Pakistan arise significantly if not exclusively from a problem of community definition: is Kashmir a part of the Indian Union, or should it become an independent state (on the grounds that it is a unique and separate "community") or a part of Pakistan (on the grounds that it is part of the Muslim "community" that defines Pakistan)?

The problem of interstate war, defined as the use of organized armed forces by one state against another(s), is not the critical problem facing most Third World and post–Socialist states. It is there in some areas at some times—particularly in the Middle East—but it is not a ubiquitous phenomenon as was war in the eighteenth, nineteenth, and first half of the twentieth centuries in the European and Cold War contexts. If this generalization is essentially correct, then International Relations Theory as it has developed over the past 250 years may be of limited relevance in helping to explain the crucial issues facing contemporary Third World and post–Socialist states. Their essential analytical and political problems are in contrast to classical International Relations Theory's focus on interstate wars; first, the definition and integration of political communities; second, the sustenance of territorial coherence or maintenance of state integrity; third, developing principles of legitimacy; and fourth, economic, social, and political development. These issues are all related in a broader *problematique,* the state-building and sustenance project. External actors are involved in all of these issues, but their role is seldom crucial. If the critical problems facing states during the time of Rousseau and the Mills were deflecting external threats and building systems of peace, their contemporary counterparts are primarily transforming fictional states into real states.

It is not accidental that dependency theory, a set of explanations of the main predicaments of Third World countries, originated in South America and swept the intellectual horizons of many governments, culminating in demands for a New International Economic Order in the 1970s and 1980s. This theory—or better, a set of hypotheses and historical explanations—reflected some of the alternative and different priorities and problems of the Third World. The key problems were state coherence, economic autonomy, and cultural integrity. No dependency theorist considered war *between* peripheral states to be a problem requiring diagnosis. If there was any consideration of security issues from the dependency perspective, it was only to underline the Great Powers' propensity to intervene militarily to squelch challenges to their economic, political, and cultural paramountcy in the Third World.[8] What mattered to academic dependency theorists and many governments of the Third World was very different from what mattered to Western International Relations theorists and to the masterminds of deterrence theory and the engineers of Cold War diplomacy.

Yet, during the height of the Cold War, particularly in the 1960s, some strategic thinkers began to contemplate the phenomenon of "peoples' wars." The sources of these wars were assumed rather than demonstrated: they grew out of popular frustrations occasioned by underdevelopment, by nationalism, and most prominently, by the appeals of communism. One did not have to go far beyond Moscow, Beijing, or Havana to locate the sources of the problem. In other words, analysts commonly associated Third World insurgencies with Cold War competition. Most of the literature was short on diagnosis of causes and long on solutions. Its purpose was to help fashion successful anti-insurgency policies. The primary empirical cases were Malaya, the Philippines, and Vietnam, all locations where insurgencies were motivated in part by Marxism-Leninism.[9] Areas of chronic warfare, such as the Sudan, Ethiopia, Sri Lanka, and Myanmar, were seldom mentioned in this literature. This reveals a "if it isn't Communist-inspired, it isn't worth analyzing" syndrome.

The lack of match between traditional International Relations Theory concerns and priorities in the Third World became apparent in Western academia only after the end of the Cold War. All of a sudden, analysts discovered "ethnic wars"—supposedly a new phenomenon of international politics, and, again reflecting center-periphery mental constructs, supposedly a phenomenon that was a *result of* the end of the Cold War. But such wars, to the extent that they are even ethnic, are not at all new in the Third World. Eritreans began their long war of secession in 1961; domestic wars have raged in Myanmar since 1962; Cyprus was effectively partitioned in 1964; Biafra fought to secede from Nigeria in 1967; Sudan has been in a state of civil war since 1955; Lebanon collapsed into a melange of warlords and Syrian satrapies in 1976; the Tamil armed secession movement started in 1983, long before the fall of the Berlin Wall. The list of wars within states is long, and they long antedate the end of the Cold War. While some of these wars and their legacies of humanitarian emergencies and disasters were sustained by outside powers, their essential etiology resides within the states themselves. One cannot make a credible case that any of them reflected Cold War imperatives, balances of power, deterrence, collective security, or any of the other ideas and practices associated with traditional European and Cold War diplomacy and their theoretical explanations. For the problem of war in the Third World and in some of the post–Socialist states is not one of the relations between states, but of relations within states.

The intellectual limitations reflected in Western approaches to war in the Third World were not confined just to theorists of International Relations or security analysts. The transnational peace movement was similarly focused on nuclear weapons and Cold War competition. While peace activists promoted nuclear arms control and disarmament to prevent a war that *might* happen, millions of people were dying in the Third World from sources that had no connection with nuclear weapons, NATO, or the Warsaw Pact. The peace movement adhered to the assumption that weapons cause wars. In the Third World, however, weapons are just symptoms of a much more profound problem of state incoherence. Whether theorists of International Relations, security analysts, or peace activists, all assumed that war was a problem of relations between states. They all assumed statehood, and they all argued about the concepts of deterrence, balance, and security dilemmas, whereas in the Third World the fundamental issues were the state in general, the relations between communities within states, and relations between those communities and the state. One cannot understand Cyprus, Sri Lanka, Myanmar, Rwanda, and Burundi and numerous parallels elsewhere in the Third World and some post–Socialist states by starting with the assumption that they are states in the classical sense. International Relations Theory, whether of the eighteenth- or twentieth-century varieties, assumes the state. To diagnose the source of war in the Third World and elsewhere, however, we must turn a taken-for-granted assumption into a problem. Regrettably the vast literature on the state, much of it related to political philosophy, does not help us a great deal.

This literature delves into the question of origins, functions, authority patterns, representation, law, bases of legitimacy, and the like. These analyses are all based on the prototypical European or North American state. The social basis of the state—the political community—is assumed or at least it is not problematized. The "commonwealth," whose members forge the social contract in the works of Hobbes, Locke, and Rousseau is taken for granted. Marx had some ideas on nationality, but his state is the executive committee of the owners of the means of production within states as they existed in late-nineteenth-century Europe. The works of Bentham, the Mills, Hobson, Carr, Morgenthau, Quincy Wright, Bull, Keohane, Waltz, and all those whose analyses derive from their intellectual innovations follow in the tradition of taking states and their underlying communities for granted. Only in the thinking and diplomacy of Woodrow Wilson and in the scholarship of Karl Deutsch is the problem of community—the basis of the state—addressed seriously. Wilson arrived at the fateful view that states ought to be based on "natural" communities, while Deutsch argued by implication that political organizations should reflect communities founded on empathy, trust, and identification. But like their theoretical contemporaries, they had in their gaze primarily to the European and North American surroundings.

Assessing Explanations of Internal War

With the end of the Cold War, Western analysts suddenly discovered "ethnic wars." The new master explanatory variable of ethnicity replaced communism as the source of trouble in the peripheries. There were, of course, numerous examples of armed conflicts that had an ethnic dimension to them. And in the event that ethnicity was not the sole or major fracture point in a conflict, the media incorrectly emphasized the ethnic dimension and characterized wars as essentially the playing out of ancient sociocultural animosities.[10] Scholarly debates then revolved around the question of whether ethnic identities are "primordial," socially constructed, or situationally created by political opportunists.[11] This question naturally arose from the puzzling observation that communal groups frequently live in reasonable harmony for long periods (the Muslims and Serbs in Sarajevo), intermarry, and share common languages and sometimes even religions. The problem with the "ethnic wars" literature is that most Third World (and other) states contain many communities, but most of the time, the majority of them are not at war with each other. Another problem is that many internal wars do not revolve primarily around social cleavages based on ethnicity.

The next step was then to try to identify those conditions under which ethnic groups are likely to take up arms. The answer was in the face of collapsing central authority.[12] This explanation grew out of the post–Cold War headlines: the sudden surge of communal fighting in ex-Yugoslavia and in the former Soviet republics. All of them seemed to coincide with the collapse of Communist authority. Others argued, on the other hand, that ethnic tensions had persisted through the decades of Communist rule, but were now emerging when the iron grip of Communist parties was removed. In other words, these areas were returning to old forms. These are two competing explanations. The first claims that political opportunists exacerbate ethnic tensions and promise to provide security for communal groups against their ostensible "enemies." Warlords, gangsters, and proto-governments provide the security function where state authority has collapsed. The second claims that ethnic tensions are indeed primordial rather than situational, that they were simply repressed under Communist rule, and reemerged when that rule collapsed. It is not so much a new emergency situation as a return to more traditional patterns of social animosities that existed in pre-Communist Eastern Europe.

These competing explanations are not generalizable to all domestic armed conflicts in the Third World and post-Communist states. There have been plenty of communally based armed conflicts that did not arise from the collapse of central authority (Eritrea, Rwanda, Burundi, Sri Lanka, Punjab, and so on). Hence, while these analyses may help us understand situations such as those in ex-Yugoslavia, Nagorno-Karabakh, or Abkhazia, they do not provide the foundations for a comprehensive diagnosis of the problem of war within states.

There are other perspectives—though not derived from International Relations Theory—that provide additional diagnoses of Third World domestic wars. These employ three different levels of aggregation or analysis: first, individual psychology; second, intergroup dynamics; and third, systemic characteristics. Each opens a path for causal analysis that goes beyond the limited explanations of "ethnic" wars outlined earlier.

Steven David has presented one approach based on essentialist and fixed personality traits. He adopts a Hobbesian psychology to show how people covet others' belongings and resources, and given the opportunities, particularly in the absence of strong government authority, they may employ force to obtain them. He suggests that, given human greed, cost-benefit calculations will always prevail on the side of opportunity. The role of government, à la Hobbes, is to provide a deterrent and thus to manipulate individuals' cost-benefit calculations to the point where there are no probable benefits to be gained from attacking one's neighbors. In this explanation, the Leviathan plays the role of the social peacekeeper. Following the 1993 analysis of Posen and others, David then argues that one is most likely to see the outbreak of social violence in an environment where political authority has collapsed or where it is weak.

There are a number of cases of internal war in Third World and post-Communist states where this form of explanation has empirical support. Somalia is a prime example. (It is also an example that shows that ethnicity is not always a major source of conflict. The Somalis constitute a single *ethnie*). Lebanon after 1976 is another example where weak central authority was unable to contain the violence among sectarian groups that had armed themselves sufficiently to challenge any attempt at social peacekeeping.

A second analytical path, popular in the 1960s and 1970s, emphasizes intergroup dynamics and concepts of relative deprivation and social frustration.[13] David reviews this literature, so we need not retrace this territory. While offering numerous avenues for exploration and diagnosis, David points out that these approaches to the subject are often contradictory: "Is internal war the result of individual or group calculation? Is it rational and purposeful or emotional and nihilistic? Do people rebel because they believe the government's coercive power is on the wane or because they no longer view its exercise of power as legitimate?"[14]

There is also the problem of nonevents. When perceptions of relative deprivation are notable, when public authority is scarce, and when there are traditional hostilities between social groups, internal war or even lesser levels of violence may not always occur (consider Malaysia from 1962 to 1967). Contrary to popular belief, violence has occurred when few or none of these characteristics exist (for example, Bougainville today).

Others have noted systemic conditions as sources of intergroup violence and internal wars. The most popular today include the various studies that link environmental degradation to domestic war.[15] More general analyses of the world capitalist system seek to demonstrate the connection between foreign capital penetration and state weakness, or World Bank and IMF "structural adjustment" policies, and armed public resistance in poor countries. As with the other forms of explanation, however, these offer insights but they do not account for variance in the outcome: the incidence or nonincidence of armed violence within states. Peru in the late 1980s and early 1990s is sometimes cited as a case where economic austerity programs coincided with insurrection, in this case the Sendero Luminoso. But similar programs in Chile and Ecuador, as well as in some African states, did not result in armed uprisings.

With so many competing explanatory paths, it is not possible at this stage to develop an overarching explanation of the phenomenon of internal war. Clearly, all the approaches listed earlier are probabilistic. They highlight certain conditions that increase the likelihood of violence and war, but there are no firm causal connections because none can satisfactorily explain variance in the dependent variable. Some conditions may be necessary, but few are sufficient. Consider the number of counterintuitive examples. If the Hobbesian-psychological explanation was sufficient, we would have had far more internal wars, given that the normal condition for many Third World states is weakness, lack of government legitimacy, and political ineffectiveness. Relative deprivation theories can only tell part of the story because different individuals handle their perceptions in many different ways, only one of which may be to take up arms. There are numerous people in the United States, for example, who feel deprived compared to others, whose expectations may be constantly frustrated, and who have withdrawn their loyalty to the American government. But not all join local militias; not all bomb federal buildings; and not all withhold tax payments. Some enter convents or monasteries; others migrate abroad; yet others will organize or join protest parties. There is no determinate outcome of feelings of relative deprivation. Rapidly declining economic conditions correlate with the incidence of domestic unrest, but causal statements are not possible.

Primordial theories of ethnicity are inadequate because, among other faults, they ignore political context and social variation. Most communities in most multicommunity states peacefully coexist most of the time. Group identities are now established in the literature to be both "imagined" and socially constructed.[16] Identity is a variable. But what does this tell us about the dynamics of intergroup relations, particularly relations that end in violence? Not a great deal. Introduction of the concept of the "Other," so popular in contemporary postmodernist and critical studies, does not help for the same reasons that notions of primordial ethnicity fail as an explanatory system.[17] Everyone identifies groups to which they do not belong as the "Other." But this does not allow us to make predictions about resulting attitudes, much less about behavior. Some people embrace the "Other" to the point of engaging in rapturous admiration of their culture, learning their language, promoting their political system(s)—in general, integrating. Other people adopt racist and belligerent attitudes toward the "Other," but probably not to all relevant "Others." Again, there is no determinate outcome of differences between groups. The high variability of intergroup relations is revealed in dozens of past and contemporary examples. The first contacts between indigenous populations and the exploring and colonizing Portuguese, Dutch, and Spanish in the fifteenth and sixteenth centuries ranged from peaceful trade, exchange, and even integration (the Portuguese in India, Italian priests in China), through carefully regulated and circumscribed contacts (Japan), to armed resistance and war, as in Australia, Mexico, and Peru (for numerous examples of the variation, see the studies in Schwartz's *Implicit Understandings*). Muslims and Hindus butchered each other by the millions during the bloody partition of India in 1947. Since then, in most communities, Hindus and Muslims usually coexist peacefully. In the 1960s, politicians convinced a large number of tribal groups in Nigeria that they were "Ibos," and then mobilized them to fight a war of secession from the federation. Most of these "Ibos" had no such identity previously, but once their lives and security depended upon such an identity, they quickly became "Ibos." Although some anthropologists and ethnologists argue that there are no clear or consistent physical distinctions between Hutus and Tutsis—the groups are not two distinct ethnic communities—government propaganda in Rwanda during the 1970s and 1980s managed to convince a large number that there are significant differences between them.[18] In April 1994, many of those Hutus who believed the distinction went to work to slaughter Tutsis.

Critique: The Benign State

There are, then, important problems of logic in these competing explanations of the internal war phenomenon. What unites most of them, however, is their relatively benign characterization of the state. Steven David's analysis, for example, provides a solution to the problem of internal war from his realist interpretation of the human condition in the absence of a state. Following Hobbes, he assumes that the main function of the state is to alter the cost-benefit calculations of citizens to the point where the opportunities for individual or group violence as a means of obtaining gains are reduced to almost zero. The state, in this view, is the great arbiter of citizens' quarrels. It is, as Hobbes's famous portrait of the Leviathan suggests, a disinterested judge of private disagreements. It also possesses the authority and the legitimacy, provided through the social contract, to impose order on society. It does this by first disarming the society (a process that took several centuries in Europe and is certainly not accomplished in many Third World countries today) and second by arming itself with a military, police forces, and a judiciary.

The Hobbesian view of the state may help resolve problems of conflict between two or more communities within the same state. The relative pacification of Hindus and Muslims in most of India since independence has been due in part to the well-trained and equipped Indian police and army. In societies where communities do not accept each other's legitimacy (elsewhere I have termed this the problem of "horizontal" legitimacy), the state may play a key role in maintaining order and preventing intercommunal violence.[19]

But in many Third World and post–Socialist states, the real problem is not between communities within the state, *but between the regime and those communities*. The state itself becomes a major threat to the well-being and security of communities. In order to protect themselves against the depredations of the state, community members arm themselves or in other ways resist. The history of violence within states since 1945 (and many cases prior to 1945) arises not directly from Hobbesian greed, ethnicity, dealing with the "Other," relative deprivation, or outbursts of anomie and angst. It has to do with the manner in which governments deal with their populations. And in many cases, it is the state—or regime acting in the name of the state and its "nation-building" project—that launches the internal war. In fact, far more people in the twentieth century have been killed by their own governments than by foreign soldiers or by members of other communities within the state. According to Rummel's 1994 data, international wars since 1945 have cost 30 million lives, while "democides" within countries account for about 130 million deaths—a ratio of 4.3 individuals killed by their governments to one soldier-caused battle casualties.[20] We know the major mass-murderers of citizens: Stalin, Hitler, Mao Tse-tung, Chaing Kai-shek, Lenin, and Pol Pot. Lesser known mass killers include Macias Nguema of Equatorial Guinea, the Indonesian military officials who, in 1965 and 1966 either killed or stood by while their compatriots massacred about 250,000, and their dispatching of about 150,000 East Timorese between 1975 and 1987; Turkey's massacre of about 1.5 million Armenians during World War I; Idi Amin's slaughter (some by personal hand) of about 300,000 fellow Ugandans, and the Tutsi killing of about 150,000 in Burundi in 1971 and 1972. It was a government-trained and organized militia in Rwanda in 1994 that launched the genocide of the Tutsis. The state, rather than ethnic communities, has often been the main threat to the lives and security of its own citizens. This was not what Hobbes had in mind when he constructed the Leviathan, authorized to punish those who would upset public order.

The basic conditions underlying these wars is the systematic exclusion of individuals and groups from access to government positions, influence, and allocations.[21] There is, in brief, differential treatment of specified groups by governments, which means that there are fundamental problems of justice underlying armed conflict. In these cases, the state is "captured" by one group for the purpose of advancing its interests, opportunities, and benefits. These are achieved primarily by exclusion of others. Both access to decision making and allocation of rewards through various public policies are fundamentally conditioned by group affiliation rather than by merit. The varieties of exclusion and discrimination are numerous. I list here several of the more notorious practices found commonly in Third World and former Socialist states, with some examples.

1. Formal exclusion of access to decision centers:
   - Apartheid in South Africa.
   - Ethiopia disbanded the Eritrean parliament, shut down newspapers, and dissolved trade unions from 1955 to 1960.
   - Croatia passed a constitutional law in 1991 declaring Serbs a "national minority" and subsequently the government fired Serb incumbents from civil service and other state-supplied positions.
2. The government uses the state and its resources to enrich itself, and denies resources to specified groups within the society:
   - The Duvalliers in Haiti not only enriched themselves by plundering the national treasury, but also systematically looted foreign aid donations for their private gain.
   - The late leader of Zaire amassed a fortune through plundering the country's population. It was used to purchase the loyalty of a few.
   - The government of Pakistan systematically discriminated against eastern Pakistanis (Bengalis) in terms of government employment and allocation of government funds and services.[22]
3. The government appropriates lands and other resources for its "development" projects and displaces local populations—often without compensation.
   - In the nineteenth century, settler governments in the United States, Canada, Australia, and New Zealand systematically broke treaty obligations and forced indigenous populations onto reserves and other suboptimal territories.
   - For the past 30 years, the Muslim Arab–dominated government of Sudan has appropriated lands and resources traditionally used by Neolithic and other tribes in the south.[23]
4. The government adopts exclusionary policies to deny social and economic opportunities for specified groups:
   - In 1971 the government of Sri Lanka drastically reduced the numbers of Tamils who would be admitted to state universities. In 1972 and 1978 it adopted constitutions making Sinhalese the sole official language of the country and Buddhism the official state religion.[24]
   - The government of Sudan has sought to impose the Sharia on non-Muslims. Those refusing conversion are denied access to almost all government-sponsored services.
5. Government-sponsored or -organized physical attacks against specific groups:

- In the nineteenth century, the governments of Argentina and Tasmania paid a bounty for citizens to kill indigenous populations.
- In Burundi in 1972 the government launched massacres of Hutus, with up to 200,000 casualties and a massive flow of refugees to neighboring Rwanda, Zaire, and Tanzania.[25]
- Idi Amin in Uganda destroyed tribal and other groups that offered resistance to his rule.
- The LTTE (Tamil Tigers) physically removed Muslim populations from areas under their control.[26] About 66,000 people were involved.
- In Burma in 1962 the Hindu community was dispossessed of its physical and financial assets and expelled to India.
- The Hutu-dominated government of Rwanda from 1962 to 1973 imprisoned, killed, or forced into exile virtually all Tutsi power-holders and politicians, as well as many moderate Hutus.[27]
- In Cambodia in 1976 the government launched a systematic program to eliminate all "bourgeois" elements in the society. More than one million perished.
- In El Salvador during the 1980s government-sponsored and -organized death squads eliminated "leftist" activists and frequently their family members. About 70,000 perished in this manner.
- In Rwanda in 1994 Hutu militias were trained and organized to slaughter Tutsis. Government radio programs encouraged ordinary Hutu civilians to follow the example of the militias.

The list of state-organized exclusionary, arbitrary, and violent policies is lengthy. The items noted are just indicative of the range of possibilities. It is clear from these situations that the state in many Third World countries, as it was in Nazi Germany, Mao's China, or Soviet Russia, is much more than a mere disinterested Leviathan-type arbiter between individuals or social groups. It is the instrument of certain groups and categories that have captured it and then use its military and police power, and sometimes constitutional or other forms of legislation, to enrich itself, to exclude others from political participation and the distribution of government rewards, and to attack distinct communities, sometimes with genocidal results. While in these situations the state is very weak in the sense of having little or no legitimacy, it is often very powerful in its command over the instruments of social surveillance, coercion, and terror. The main options for those who are the target of government discrimination and threats are to go underground, to flee the country, or to resist with arms.[28]

The Realist-inspired explanations of Posen and David, while relevant perhaps in identifying key causal sources of communal armed conflict in the former Yugoslavia and other post–Socialist states, has not been central to most internal wars elsewhere. Many wars erupted where there was no notable decline of government authority over rival communities. The victims in the examples I have cited did not seek security from other communal groups. They held ordinary aspirations for political participation, and maintained normal expectations of receiving government services in exchange for tax and other extractions. The threats to their security came not from other groups or communities, but from the state. The Hobbesian analogy of citizen against citizen in the absence of a Leviathan does not hold in these numerous cases.

The role of ideas is also missing in the realist and other theories of domestic war. Most of the explanatory systems, whether they emphasize rational choice theories of the Hobbesian type or more irrational forms of hatred and nihilism, are ultimately materialist: people rebel because they suffer relative economic losses and status (relative deprivation), because they unsuccessfully seek opportunities to better their life, or because they fear the state or other communal groups. But rebellions may also be fueled by ideas and ideologies. This point hardly needs elaboration but it is remarkably overlooked in most theories of International Relations, as well as in theories of revolution and in explanations of wars within states. In Cambodia, Pol Pot's interpretations of Marxism-Leninism helped him concoct the idea that the country must be purged of bourgeois elements. In many Muslim countries today, religious activists rail against Western conceptions of the state and deny that present secular authorities have any right to rule. They claim that power and legitimacy do not emanate from the people, as most Western constitutions aver, but from God (note the similarity to seventeenth-century ideas of divine right). The purpose of groups at war against the state in Algeria, Egypt, Lebanon, Afghanistan, and elsewhere is to destroy the modern secular state and to replace it with an appropriately governed instrument of God. Many, of course, are duped or coerced into following these programs. But probably the majority are true believers whose dedication and loyalty cannot be reduced to crude loss/gain calculations or to psychologisms about individual angst. While many in the West may not find ideological arguments or explanations compelling, we should recall that in the sixteenth and seventeenth centuries most budding states in Europe were torn apart by internal wars fought over religious ideas. Hobbes was an observer of them.

Tipping Events

Another problem remains. Even where governments employ exclusionist policies, or where authority breaks down and communal groups threaten each other, the outcome of violence and particularly war (which implies a certain degree of planning and organization, as opposed to spontaneous out-bursts such as riots) is not certain. We are still speaking in terms of proba-bilities. But to repeat: we can observe situations such as those listed on pages 115–116 that did not result in war, or even in armed resistance. There was none, for example, in Argentina during the military regime's "dirty war" in the 1980s; nor among blacks in the United States after the Civil War; nor among numerous indigenous peoples and minorities whose livelihood and cultures are often threatened by state-sponsored "development" programs. We need, then, to locate some triggering device that alters the situation from one of threat, fear, and coercion to open violence.

Russell Hardin, in *One for All: The Logic of Group Violence,* provides one important clue in what he calls "tipping events." These are usually sudden changes, even random events, that fundamentally alter the constellation of forces among social groups, including the state. It is difficult to be precise about their quality, but Hardin and others argue that in certain circumstances long-standing relationships disintegrate and people are literally forced to take sides in a logic of "kill or be killed."[29] This situation helps explain how, for example, Serbs and Muslims in Bosnia who had cohabited in communities for decades and centuries, worked together, and commonly intermarried, all of a sudden began to kill each other—even neighbors—and to participate in acts of ethnic cleansing and other atrocities. While this example does not match all "tipping events," the structural features are often similar: one act of violence, even an accidental one, begins a chain reaction based on fear, where individuals are literally forced to take sides if they wish to survive. Several ex-amples will illustrate the nature and consequences of "tipping events."

- In 1972 a small armed *incursion* from a neighboring state into Burundi was the event that led to a mass slaughter of Hutus by the government army, with up to 150,000 casualties.
- In July of 1983, a small *ambush* of government forces by Tamil dissi-dents, in which only 13 soldiers died, led to a government-organized pogrom of Tamils in which up to 400 were killed. The event marks the beginning of the LTTE war of secession that continues to rage.
- The *plebiscite* on independence held in Bosnia in April 1992 officially changed the Serbian population from a majority within Yugoslavia into a minority within Bosnia. This was the signal for the uprising that be-came an armed attempt at secession.[30]
- In 1991, the Croatian parliament *passed a constitutional law* declaring the Serbian population a "national minority," thus the object of differ-ential treatment. Subsequent dismissal of Serbs from government posi-tions led to the armed attempt at secession of the Serbian population in Krajina.

- Perhaps the most famous recent "tipping event" was the April 1994 *downing of the aircraft* containing the Hutu president of Rwanda returning home from a peace conference in Tanzania to end the guerrilla war fought by Tutsis against the regime. This was the signal for the massive genocide that the Hutus launched against Tutsis throughout the country.

Causes, Sources, and Prescriptions

This chapter has criticized some of the many explanations of internal wars, a phenomenon that long preceded the end of the Cold War, but which seems to have become a permanent part of the contemporary international landscape. Around the world today, there are armed struggles ranging from Bougainville in the South Pacific, through the lengthy wars in Myanmar, the Sri Lanka secession war, the armed chaos in Afghanistan, civil war in Tajikistan, more than 30 years of civil war in Sudan, numerous armed resistance or secessionist movements in Africa, the collapse of Liberia, and the continued partition of Cyprus—just to mention the better-known contemporary wars. Others, after years of fighting, have finally come to an end, although these "wars of a third kind" or "wars of national debilitation" have a way of waxing and waning despite cease-fires and final peace accords.[31] However, in recent years, the Moros in the Philippines have made peace with the central authorities; Basques in Spain are less active, if not resigned to their continued integration into the Spanish state; peace is an on-and-off proposition in Northern Ireland; and there is painfully slow accommodation being achieved between the Palestinians and Israel. While the evidence suggests that most internal wars are terminated by military defeat rather than through negotiation (is armed secession ever negotiable?), the termination of these wars always involves a lengthy process.

And so do their origins. Just as analysts have chronicled numerous causes of interstate wars, only to find that there is no agreement on a single source, so there are numerous processes within states that increase the probabilities of internal wars. Process is the key word here. There is seldom a single source or situation that inevitably leads to armed violence between communities or between a community and the state. Various processes and conditions combine in various ways to create explosive situations. "Tipping events" significantly increase the risks of the outbreak of violence, and, ultimately, of war. The task now, since we already have a roster of competing explanations of internal war, is to reconceptualize the problem and to see how variables interact. In my work, I have emphasized the weakness of horizontal and vertical legitimacy as prime conditions that set the stage of "tipping events," but a complete explanatory narrative has to locate other domestic and external sources. To this point, we have identified numerous necessary conditions (of which state weakness—low horizontal and vertical legitimacy—is surely one), but they are seldom sufficient. Perhaps it is time to change how the problem is framed from "why" questions to "how" questions: How is it possible that a society in a relative condition of peace breaks down into wars and genocide? And, at the individual level, how do "citizens" turn into warriors and murderers? Realist-type explanations, as Steven David acknowledges, provide insights but few certainties. Professor Ayoob's analysis highlights the great difficulties facing weak states and suggests with reasonable evidence that the processes of democratization may in fact exacerbate problems rather than ameliorate them.[32] There was a significant increase in ethnic mobilization and conflict that coincided with democratization in various areas of the world. However, it is questionable whether there is a direct causal connection between the two phenomena.[33] What both essays share in common is their privileging of the Western conception of the state when it comes to solutions.

Steven David's prescription for the problem of the weak state is to strengthen it, to create a genuine Hobbesian Leviathan. While it may have been historically a solution in the reasonably homogenous societies of Western Europe, there are serious difficulties about this path as a solution to problems of some contemporary multicommunal societies. Perhaps the problem is not to try to solve all these problems within the context of the Western-type state. It may be time to rethink the nature of political community and organization in the Third World and in some post–Socialist states, to open up fundamental questions, and not just to rely on solutions that approximate the Western experience of the state over the last three or four centuries.

The fundamental problem is the nature of states, the relations between communities in states, and the relations between governments and the communities over whom they claim the right to rule. Western commentators, as well as the leaders of various "national liberation" movements, have assumed uncritically that all former colonial societies must transform themselves into the Western-state template. But what was assumed in the heyday of imperial collapse, or "decolonization" as it was portrayed in most of the discourse, has now become problematic. We must ask the question if it is "normal," appropriate, or even desirable that former colonies, which were created for reasons that had nothing to do with statehood, should now become states. For some former colonies, the liberal conception of the state as encompassing a community of *citizens* regardless of their natural or primordial affiliations, seems to have worked reasonably well. Despite continuing ethnic tensions and difficulties, Malaysia, Singapore, Fiji, the Commonwealth Caribbean, and many other former colonies are today more or less thriving as coherent states. Identities of nationality and civic pride have developed to provide a basis for political authority and reasonable social solidarity. But this is not the case in a large number of countries, stretching from Bougainville in the Pacific, through Myanmar, most of South Asia, some portions of the Middle East, and large swaths of Africa. There are compelling reasons to doubt whether Afghanistan, Sudan, Rwanda, Nigeria, and many others will ever become normal states in the sense of internal coherence, popular legitimacy of rulers, and the development of a sense of citizenship that can sustain enduring legitimate rule.

But merely to raise the question of the appropriateness of the state is to invite serious questions from International Relations scholars—and probably experts on comparative politics as well. Kenneth Waltz, in *Theory of International Politics,* has made the case that there are strong pressures for organizational forms to reproduce themselves. The historical record is on Waltz's side: half a millennium ago, or even less, the world was populated by an immense variety of political formats ranging from private feudal lordships, through tribal organizations, city-states, multicommunity empires, to hereditary kingdoms and even a few republics. A brief list of ruling types suggests the variety: kings, dukes, margraves, doges, efendis, emperors, chiefs, "sons of heaven," caudillos, presidents, prime ministers, and sultans. Since then, the heterogeneity of political forms has swiftly (in historical terms) been reduced to only one kind that has official standing in the international community: the territorial state.[34] With the demise of the Soviet Union, and the admission of Monaco to the United Nations, we may have seen the last of multicommunity empires and feudal remnants. The territorial state has persisted, while most other forms of political organization have not. The pressures for emulation of the economic, military, and social organization of modern states are immense and compelling.[35] But the *persistence* of states is not the same as *success.* Many post–1945 states have been in a condition of almost chronic warfare, often pitting governments against their own populations. Can we call them "successes," when in the name of state integrity and coherence, governments systematically disenfranchise large proportions of their citizenry, conduct dirty wars against dissenters, expel minorities, and even engage in genocidal policies?[36]

In many parts of the world, there is not yet a reasonable concordance between the structure and nature of the society within the state, and the state itself. While, from an external point of view, today we have only prime ministers and presidents remaining, in fact in many countries clan leaders, efendis, mullahs, caudillos, warlords, and other types of local rulers prevail.[37] Even in some of the former Soviet republics, where for more than seven decades government was centralized, developed, and all-embracing under the auspices of Communist parties, locally based, factional leaders have come to prevail. One observer of recent events in Tajikistan has noted, for example, that "You still don't have a real state here. It is a collection of various forces fighting for power."[38] All of these sap the legitimacy of those who claim the right to rule the Western-style state. And despite decades of Western support of the great "nation-building" enterprise, in many areas it has failed. It is not easy to build an entity called "Afghanistan" when the only meaningful political authority in it resides among various cross-cutting sectarian, tribal, and ethnic communities and associations, most of them at war with each other.

Fundamental state weakness—a legitimacy deficit—is easy to chronicle. But instead of examining all of its indicators, we can take just one profound illustration. Consider the practice of state recognition. Writing in 1955 before most colonies had achieved independence, Quincy Wright enunciated the traditional requirements for "recognizing new states and emancipating dependencies, and the policy of international organizations in admitting states to membership and in emancipating mandates and trusteeships." These included first, clearly established boundaries and reasonable prospects of maintaining them; second, an administration with de facto capacity to govern the area; third, laws and institutions capable of giving reasonable protection to aliens and minorities and of maintaining reasonable standards of justice among all inhabitants, and fourth, a public opinion, and institutions for manifesting it, which gives reasonable indication of a desire for independence and a *reasonable assurance of the permanence of the two preceding conditions* (my emphasis).[39]

In 1955, these criteria reflected not only an evaluation of the "facts on the ground" in European experience and policy, but also a normative statement of what states should be. How many states can meet these criteria today? Can "modern" Afghanistan, Liberia, Somalia, or Sudan meet *any* of them? Can Iraq, Myanmar, Sri Lanka, Nigeria, Burundi, Algeria, Israel, Indonesia, Guatemala, or Kampuchea meet most of them? Can Yugoslavia, Croatia, Bosnia, Tajikistan, Estonia, and many others meet the third criterion? In brief, a very high proportion of today's 185 UN members cannot meet traditional criteria of what constitutes a state. And there is little reason to expect that many of them will be able to meet most of the criteria in the foreseeable future. Are there any reasonable alternatives to the Western-type state? Probably not, but whether from the perspective of International Relations (which trains us to look only for states) or comparative politics (which shares a similar bias), it might be worthwhile to look around. We already have the phenomenon of de facto states, communities that have many of the attributes of statehood in terms of coherence and legitimacy, but which do not have international recognition.[40] Somaliland, the Palestinians, the Turkish Republic of Cyprus, and a few others come to mind. However, lend-ing support to the Waltzian thesis of state reproduction, the purpose of these associations is to become states, not to offer alternatives to the state. It is highly unlikely, for example, that the Palestinians will eventually settle for some halfway house between being a "people" and being a state.

Elsewhere, however, there is the case of Somalia. It has collapsed as a state, yet life continues in a shifting pattern of localized political authority combined with highly innovative forms of economic activity that link local pastoralists to the outside world. There may be quite a few Somalis who are convinced that life is better today in the absence of a state than it was when today's fiction called Somalia was an actual state.[41] A single example does not offer a true alternative, but whether we like it or not, in some areas of the world, the fictional territorial, postcolonial state is becoming "unbundled" and a few postcolonial polities were probably never "bundled" initially.[42] We see the results today. Thus, it may help to begin serious thought about re-configuring political communities in such a manner as to reduce the risks of domestic wars and their consequent humanitarian disasters.

International Relations Theory and Internal War

International Relations Theory assumes both the state and legitimate rule. The traditional problems for International Relations scholars begin only after sovereignty is assumed or established. As demonstrated in the International Relations discipline's designation of the Treaties of Westphalia as the beginning of modern International Relations, the field of study could only develop after the principle of sovereignty had become a foundational rule of the system. It should not surprise us, therefore, that scholars in this field have little to tell us about what is *pre-sovereign*. As Robert Jackson has so well put it in *Quasi-States: Sovereignty, International Relations and the Third World*, many of the states of the Third World are only "quasi-states." Although they are internationally recognized as states, they do not contain the "stuff" of sovereignty in the domestic realm. Pre-sovereigns may become a problem in International Relations, as is seen in the myriads of studies that today examine the pros and cons of humanitarian interventions, but these interventions are results, not causes. If we are in the realm of etiology, it does not do much good to begin with results rather than with sources and causes. Just as historical sociologists are probably better equipped than international theorists to enlighten us on the processes of state formation in thirteenth- to seventeenth-century Europe, so economists, sociologists, comparativists, and area experts might be able to offer better avenues for diagnosis than experts—and particularly theorists—of International Relations. In analyzing domestic armed conflicts, rule and statehood *are* the problems; they cannot be assumed. When we explore contemporary domestic wars, we are in a sense in the times and locations of pre-sovereignty. International Relations is in the arena of post-sovereignty.

International Relations Theory, then, does not have a good deal to offer in the way of analytical tools and suggestive analogies for exploring the etiology of domestic wars. Many have observed that the anarchy principle and its resulting security dilemma might be, today, more applicable to the internal realm of weak and collapsing states than to the International Relations among the industrial countries.[43] But even this gets us only part of the way; it may help us understand the situations characteristic of collapsing states or even of very weak states. But it is not the condition surrounding many domestic wars, where authority continues to exist, however illegitimate. It is not, therefore, a problem of "governance without government" in the sense that this idea can be and has been applied to international relations.[44] There is both governance *and* government in most weak states, and so anarchy is not always the correct analogy. To repeat, the fundamental problems link the issues of legitimacy and justice to the three-cornered relationships between communities, and between communities and the state. The fundamental problem is the denial or withholding of legitimacy by one community toward another, or from various communities to the state. Absent vertical and horizontal legitimacy, the forces of fragmentation, disintegration, and secession, all surrounded by some manufactured "identity," begin the process of social breakdown that, in the face of a "tipping event" leads to organized violence.

According to Mohammed Ayoob's 1995 analysis, these matters are part of the larger *problematique* of state building. The difficulties facing post–1945 states are similar to those present in the great state-building project of Europe that began in the sixteenth century and that was attended by innumerable civil and international wars. The parallels are apt, although there are also fundamental differences that must be noted. But the larger point in Ayoob's analysis helps lead to a similar conclusion. Existing theories of International Relations do not have a great deal to offer by way of suggestive concepts or general approaches to the problem of wars in post–1945 states. Neoliberalism and neorealism are particularly deficient because they arose in the context of European and Cold War international politics, where problems in the peripheries had no independent or significant ontological status. The parochialism of these theories has not been reduced either by dependency theory or by the end of the Cold War.

On the other hand, we should not overstate the case of irrelevance, for the security problems of many new states are not exclusively domestic. There are ongoing security dilemmas, as between India and Pakistan and Israel and its neighbors, that display many of the characteristics associated with realism. The Muslim states of the former Soviet Union, for example, have become playgrounds for competitive strategic and commercial rivalry featuring Turkish, Iranian, Russian, and American players. Competitive arming and rearming feed suspicions and territorial conflicts in Asia. A resulting need for an Asian "security architecture" is expressed in numerous publications and government policy papers. There is much evidence that the end of the Cold War did not end power-seeking behavior in the international system.

Yet, if present trends continue, the main sources of killing and the floods of refugees will be found in the weaknesses of many post-1945 states. Burundi remains at the precipice. The civil wars of the 1970s and 1980s in the Sudan, Afghanistan, Myanmar, East Timor, and elsewhere continue apace, with new wars sprouting in Bougainville, some former Soviet republics, and in the former Yugoslavia. All these violent conflicts have their roots in questions of community and legitimacy, questions that are ignored or assumed in contemporary theories of International Relations. Until those theories address the issue of the origins of the state, and the relationship between community and state, they will remain in the peripheries of relevance to the problem of war in the post–Cold War era.

Notes

1. George Modelski, "Kautilya: Foreign Policy and International System in the Hindu World," *American Political Science Review*, vol. 58 (1964), pps. 549–60; Joel Larus, ed., *Comparative World Politics: Readings in Western and Pre-modern Non-Western International Relations* (Belmont, CA: Wadsworth, 1964).

2. K. J. Holsti, *The State, War, and the State of War* (Cambridge: Cambridge University Press, 1996), chap. 2.

3. Aside from the Marxist-inspired literature on imperialism, few studies have figured prominently in the English-language literature on International Relations. The most-cited works are Parker T. Moon, *Imperialism and World Politics* (NY: Macmillan, 1926); George Lichtheim, *Imperialism* (NY: Praeger, 1971); and a chapter in Quincy Wright, *The Study of International Relations* (NY: Appleton-Century-Crofts, 1955). None examines the problem from the perspective of the colonized, however.

4. Kenneth Waltz, *Theory of International Politics* (Reading, MA: Addison-Wesley, 1979), p. 72.

5. This deficiency may also relate to the scholarly habits of many Americans, which is to ignore ideas and perspectives from elsewhere. Susan Strange (1995: 165) has claimed in her inimitably forward style that "academic writing by the great majority of Americans is blissfully and habitually deaf and blind to the ideas and perceptions of the outside world." Susan Strange, "Political Economy and International Relations," in *International Relations Today*, eds. Ken Booth and Steve Smith (Cambridge: Polity Press, 1995), p. 165.

6. K. J. Holsti, "War, Peace, and the State of the State," *International Political Science Review*, vol. 16, no. 4 (1995), pps. 319–26; K. J. Holsti, *The State, War,*

and the State of War, chap. 2. See also, for comparison, Julian Saurin, "The End of International Relations? The State and International Theory in the Age of Globalization," in *Boundaries in Question: New Directions in International Relations,* eds., Andrew Linklater and John Macmillan (NY: Pinter, 1995), pps. 244–61, see esp. p. 247.

7. James M. Goldeiger and Michael McFaul, "A Tale of Two Worlds: Core and Periphery in the Post–Cold War Era," *International Organization,* vol. 46, no. 2 (1992), pps. 467–92; Max Singer and Aaron Wildavsky, *The Real World Order: Zones of Peace, Zones of Turmoil,* revised edition (Chatham, NJ: Chatham House Publishers, 1996).

8. Johan Galtung, "A Structural Theory of Imperialism," *Journal of Peace Research,* vol. 8 (1971), pps. 81–117.

9. Brian Crozier, *The Rebels: A Study of Post-War Insurrections* (Boston: Beacon Press, 1960); Franklin M. Osanka, ed., *Modern Guerrilla Warfare: Fighting Communist Guerrilla Movements, 1941–1961* (NY: The Free Press, 1962).

10. John Schoeberlein-Engel, "Conflict in Tajikistan and Central Asia: The Myth of Ethnic Animosity," *Harvard Middle Eastern and Islamic Review,* vol. 1 (1995), pps. 1–55.

11. Benedict Anderson, *Imagined Communities: Reflections on the Origin and Spread of Nationalism* (London: Verso Press, 1983); Paul Brass, ed., *Ethnic Groups and the State* (London: Croom Helm, 1985); see also Yosef Lapid, "Culture's Ship: Returns and Departures in International Relations Theory," in *The Return of Culture and Identity in IR Theory,* eds., Yosef Lapid and Friedrich Kratochwil (Boulder, CO: Lynne Rienner, 1996), pps. 3–20.

12. Barry R. Posen, "The Security Dilemma and Ethnic Conflict," in *Ethnic Conflict and International Security,* ed., Michael E. Brown (Princeton, NJ: Princeton University Press, 1993), pps. 103–24; Jack Snyder, "Nationalism and the Crisis of the Post-Soviet State," in *Ethnic Conflict and International Security,* ed., Michael E. Brown (Princeton, NJ: Princeton University Press, 1993), pps. 79–102. For a critique of Posen's realist-type analysis, see Yosef Lapid, "Culture's Ship," in *The Return of Culture and Identity in IR Theory,* eds., Yosef Lapid and Friedrich Kratochwil, pps., 112–14.

13. Lewis Coser, *The Functions of Group Conflict* (NY: The Free Press, 1964); Ted Robert Gurr, *Why Men Rebel* (Princeton, NJ: Princeton University Press, 1970).

14. Steven R. David, "The Primacy of Internal War," paper presented at the annual meeting, International Studies Association, San Diego, CA, 1996. The quote is from p. 16.

15. Ted Robert Gurr, "On the Political Consequences of Scarcity and Economic Decline," *International Studies Quarterly,* vol. 29, no.1 (1985), pps. 51–75; Thomas F. Homer-Dixon, "Environmental Scarcities and Violent Conflict: Evidence from Cases," *International Security,* vol. 19, no.1 (1994), pps. 5–40; Mark Levy, "Is the Environment a National Security Issue?" *International Security,* vol. 20, no. 2 (1995), pps. 35–62; Shin-wha Lee, "Not a One-Time Event: Environmental Change, Ethnic Rivalry, and Violent Conflict in the Third World," paper presented at the annual meeting, International Studies Association, San Diego, CA, 1996.

16. Benedict Anderson, *Imagined Communities: Reflections on the Origin and Spread of Nationalism* (London: Verso Press, 1983).

17. Edward Said, *Orientalism* (NY: Pantheon, 1978).

18. Peter Uvin, "Development, Aid and Conflict," paper presented at the conference "The Political Economy of Humanitarian Emergencies," United Nations University/World Institute for Development Economics Research, Helsinki, 1996, pps. 4–6.

19. K. J. Holsti, *The State, War, and the State of War,* chap. 5.

20. Rudolph J. Rummel, *Death by Government* (New Brunswick, NJ, and London: Transaction Publishers, 1994), p. 15.

21. Russell Hardin, *One for All: The Logic of Group Conflict* (Princeton, NJ: Princeton University Press, 1995).

22. Wayne Nafziger and William Richter, "Biafra and Bangladesh: The Political Economy of Secession," *Journal of Peace Research,* vol. 13, no. 2 (1976), pps. 91–109.

23. Shin-wha Lee, "Not a One-Time Event," pps. 16–22.

24. Ishtiaq Ahmed, *State, Nation and Ethnicity in Contemporary South Asia* (NY: Pinter, 1996), pps. 246, 253.

25. Patrick D. Gaffney, "Burundi in the Balance: Humanitarian Crisis or Genocidal Disaster?" paper presented at the conference "The Political Economy of Humanitarian Emergencies," United Nations University/World Institute for Development Economics Research, Helsinki, 1996.

26. Ishtiaq Ahmed, *State, Nation and Ethnicity;* Scott Pegg, "On the Margins: International Society and the *de facto* State," Ph.D. diss., University of British Columbia, 1997, pps. 101, 106.

27. Peter Uvin, "Development, Aid and Conflict," p. 8.

28. K. J. Holsti, *The State, War, and the State of War,* ch. 6.

29. Russell Hardin, *One for All;* Michael Ignatieff, *Blood and Belonging: Journeys into the New Nationalism* (NY: Farrar, Strauss, and Giroux, 1993).

30. There is much evidence to suggest that the violent secessionist movement had been planned and organized—partly by Serbia—for some time before the plebiscite. It is questionable, however, whether the Bosnian Serbs would have launched the war in the absence of a Bosnian declaration of independence.

31. Edward E. Rice, *Wars of the Third Kind: Conflict in Underdeveloped Countries* (Berkeley, CA: University of California Press, 1988); Leslie Gelb, "Quelling the Teacup Wars," *Foreign Affairs,* vol. 73, no. 6 (1994), pps. 2–6.

32. Mohammed Ayoob, "State Making, State Breaking, and State Failure," in *Managing Global Chaos: Sources of and Responses to International Conflict,* eds., Chester A. Crocker and Fen Osler Hampson with Pamela Aall (Washington, DC: United States Institute for Peace Press, 1996), pps. 37–52.

33. Ted Robert Gurr, "Ethnopolitical Conflict in the 1990s: Patterns and Trends," paper presented at the conference "The Political Economy of Humanitarian Emergencies," United Nations University/World Institute for Development Economics Research, Helsinki, 1996, p. 17.

34. There are many other types of authority structures in the world, or what Ferguson and Mansbach have called "polities." Yale H. Ferguson and Richard W.

Mansbach, "The Past as Prelude to the Future? Identities and Loyalties in Global Politics," in *The Return of Culture and Identity in IR Theory*, eds., Yosef Lapid and Friedrich Kratochwil (Boulder, CO: Lynn Rienner, 1996), pps. 21–44. However, few of these have formal standing in international law, and none has official representation in most international organizations.

35. A postmodernist-type analysis suggests that the universalization of the state format did not come from emulation of the successful, or from material conditions. Rather, it came from a forceful expansion of European ideas of destiny and superiority of the Self over the Other. This is seen, for example, in numerous statements by Hegel. Bartelson quotes Hegel as stating "[w]hether in its transcendental or empirical mode of being . . . [the state and the states system] stands to the non-European arena as Same to Other; the ideal unity of sovereignty and anarchy is historically destined to spread, and sweep away all other inferior forms of political organization." Jens Bartelson, *A Genealogy of Sovereignty* (Cambridge: Cambridge University Press, 1995), p. 230. João Resende-Santos, "Anarchy and the Emulation of Military Systems: Military Organization and Technology in South America, 1870–1930," *Realism: Restatements and Renewal*, special issue of *Security Studies*, vol. 5, no. 3 (1996), pps. 193–260.

36. Julian Saurin, "The End of International Relations?" in *Boundaries in Question*, eds., Andrew Linklater and John Macmillan, pps. 244–61.

37. Joel Migdal, *Strong Societies and Weak States: State-Society Relations and State Capabilities in the Third World* (Princeton, NJ: Princeton University Press, 1988); Yale H. Ferguson and Richard W. Mansbach, "The Past as Prelude to the Future? Identities and Loyalties in Global Politics," in *The Return of Culture and Identity in IR Theory*, eds., Yosef Lapid and Friedrich Kratochwil (Boulder, CO: Lynne Rienner Publishers, 1996), pps. 21–46.

38. Steve Levine, "Tajiks Talk of Peace between Battles," *The New York Times*, January 6, 1997, p. 4.

39. Quincy Wright, *The Study of International Relations* (NY: Appleton-Century-Crofts, 1955), p. 185.

40. Scott Pegg, "On the Margins."

41. There is a developing literature on alternatives to the state, including the "emergence of a new form of state and thus states system, which breaks down the spatial coincidence between state-as-actor and state-as-structure." Alexander Wendt, "Identity and Structural Change in International Politics," in *The Return of Culture and Identity in IR Theory*, eds., Yosef Lapid and Friedrich Kratochwil (Boulder, CO: Lynne Rienner, 1996), p. 61. However, most of this discussion alludes to derogation of state authority to international bodies, not to the development of "micro-authorities" at local levels, as has been seen in Somalia and Liberia recently.

42. John Ruggie, "Territoriality and Beyond: Problematizing Modernity in International Relations," *International Organization*, vol. 47, no. 1 (1993), pps. 139–74.

43. Bahgat Korany, "Strategic Studies and the Third World: A Critical Evaluation," *International Social Science Journal*, vol. 38, no. 4 (1986), pps. 547–62; Barry Buzan, *People, State and Fear: The National Security Problem in International Rela-*

tions (Chapel Hill, NC: University of North Carolina Press, 1983); K. J. Holsti, "International Theory and War in the Third World," in *The Insecurity Dilemma,* ed., Brian Job (Boulder, CO: Lynne Rienner Publishers, 1992), pps. 37–60.

44. James N. Rosenau and Otto Czempiel, eds., *Governance without Government: Order and Change in World Politics* (Cambridge, MA: Cambridge University Press, 1992).

Bibliography

Ahmed, Ishtiaq. *State, Nation and Ethnicity in Contemporary South Asia.* New York: Pinter, 1996.

Anderson, Benedict. *Imagined Communities: Reflections on the Origin and Spread of Nationalism.* London: Verso Press, 1983.

Ayoob, Mohammed. "State Making, State Breaking, and State Failure." In *Managing Global Chaos: Sources of and Responses to International Conflict.* Eds. Chester A. Crocker and Fen Osler Hampson with Pamela Aall. Washington, DC: United States Institute for Peace Press, 1996, pps. 37–52.

———. *The Third World Security Predicament: State Making, Regional Conflict, and the International System.* Boulder, CO: Lynne Rienner, 1995.

Bartelson, Jens. *A Genealogy of Sovereignty.* Cambridge: Cambridge University Press, 1995.

Brass, Paul, ed. *Ethnic Groups and the State.* London: Croom Helm, 1995.

Bull, Hedley. *The Anarchical Society.* London: Macmillan, 1978.

Buzan, Barry. *People, States and Fear: The National Security Problem in International Relations.* Chapel Hill, NC: University of North Carolina Press, 1983.

Coser, Lewis. *The Functions of Group Conflict.* New York: The Free Press, 1964.

Crozier, Brian. *The Rebels: A Study of Post-War Insurrections.* Boston: Beacon Press, 1960.

David, Steven R. "The Primacy of Internal War." Paper presented at the annual meeting, International Studies Association, San Diego, CA, 1996.

Deutsch, Karl W. *Political Community at the International Level: Problems of Definition and Measurement.* Garden City, NY: Doubleday, 1954.

Ferguson, Yale H., and Richard W. Mansbach. "The Past as Prelude to the Future? Identities and Loyalties in Global Politics." In *The Return of Culture and Identity in IR Theory.* Eds. Yosef Lapid and Friedrich Kratochwil. Boulder, CO: Lynne Rienner Publishers, 1996, pps. 21–46.

Gaffney, Patrick D. "Burundi in the Balance: Humanitarian Crisis or Genocidal Disaster?" Paper presented at the conference "The Political Economy of Humanitarian Emergencies." United Nations University/World Institute for Development Economics Research. Helsinki, 1996.

Galtung, Johan. "A Structural Theory of Imperialism." *Journal of Peace Research.* Vol. 8 (1971), pps. 81–117.

Gelb, Leslie. "Quelling the Teacup Wars." *Foreign Affairs.* Vol. 73, no. 6 (1994), pps. 2–6.

Goldgeier, James M. and Michael McFaul. "A Tale of Two Worlds: Core and Periphery in the Post–Cold War Era." *International Organization.* Vol. 46, no. 2 (1992), pps. 467–92.

Gurr, Ted Robert. "Ethnopolitical Conflict in the 1990s: Patterns and Trends." Paper presented at the conference "The Political Economy of Humanitarian Emergencies." United Nations University/World Institute for Development Economics Research. Helsinki, 1996.

———. "On the Political Consequences of Scarcity and Economic Decline." *International Studies Quarterly.* Vol. 29, no. 1 (1985), pps. 51–75.

———. *Why Men Rebel.* Princeton, NJ: Princeton University Press, 1970.

Hardin, Russell. *One for All: The Logic of Group Conflict.* Princeton, NJ: Princeton University Press, 1995.

Hobson, J. A. *Imperialism: A Study.* London: Allen & Unwin, 1938.

Holsti, K. J. *The State, War, and the State of War.* Cambridge: Cambridge University Press, 1996.

———. "War, Peace, and the State of the State." *International Political Science Review.* Vol. 16, no. 4 (1995), pps. 319–39.

———. "International Theory and War in the Third World." In *The Insecurity Dilemma.* Ed. Brian Job. Boulder, CO: Lynne Rienner Publishers, 1992.

Homer-Dixon, Thomas F. "Environmental Scarcities and Violent Conflict: Evidence from Cases." *International Security.* Vol 19, no. 1 (1994), pps. 5–40.

Ignatieff, Michael. *Blood and Belonging: Journeys into the New Nationalism.* NY: Farrar, Strauss, and Giroux, 1993.

Jackson, Robert H. *Quasi-states: Sovereignty, International Relations and the Third World.* Cambridge: Cambridge University Press, 1990.

Korany, Bahgat. "Strategic Studies and the Third World: A Critical Evaluation." *International Social Science Journal.* Vol. 38, no. 4 (1986), pps. 547–62.

Krause, Keith. "Insecurity and State Formation in the Global Military Order." *European Journal of International Relations.* Vol. 2, no. 3 (1996), pps. 319–54.

Lapid, Yosef. "Culture's Ship: Returns and Departures in International Relations Theory." In *The Return of Culture and Identity in IR Theory.* Eds. Yosef Lapid and Friedrich Kratochwil. Boulder, CO: Lynne Rienner, 1996, pps. 3–20.

Larus, Joel, ed. *Comparative World Politics: Readings in Western and Pre-modern Non-Western International Relations.* Belmont, CA: Wadsworth, 1964.

Lee, Shin-wha. "Not a One-Time Event: Environmental Change, Ethnic Rivalry, and Violent Conflict in the Third World." Paper presented at the annual meeting, International Studies Association, San Diego, CA, 1996.

Lenin, V. I. *Imperialism: The Highest Stage of Capitalism.* NY: International Publishers, 1939.

LeVine, Steve. "Tajiks Talk of Peace between Battles." *New York Times,* January 6, 1997, p. 4.

Levy, Mark. "Is the Environment a National Security Issue?" *International Security.* Vol. 20, no. 2 (1995), pps. 35–62.

Lichtheim, George. *Imperialism.* NY: Praeger, 1971.

Migdal, Joel. *Strong Societies and Weak States: State-Society Relations and State Capabilities in the Third World.* Princeton, NJ: Princeton University Press, 1988.

Modelski, George. "Kautilya: Foreign Policy and International System in the Ancient Hindu World." *American Political Science Review.* Vol. 58, (1964), pps. 549–60.

Moon, Parker T. *Imperialism and World Politics*. NY: Macmillan, 1926.

Nafziger, Wayne, and William Richter. "Biafra and Bangladesh: The Political Economy of Secession." *Journal of Peace Research*. Vol. 13, no. 2 (1976), pps. 91–109.

Osanka, Franklin M., ed. *Modern Guerrilla Warfare: Fighting Communist Guerrilla Movements, 1941–1961*. NY: The Free Press, 1962.

Pegg, Scott. "On the Margins: International Society and the *de facto* State." Ph.D. diss., University of British Columbia, 1997.

Posen, Barry R. "The Security Dilemma and Ethic Conflict." In *Ethnic Conflict and International Security*. Ed. Michael E. Brown. Princeton, NJ: Princeton University Press, 1993, pps. 103–24.

Resende-Santos, João. "Anarchy and the Emulation of Military Systems: Military Organization and Technology in South America, 1870–1930." *Realism: Restatements and Renewal*. Special issue of *Security Studies*. Vol. 5, no. 3 (1996), pps. 193–260.

Rice, Edward E. *Wars of the Third Kind: Conflict in Underdeveloped Countries*. Berkeley, CA: University of California Press, 1988.

Rosenau, James N. and Otto Czempiel, eds. *Governance without Government: Order and Change in World Politics*. Cambridge: Cambridge University Press, 1992.

Ruggie, John. "Territoriality and Beyond: Problematizing Modernity in International Relations." *International Organization*. Vol. 47, no.1 (1993), pps. 139–74.

Rule, James B. *Theories of Civil Violence*. Berkeley, CA: University of California Press, 1988.

Rummel, Rudolph J. *Death by Government*. London: Transaction Publishers, 1994.

Said, Edward. *Orientalism*. NY: Pantheon, 1978.

Saurin, Julian. "The End of International Relations? The State and International Theory in the Age of Globalization." In *Boundaries in Question: New Directions in International Relations*. Eds. Andrew Linklater and John Macmillan. NY: Pinter, 1995, pps. 244–61.

Schoeberlein-Engel, John. "Conflict in Tajikistan and Central Asia: The Myth of Ethnic Animosity." *Harvard Middle Eastern and Islamic Review*, Vol. 1 (1994), pps. 1–55.

Schwartz, Stuart B., ed. *Implicit Understandings: Observing, Reporting, and Reflecting on the Encounters Between Europeans and Other Peoples in the Early Modern Era*. Cambridge: Cambridge University Press, 1994.

Singer, Max, and Aaron Wildavsky. *The Real World Order: Zones of Peace, Zones of Turmoil*, Revised ed. Chatham, NJ: Chatham House Publishers, 1996.

Snyder, Jack. "Nationalism and the Crisis of the Post-Soviet State." *Ethnic Conflict and International Security*. Ed. Michael E. Brown. Princeton, NJ: Princeton University Press, 1993, pps. 77–102.

Strange, Susan. "Political Economy and International Relations." In *International Relations Theory Today*. Eds. Ken Booth and Steve Smith. Cambridge: Polity Press, 1995, ch. 7.

Uvin, Peter. "Development, Aid and Conflict." Paper presented at conference "The Political Economy of Humanitarian Emergencies." United Nations University/World Institute for Development Economics Research. Helsinki, 1996.

Waltz, Kenneth. *Theory of International Politics.* Reading, MA: Addison-Wesley, 1979.

Wendt, Alexander. "Identity and Structural Change in International Politics." In *The Return of Culture and Identity in IR Theory.* Eds. Yosef Lapid and Friedrich Kratochwil. Boulder, CO: Lynne Rienner Publishers, 1996, pps. 47–64.

Wright, Quincy. *The Study of International Relations.* NY: Appleton-Century-Crofts, 1955.

SIX

Third World Thinking and Contemporary International Relations[1]

Donald J. Puchala

Salman Rushdie

One could, as Timothy Brennan recommends, interpret Salman Rushdie's *The Satanic Verses,* as "a novel that is, after all, primarily about a very secular England."[2] Like several of Rushdie's other writings, this controversial novel is about immigrant ordeals in British society, and his criticisms of the Thatcher-constructed environment are stinging. But almost no one who read the book, read it for its British content, and countless others who reacted without reading the novel were ever aware that it had British content. Instead, *The Satanic Verses* became in 1988–89, and still remains, an extraordinarily powerful symbol of what we may term a "West-non-West" cultural cleavage that is emerging as a central fault line in contemporary International Relations.

The events and implications of the Rushdie affair are well known. The publication of Rushdie's *The Satanic Verses* in 1988, set off a chain of events that reverberated around the world. Parts of the novel were read by Muslims as blasphemous insults to their faith of the most serious kind. "The real equivalent of comparative blasphemy would be in portraying the Virgin Mary as a prostitute, and Jesus as the son of one of her sexual clients," said Ali Mazrui, and his comments were not among the most disparaging that were offered.[3] Other Muslim critics took Rushdie to task as a "self-hater eager to ingratiate himself with the colonizer," as someone who put commercial success above honor, someone who stooped to writing in English about sacred matters that could not and should not be discussed in that language, someone who had engaged in "literary terrorism" against Islamic societies and in "literary colonialism" more generally, and, most dramatically, someone who had committed high treason under Islamic law.[4] For this treasonous act, Salman Rushdie and his publishers were sentenced to death on February 14, 1989, under a fatwa issued by Iran's Ayatollah Khomeini, who asked "all Muslims to execute them wherever they find them."[5] Khomeini's fatwa prompted V. S. Naipaul to call the episode "an extreme form of literary criticism."[6]

Rushdie went into hiding. Meanwhile, sales of *The Satanic Verses* were banned in most Muslim countries, rioting in protest of sales in the West erupted in several countries, including India and Pakistan, dozens of people were killed in these incidents, book burnings took place in Muslim immigrant communities in Western countries, and diplomatic protests were directed at London by Arab and Islamic governments, variously demanding the banning of *The Satanic Verses*. At the same time Muslim countries fell out among themselves both over the rectitude of the Ayatollah's fatwa, and over how quickly and how harshly those among them had moved to condemn Rushdie and *The Satanic Verses*. Saudi Arabia, for example, came under heavy criticism from Arab neighbors for moving too slowly and irresolutely against the infamous book.[7]

The British, American, and other Western governments reacted to the Ayatollah's fatwa and the Muslim protests with strong affirmations of Rushdie's right to freedom of speech, with his publishers' right to freedom of the press, with determined condemnation of Iran's intrusion upon British sovereignty, and with every intention of enforcing respect for international law. Both the Islamic outrage over Rushdie's book, and, more particularly, the extraterritorial death sentence by the Ayatollah Khomeini were widely interpreted in the West as immoral, illegal, and therefore unconscionable. They offended basic Western values and confirmed stereotypes of Third World extremism and propensities to violence. The United Kingdom ultimately severed diplomatic relations with Tehran over the Rushdie affair. Leading Islamic spokesmen reacted to the entire turn of events with a certain satisfaction at having delivered the message to the West that the Muslim religion could not be defamed without serious consequences and that the West had been prevented "from using the Rushdie affair to infiltrate its ideas of human rights into the Islamic world."[8]

From the Tiny Tip toward the Larger Iceberg

Among the more revealing musings on the Rushdie affair were those of Edward Said, who remarked, sometime after the incident had run its immediate course, that neither "Iran's official reaction to the Rushdie novel . . .

or the public and private expression of outrage in the West against the fatwa is intelligible . . . without reference to the overall logic and the minute articulations and reactions set in motion by the overbearing system."[9] It is this "overbearing system" that this chapter seeks to examine, largely from the perspective of those, like Said, who find it overbearing. In many ways the Rushdie affair was a microcosmic sounding of themes and interpretations contained in the perspectives of thinkers in today's Third World who write about International Relations. We find in the Rushdie affair for example: first, a politicized cleavage and confrontation along cultural fault lines that perceptibly separate the non-West from the West; second, high degrees of "Orientalist" and "Occidentalist" stereotyping; third, another politicized cultural cleavage within the involved group of Third World societies that separates moderate, western-leaning actors from radical, Western-hostile ones; fourth, yet another politicized cultural cleavage within each involved Third World society that separates moderns from traditionals; fifth, an ethos or atmosphere of antihegemonic struggle shared by many Third World participants; next, a condoning orientation on the part of some Third World agents toward deconstruction, retribution, and violence; and finally, a battle of books or texts that involves fundamental values, references to Gods, interpretations of history, uses of language, and definitions of literature, all amounting to what might be called a "clashing of civilizations."[10]

For purposes of this chapter, let us define the Third World as mainly those societies that are outside of Europe and its cultural enclaves in North America, Australia, and New Zealand. But, let us also note, and emphasize, that the designation Third World as employed in here is much more a state of mind—a perspective, interpretation, critique, or weltanschauung—than a geographical sphere. Many of the ideas discussed in this chapter, for example, are the inspirations of writers living and working within the unassimilated immigrant enclaves of Africans, Asians, Middle Easterners, and Latins found within Europe, the United States, Canada, Australia, and New Zealand. In the same way, in this chapter the Third World is contrasted with the West, which again, is a state of mind and not a condition of geography. It must include, for example, the perspectives of the bourgeois strata and other Westernized or comprador groups found today within all Third World societies. Accordingly, interactions between the Third World and the West may therefore take place *between* predominantly Third World and predominantly Western societies as well as *within* both. The relevant frontiers across which interactions between the Third World and the West occur are political-ideological and cultural rather than geopolitical and they do not necessarily correspond to the world of states as depicted on political maps. Naturally, there is great diversity within both the Third World and the West, but there is also sufficient commonality within both to render them ontologically meaningful and analytically useful. Finally, it needs to be pointed out that there are fundamental conceptual problems with the designations Third World and West inasmuch as they are both hangovers from the analytical vocabulary of the Cold War. Neither satisfactorily identifies either of the ideological configurations discussed here and having to use them for want of better concepts blunts rather than sharpens analysis.[11]

In this chapter I am going to try to explain the Third World's thinking about International Relations, but I enter upon this undertaking with considerable trepidation. I am sensitive to the fact that I am a Westerner, that I risk falling into Orientalist intellectual traps, and that there are very possibly important aspects of Third World thinking that I cannot fully understand regardless of the effort invested in study.[12] Generally speaking, Westerners, and Americans in particular, have not proven themselves especially successful at fathoming the depths of non-Western cultures and ideologies (though neither have Third World analysts done very well at understanding the West).[13]

There are also problems of validity and meaning inherent in this exercise. A great many of the Third World authors, such as Frantz Fanon, C. L. R. James, Basil Davidson, Amilcar Cabral, Ngugi wa Thiong'o, Lee Kuan Yew, and Muhammed Hussein Fadlallah, whose thinking is reviewed in this chapter might be considered radicals who espouse views distant even from Third World mainstreams, and the same might be said for many of the Western commentators, such as Barbara Harlow, Immanuel Wallerstein, William Pfaff, and Timothy Brennan, with respect to their own societies' critical mainstreams. But, who defines the mainstreams, and, more important, what determines the historical significance of ideas? "The temptation for metropolitan audiences," Said notes, "has usually been to rule that these books . . . are merely evidence of native literature written by 'native informants,' rather than coeval contributions to knowledge," and to therefore dismiss them.[14] More poignantly, concerning some of the Islamic spokesmen, Judith Miller observes that: "For American and European officials charged with protecting Western interests abroad, their names evoke images of car bombs, murder, and young, bearded holy warriors bent on historic revenge. In Arab capitals, they represent the militant Islamic revival feared by conservative rulers and prayed for by the millions of unhappily ruled, the futureless young, the poor, the dispossessed—those the Muslims call 'the disinherited.'"[15]

It is never easy to identify beforehand ideas destined to affect history, partly because such ideas are usually revolutionary, and complacent elements of the status quo tend seldom to take them seriously until it is too late. Every great revolution is an intellectual surprise when it happens. Still, countless other revolutionary ideas have dissolved into history, as well might all of those examined in this chapter.

There is also the question of perspective. A good deal of what Third World theorists are propounding and prescribing is inimicable to Western values and threatening to Western interests, and many Third World doctrines, firmly endorsed, leave little room for dialogue or compromise. My intellectual standpoint, I find, is close to that of Adda Bozeman, who is deeply bothered by Third World challenges to Western values, but who nevertheless insists that we in the West must, in our own interest, understand and continually take account of non-Western thinking. "[B]ecause we do not understand 'others' in the world on their own terms, and because both our collective self-view and our worldview are decidedly unrealistic, . . . we do not have the knowledge upon which our foreign relations can rest securely in war and peace."[16] Inasmuch as others who hold strong beliefs can be expected to act in accord with them, it is incumbent upon us, who might be the subjects of others' actions, to understand their beliefs.

Finally, there is the question of comprehensiveness. There is a great deal of Third World political thinking that is not reviewed in this chapter, and obvious omissions certainly raise questions about bias and generalizability. Many Chinese notions about the structure and process of International Relations are touched upon in only a very cursory way here, and Japanese and Korean thinking are passed over completely. Leaving out these important East Asian perspectives was a matter of the time I had available for research and writing, and continuing research will certainly take them seriously into account. Also omitted are most of the nonradical, Third World views—the moderates, modernists, secularists, and globalists, and most of the Westernized and social science socialized products of American graduate schools who today staff the political science departments of Third World universities. These people are individually and collectively vilified by those theorists about whom I discuss in this chapter. How representative Third World radical thinking is today, is difficult to determine. That its main themes recur in the analyses and pronouncements of Islamic fundamentalists, Arab nationalists, American Black nationalists, Iranian revolutionaries, Hindu fundamentalists, Chinese Marxists, Chiapas leaders, Shining Path and Tupac Amaru guerrillas, Singaporian officials, Lebanese poets, African dramatists, South American novelists, Caribbean political theorists, and Indian and Chinese filmmakers, suggests that such thinking is fairly widespread. The themes resonate among young people, poor people, and angry people, of which there are many in the Third World.

Third World Worldviews

Third World thinking about International Relations is best treated as a set of normative themes that collectively embody a description and evaluation of world affairs as well as prescriptions for action. Prominent among these themes are bifurcation, Western culpability and cultural inadequacy, neo-colonialism, emancipation, and struggle.

Bifurcation

In the Third World worldview the only centrally significant subdivision of humanity and its constituent social units is the bifurcation "non-West/West." The distinction drawn by Third World writers is essentially cultural, through the two respective cultural communities—that is, the Third World and the West—also have distinguishing social, political, and economic attributes. It is acknowledged that the Third World is not a homogenous cultural community, but this is less important for the non-Western writers than their firm belief that the West *is* such a homogeneous community and that it must therefore be confronted in solidarity. Diversity in the world outside the West is inconsequential in the face of the much more profound cleavage between all Third World peoples and those in the West. C. L. R. James speaks of "mighty opposites," Ngugi wa Thiong'o sees "two mutually opposed forces," while Fanon observes "two forces, opposed to each other by their very nature." Jean-Paul Sartre opens his sympathetic preface to Fanon's *The Wretched of the Earth* by observing that "not so very long ago, the earth numbered two thousand million inhabitants: five hundred million men, and one thousand five hundred million natives." Muhammad Iqbal, symbolizing the Third World as "Syria," described this bifurcation of humanity in four ironic lines:

> This land of Syria gave the West a Prophet
> Of purity and pity and innocence;
> And Syria from the West as recompense
> Gets dice and drink and troops of prostitutes.[17]

Canadian author Rhoda E. Howard calls the bifurcated worldview of the Third World Occidentalism. Referring to the West's caricatured and self-serving image of the East that Edward Said labeled Orientalism, Howard observes that the Third World's image of the West is Orientalism's obverse. "In the Occidentalist vision," she writes, "the West is unchanging, monolithic, and completely defined by its cultural attributes."[18] To which Said himself adds that "Muslims or Africans or Indians or Japanese . . . attack the West, or Americanization, or imperialism, with little more attention to detail, critical differentiation, discrimination, and distinction than has been lavished on them by the West."[19] The vision is Gramscian: the West and its culture are deemed to represent a global hegemony, frequently shorthandedly labeled "imperialism," that is relatively undiminished even with the formal

passing of colonialism. It is reinforced by the global reach of Western public and private institutions—international organizations, international law
and diplomacy, the CIA, MNCs, Christian churches, the media, films, and
the like—and it is abetted by quisling, Westernized classes and governments
within Third World countries who share in the exploitation of peasants and
workers and the destruction of traditional cultures. From this vision there
follows a riveting obsession with the West, largely to the exclusion of other
international agents or arenas. For Third World writers, non-West/West interactions constitute if not most of International Relations, then at least
everything that is significant in contemporary International Relations.

Western Culpability and Cultural Inadequacy

Along with the Third World's preoccupations with the West goes a bitter
criticism. "Listen to the white world," writes the West Indian poet Aimé
Césaire,

> its horrible exhaustion from its
>   immense labours
> its rebellious joints cracking under
>   the pitiless stars
> its blue steel rigidities, cutting
>   through the mysteries of the flesh
> listen to their vainglorious conquests
>   trumpeting their defeats
> listen to the grandiose alibis of their
>   pitiful floundering[20]

Or, even more bitingly, in the words of the Senegalese poet David Diop:

> In those days
> When civilization kicked us in the face
> When holy water slapped our cringing brows
> The vultures built in the shadow of their talons
> The bloodstained monument of tutelage
> In those days
> There was painful laughter on the metallic hell of the roads
> And the monotonous rhythm of the paternoster
> Drowned the howling on the plantations
> O the bitter memories of extorted kisses
> Of promises broken at the point of a gun

> Of foreigners who did not seem human
> Who knew all the books but did not know love[21]

The heart of the Third World's indictment of the West is the historical fact that Europeans and later Americans were perpetrators of imperialism and colonizers who purposefully, and often brutally, subjugated large portions of the non-European world between the early sixteenth and the mid-twentieth centuries. Westerners are seen to have exploited and enslaved people, extracted wealth, appropriated property, destroyed communities and displaced governments—selfishly, insensitively, arrogantly, and unjustifiably. But even more devastatingly, and more importantly in the context of present-day critical thinking, Westerners are accused of having ripped away the cultures, silenced the languages, belittled the religions, and denied the histories of native peoples.[22] Imperialism was more than alien rule: it was cultural annihilation. Westerners forcibly imposed their own norms, Gods, languages, and ways of living on non-European peoples, but then continued to treat as inferiors even those among the native peoples who assimilated.[23] For Muslim peoples the humiliation of Western imperialism was all the more devastating because what was "truly evil and unacceptable [was] the domination of infidels over true believers," which "is blasphemous and unnatural, since it leads to the corruption of religion and morality in society."[24] The ghosts of colonialism continue to haunt Third World thinking, and their mesmerizing powers should never be underestimated.

Resenting imperialism is only one part of the Third World brief against the West. Even if imperialism had never occurred, today there would still be a rejection of western culture. Many Muslims presently look askance at the West because it is Christian, and they see that religion as having lost its vigor and its purity. For their part, secular critics, like Singapore's Lee Kuan Yew, indict Western society for its moral decline and hedonism and for obvious disconnections between professed values and actual performance: "[A]s a total system, I find parts of it totally unacceptable: guns, drugs, violent crime, vagrancy, unbecoming behavior in public—in sum the breakdown of civil society. The expansion of the right of the individual to behave or misbehave as he pleases has come at the expense of orderly society."[25]

Others, such as Africa's Josiah Cobbah center their distaste for Western culture on the West's extolling of individualism at the expense of communalism, the emphasis on individual rights along with the playing down of duties and responsibilities, and the trumpeting of legal equality along with the denial of social deference, respect for status, and ascriptive hierarchy. African culture is communal and hierarchical, Cobbah points out, and "this worldview is for all intents and purposes as valid as the European theories of individualism and social contract."[26] Any number of East Asians would share Cobbah's views. Other Third World critics go on to add that the West is congenitally racist, predispositionally violent, false to its own principles regarding human equality, cynical in its claims about advancing democracy (which in itself is regarded by some as an alien and undesirable form of government), and self-deceived in its beliefs that it is democratic.[27] People in the West, critics contend, have little access to government and no voice in public policy, which is the ken of self-interested, exploiting elites. Culturally, the critics say, the West has little to offer, and indeed it represents much that must be guarded against.

Neocolonialism

Both vigilance and resistance are required among Third World peoples because Western imperialism continues in the form of neocolonialism. There is near unanimity among radical Third World thinkers—African, Asian, West Indian, Latin, and Islamic—that colonialism did not end when formal political independence was achieved. Western economic exploitation did not subside; indeed it increased under the regime of the global-reaching multinationals. Western political domination did not diminish. It continued in the context of constraining Cold War alliances, and continues today in the form of quisling elites manipulated by outsiders, international institutions controlled by the West, imposed doctrines like "parliamentary democracy" endorsed by the West, and interventions by Western-dispatched "peacekeepers" and the ever-present CIA. Neither did Western cultural hegemony end: it continues via the Western control of the world's media, the prevalence of Western languages, particularly English, and the Western near-monopoly over advanced academic training and the determination of disciplinary canons. "By now," David Gordon summarizes, "[W]estern empire in any formal sense is almost completely a matter of the past . . . but economic and cultural decolonization often remain processes that are still not complete, and political decolonization is often only a formal rather than a real accomplishment." He appropriately concludes, that this situation is "in the eyes of the Third World, a source of frustration."[28]

Much of this frustration is vented on Westernized elites within non-Western societies, and within the Third World on countries identified as having sold out to Western imperialism. National political liberation in the 1960s and 1970s and so-called reformist nationalism thereafter, the critics say, served only to install in power local elites who seek in their own interest to ingratiate themselves with the West. The West in turn supports and protects them as they consolidate power, accumulate wealth, and suppress their own people. Typical of the vitriol heaped upon postcolonial nationalist elites is C. L. R. James's reaction to the breakup of the West Indian Federation:

> A federation meant that the economic line of direction should no longer be from island to London, but from island to island. But that involved the breakup of the old colonial system. The West Indian politicians preferred the breakup of the Federation.... The Queen of England was their queen. They receive royal visits; their legislatures begin with prayers; their bills are read three times; a mace has been presented to each of these distant infants by the Mother of parliaments; their prominent citizens receive an assortment of letters after their names, and in time the prefix "Sir." This no longer lessens but intensifies the battle between the old colonial system and democracy. Long before the actual independence was granted, large numbers of the middle classes, including their politicians, wanted it out as far into the distance as possible.[29]

More succinct, though also more damning, is Ngugi's description: "The economic and political dependence of this ... neo-colonial bourgeoisie is reflected in its culture of apemanship and parrotry enforced on a restive population through police boots, barbed wire, a gowned clergy and judiciary; their ideas are spread by a corpus of state intellectuals, the academic and journalistic laureates of the neo-colonial establishment."[30]

The thrust of the critique of reformist nationalism and the elites who espouse it is that it is precisely that—reformist and not revolutionary. It seeks accommodation with former imperial masters, and in so doing tramples upon the interests of Third World peoples. Nationalism was an essential first phase of liberation from colonial domination. It sought to achieve political independence, but it was to be a first phase only, since creating a fragmented postcolonial world of small, weak, impoverished, Western-styled states was not a formula for genuine liberation. In fact, such an arrangement played directly into the hands of those in the West who were interested in perpetuating their hegemony. Liberation stalled at the nationalist phase, mainly because nationalist movements installed Westernizers into positions of political power who have not deemed it in their interest to press on with the struggle for autonomy and identity.

Particular criticism is directed toward postcolonial and other Third World governments perceived as being too close to the West. Not only are these governments seen as dominated by comprador elites, alienated from the people, but they are also identified as promoters of Western interests in regional and world affairs. For this they earn pariah status, and open themselves to externally condoned and assisted attempts at subversion. Egypt, Saudi Arabia, and Algeria under its current military government are special cases in point. They are incessantly singled out for condemnation. Mexico and Peru are also in jeopardy. Examining the fates of Westernized elites in the Third World, William Pfaff reminds his readers that "South Vietnam's leaders had represented both the strong Catholic minority in their country and the westernized middle and professional classes who had run it under the previous colonial system."[31] Everything about the South Vietnamese elite was therefore anathema to proponents of genuine liberation.

Emancipation

This is by far the most prominent, and indeed the most powerful, theme in the non-Western narrative today. As told by Third World writers, relations between their societies and the West are essentially stories about undoing dominance-subordination, gaining self-determination, and regaining self-respect, reasserting that which has been suppressed, resurrecting that which has been submerged and reclaiming that which has been stolen. The goal is independence (the eradication of dependence); the process is emancipation; the method is "resistance," which means more than "standing against" and something more like "rejecting, purging and replacing."[32]

There are several variations on the theme of emancipation. Political emancipation is, by now, a rather timeworn striving, but it receives continuing emphasis in Third World articulations. As already suggested, formal political independence is no longer the objective; independence, however, is looked upon as a sham, nationalism is seen as a Western-modeled ideological distraction, and the goal of political emancipation is the displacement of Western-inserted elites and all that they stand for. "The European elite undertook to manufacture a native elite . . . these walking lies had nothing left to say to their brothers" and they have to go.[33]

There is also in Third World rhetoric the recurrent theme of emancipation from imperially imposed borders. While talk of adjusting borders appears to be officially taboo, especially in Africa, those who find no reason to respect quisling officialdom complain of the constraining, and symbolically prisonlike, nature of the time-defiant colonial borders, which they find insulting and meaningless. Edward Said begins to pick up this emancipation theme when, in his criticism of comprador elites, he notes that "along with authorized figures . . . the newly triumphant politicians seemed to require borders and passports first of all."[34] Basil Davidson drives the point home most eloquently:

> The frontiers are there, the frontiers are sacred. What else, after all, could guarantee privilege and power to the ruling elites? Yet the peoples, it would seem, see matters differently. They have their own solutions to this carapace accepted from the colonial period. The frontiers, for them, remain a foreign

unwanted imposition. What the peoples think upon this subject is shown by their incessant emigration and immigration across these lines on the map. . . . So that while a "bourgeois Africa" hardens its frontiers . . . a "peoples'" Africa works in quite another way.[35]

What is most disagreeable in critics' eyes about national borders in the former colonial world is not only that they are meaningless in cultural, tribal, geographic, or economic terms, but that *they were drawn by the imperial powers* and are imperialism's lingering, insulting legacy. They are also moats around national elites who abet neocolonialism.

Most familiar to Western readers are the economic arguments about *dependencia*.[36] Third World prescriptions for economic emancipation still follow from an originally Leninist-inspired analysis that links pervasive poverty in many Third World countries to the workings of the world capitalist system, deemed to be collusively controlled by financial, industrial, and governmental interests in the West. Classically stated by Chile's Salvador Allende in 1972, "there is a clear-cut dialectical relationship: imperialism exists because underdevelopment exists; underdevelopment exists because imperialism exists."[37] Even though Marxist articulations have been muted since the end of the Cold War, those elements of the *dependencia* analysis that linked economic underdevelopment in Third World countries to injustices perpetrated by an economically self-interested West continue to be widely accepted. Due partly to their lack of success and partly to the fall of Marxist economics from fashion, favor for statist development strategies, aimed at insulating weaker economies and poorer people from exploiting outsiders, were abandoned in a number of Asian, African, and Latin American countries beginning in the late 1980s. For a time, not even very many Third World radicals were objecting to pursuing development via "marketization" and to economic "reform" in the interest of making marketization work. Yet, by the mid-1990s, when the socially destructive and economically stratifying implications of "reform" began to appear, particularly in Latin America and Africa, and when it also became clear that about all the West was prepared to contribute economically to the Third World in the post–Cold War era was advice, the *dependencia* drums began beating again. The West on the outside, the reformers on the inside who took their cues from the West, the International Monetary Fund and its conditionalities, the World Bank and its criteria, the Lomé regime and its insensitivies, the United States and its indifference—became the attributed causes of the wrenching conditions inflicted upon the poor people in poorer countries. Revealingly, when the Tupac Amaru guerrillas seized the Japanese ambassador's residence in Lima, Peru, and took hostages in late 1996, "abandoning economic reform" was high on their register of demands.

The Third World perception that the poor people and poorer countries of the world are economically constrained by the global hegemony of the rich remains. Calls for economic justice and the redistribution of world income are still heard, as are protests against the power and exploitative behavior of western agents and institutions. There continue to be appeals for self-reliance, proposals for economic integration, and demands for heightened Third World influence within world economic organizations. But, in recent years Third World solidarity on economic issues has waned, various countries seem to be going it alone as best they can, and economic emancipation has slipped in priority on the resistance agenda to be replaced by more culturally focused ends.

William Pfaff calls the Third World quest for cultural emancipation "moral recovery" and Benjamin Barber calls it "jihad," which he defines at one point as "a throwback to premodern times: an attempt to recapture a world that existed prior to cosmopolitan capitalism and was defined by religious mysteries, hierarchical communities, spellbinding traditions, and historical torpor." Elsewhere, he defines Jihad as an "anti-Western anti-universalist struggle," and elsewhere again as "a literal war on the values, culture, and institutions that make up liberal society."[38] While such definitions describe some of the substance of the Third World's striving for cultural emancipation, they omit the essence of the movement. What non-Western intellectuals are advocating is the *seizing back of values, traditions, and identities that they assert have been stolen from them by colonialism.* Some describe the effort as being directed toward the voicing of narratives that colonialism had silenced. Without placing the striving for cultural emancipation in the context of earlier colonial suppression and oppression, it looses its meaning, and it sheds the bitter affect that must be attached to it. Ngugi captures this well:

> The oppressed and the exploited of the earth maintain their defiance: liberty from theft. But the biggest weapon wielded and actually daily unleashed by imperialism against that collective defiance is the cultural bomb. The effect of a cultural bomb is to annihilate a people's belief in their names, in their languages, in their environment, in their heritage of struggle, in their unity, in their capacities and ultimately in themselves. It makes them see their past as one wasteland of non-achievement and it makes them want to distance themselves from that wasteland. It makes them want to identify with that which is furthest removed from themselves; for instance, with other people's languages rather than their own. It makes them identify with that which is decadent and reactionary, all those forces which would stop their own spring of life. It even plants serious doubts about the moral rightness of struggle.[39]

Cultural emancipation has several aspects, not all pursued with equal vigor everywhere. For some, and for fundamentalist Muslims in particular, cultural emancipation takes the form of the rejection of modernity, its materialistic trappings, its secular lifestyle, its strict distinction between church and state, and its cosmopolitanism. "If democracy means Western democracy," Barber observes, "and modernization means Westernization, there would seem to be little hope for reconciliation since Islam regards Western secular culture and its attending values as corrupting to and morally incompatible with its own."[40] Others in the Third World seek modernization à la carte by asserting that industrialization need be accompanied neither by Western varieties of politics nor by Western kinds of liberal, civil societies. Economic modernization, they say, is fully compatible with traditional, non-Western social and political institutions that need to be vigilantly protected as industrialization runs its course.

Some in the Third World are also deeply concerned about seizing back languages and literatures suppressed under colonialism, because, they insist, language is the vehicle of culture and to silence it is to suffocate culture and to steal identity. Ngugi, for example, in his *Decolonizing the Mind* describes how English-language education under British colonialism subordinated and stifled African culture and how the stifling effects—and therefore colonialism itself—continue as long as African teachers teach and African writers write in English. "Literature and literary studies," Barbara Harlow agrees, "as part of the academic enterprise, are being contested by the cultural and ideological expressions of resistance, armed struggle, liberation, and social revolution in those geopolitical regions referred to as the 'Third World.'"[41] "Language," says Ngugi, "has always been at the heart of the two contending social forces . . . of the twentieth century."[42] He and others see the pathway to emancipation in an all-encompassing return to native languages.

Third World intellectuals are also striving to emancipate their history, that is, to break the dominance of the West over the historical narrative, to tell stories about which Western historiography is silent, to periodize in ways that delimit eras and emphasize turning points most significant to the non-West, to cast characters—heroes and villains, nobles and knaves—in terms of their roles in the Third World rather than the Western experience, and to achieve recognition and respect for all of these enterprises. Why not periodize the last half of the twentieth century as the era that spanned from the Chinese Revolution in 1949 and includes the Vietnamese victory against the French in 1954; the independence of Ghana in 1957; the Cuban revolution in 1959; the Indian seizure of Goa in 1961; and the gaining of Algerian independence in 1962; followed by an era extending from the American withdrawal from Vietnam in 1972, which encompasses the Arab–Israeli October War of 1973; the independence of Angola; the Iranian Revolution; the independence of Namibia; and the end of apartheid?[43] And why not highlight in the narrative events such as the Bandung Conference; the Suez Crisis; the

Bay of Pigs invasion; the proliferation of independence movements and new states in the 1970s; the founding of the Non-Aligned Movement and the Group of 77; the deaths and martyrdoms of Patrice Lumumba, Che Guevara, Aimé Césaire, and Amilcar Cabral; the Sandinista victory in Nicaragua; PLO Chairman Yasser Arafat's 1974 appearance at the UN; the intifada; and the decolonization of Hong Kong? Would not the history of our time in terms of this highlighted sequence of events appear very different from conventional Western interpretations? Would not the Third World appear more accomplished, and might not Third World peoples take great pride in it? In particular, would not the International Relations of our time also appear very different from conventional Western interpretations, and would the peoples of the Third World not appear much more involved? Would such a Third World history of the last half of our century be less real than the Western narrative that centers on the rise of the superpowers after World War II, the American–Soviet Cold War, the collapse of communism, and the triumph of the West? The point is that Third World peoples want to write their own history because their identities are bound up in it. Resistance to imperialism and colonialism *is* their history and they insist that the history of the resistance must be told and taught. They tend to view the mainstream of modern International Relations as the "history of their imbrication with the West" and they will continue to resist the Western narratives that say otherwise.[44]

Many Third World writers insist that their striving after cultural emancipation is not a naive romanticism or a primitivism or nativism that seeks to re-create idyllic precolonial ways of life. These ways were not very idyllic in the first place, and to rediscover and reestablish them is in any event impossible. What the writers and thinkers are aspiring toward gets various labels— a "neocolonial antithesis," a "culture-changing process capable of assuming entirely new dimensions of independent self-realization," "moving beyond nativism," or moving toward "the full development of a new cultural hegemony." Basil Davidson, commenting on the thinking of Amilcar Cabral, observes that "a valid system to replace and overcome colonial values could never be a reversion to those of the past, even if any such reversion were in any case practicable." He goes on to quote Cabral, who argues that "while we scrap colonial culture and the negative aspects of our own culture . . . we have to create a new culture, also based on our traditions but respecting everything that the world today conquered for the service of mankind."[45] What is perceived to be at issue here is the entire superstructure of Western cultural hegemony in the world, the institutions and values of the eighteenth-century Enlightenment, the perversions and distortions that justified imperialism and its attendant atrocities, and the dehumanizing ethos of consumerist capitalism. Not only must all of this be torn down, but it must be replaced by a new cultural mode, a new human consciousness, that can only emanate from the Third World. "Objectively," says Muslim spokesman Hassan al-Turabi, "the future is ours."[46]

It must be emphasized that the main thrust in the pursuit of emancipation is not the reaping of revenge for past injustices perpetrated by the West on the non-European world. Nowhere do we find Third World theorists calling for replacing one cultural hegemony with another. If anything, they appear to be seeking justice, or at least a world environment where people do not exploit one another. More idealistically, they seek something akin to "salvation" in the sense that they believe that no habitable planet can, or will, continue to exist if perceived Western hegemony and its attendant injustices continue long into the future. International Relations simply cannot continue in its conventional power-competitive, Western-established ways. But it is not the West that is going to instigate the changes. These changes have to come from the Third World.[47]

Struggle

But, in Third World thinking, changes in International Relations, or human society, will not come swiftly, and they will not happen without conflict. Peace is seldom mentioned in Third World articulations about world affairs, nor indeed even about human affairs more generally. The prevailing image projected is that of struggle, seemingly incessant and never-ending, pressed against omnipresent, malevolent forces. "If we hadn't buried our unity," writes Lebanese poet Nizar Qabbani,

> If we hadn't ripped its young body with bayonets
> If it had stayed in our eyes
> The dogs wouldn't have savaged our flesh.
> We want an angry generation
> To plough the sky
> To blow up history
> To blow up our thoughts.
> We want a new generation
> That does not forgive mistakes
> That does not bend.
> We want a generation
> Of giants.[48]

The language of the Third World theorists is militant. The vocabulary is military: they speak of enemies, war, battlefields, assaults, victories, and defeats. They assume that struggle, conflict, and confrontation are normal modes of human affairs. As Cabral affirms, "struggle is a normal condition of all living creatures in the world. All are in struggle, all struggle."[49] Violence is also accepted, sometimes welcomed. "For if the last shall be first," Frantz Fanon implores, "this will only come to pass after a murderous and decisive struggle" between the two protagonists. "Decolonization is always a violent phenomenon." The struggle, moreover, will invariably continue for a very long time, as "centuries will be needed to humanize this world which has been forced down to animal level by imperial powers."[50] The Third World theorists therefore imagine themselves and their peoples engaged in a long war of attrition, a Gramscian "war of position," with the hegemonic West, which they will ultimately win because the mode of conflict favors them, because the advantages of youth and vigor are with them, and because they have already captured the moral high ground and their enemies have lost their legitimacy.

International Relations Theory and Third World Thinking

The experience of the Third World can be forced into the conceptual categories of conventional Western theorizing about International Relations. But the explanations that result are at least wanting in richness if not also in interpretative validity. From all that has been said in this chapter, attempting now to frame an analysis of relations between the Third World and the West in western terms would be like fishing (for insights) with an oversized net; some obvious conclusions might be netted, but more subtle ones would slip through the conceptual webbing. A realist analysis, for example, would reveal that in the world of states most of those in Asia, Africa, and Latin America are deficient in power, and most predominantly Third World societies are therefore inconsequential in world politics. Small, weak actors occupy the "empty" geostrategic space that separates the large, powerful ones, and the weak are therefore destined to have their autonomy constrained and their identities threatened as the major powers play out their perennial rivalries. The "sovereignty" of the weak states entitles them to adhere to international laws encoded long before many of them entered the international system and to be sanctioned for infracting these laws. Postrealist analyses developed around Western-inspired notions of interdependence and order prescribed by regimes would similarly diminish the significance of Third World actors who are highly vulnerable to the asymmetries of interdependence and who, under normal circumstances, can contribute little to regime-building or maintenance. Western theories explain rather well why the Third World emerged after World War II when European power collapsed, why the Third World–led drive for a New International Economic Order failed in the 1970s, why the UN is not and never was a Third World–dominated institution, why it does not really matter who occupies the office of United Nations Secretary-General, why the oil-producing countries of the Persian Gulf region are more influential than their size suggests, and why China's development should be monitored. But contemporary Western thinking about International Relations has had little to offer to explain, or to evaluate the significance of, the embittered tone, the complex motivations, the mythological underpinnings, or the historical dynamics of North-South relations. The main reason for this is that for a very long time—perhaps not since Lasswell, Northrop, Sigmund, and Bozeman—Western theorists have not been sufficiently concerned with the impacts of culture and ideas upon interactions among states and peoples.[51] When theorists assume that power moves international history, the driving force of ideas is easily ignored. In present-day Western theorizing there has been no way to fit the poets into the game matrices, and the myths and emotions that truly drive human affairs have been lost in preoccupations with the tiny corner of human behavior that turns out to be predictably rational.

In response to conceptually Western analyses, and the theories of International Relations that instruct them, a good many Third World analysts would say that there are other ways of looking at the world and that these capture social reality at least as well as, and perhaps even better than, the Western formulations. As this chapter has tried to show, many Third World theorists do not organize their worldviews in terms of familiar Western categories and concepts. "States," for example, are not very important in Third World thinking about world affairs, but "forces," "movements," "parties," "peoples," "cultures," and "civilizations" are very significant. Most states in the non-European world are looked on as creatures of colonialism, entirely artificial culturally, and therefore appropriately downgraded. In the same way, "sovereignty" for some Third World thinkers is a suspect notion, not only because it is meaningless for the small, weak, porous, political entities of the Third World in every practical sense, but also because it enmeshes the decolonized areas and peoples in a biased and constraining, Western-devised international legal order.[52] Similarly, in Third World thinking, state-to-state interactions constitute far less of the substance, and less important aspects, of world affairs than do other kinds of interactions, including intrastate interactions that are actually international because they are intercultural or intercommunal. "Power" likewise explains little, because in Third World thinking powerlessness is a constant and not a variable; the West has most of the power, yet significant change has occurred in relations between the West and the Third World over the last half century so that changing power is not the reason for changing relations. So too in Third World thinking is the unequal distribution of the world's wealth taken as a constant and not a variable. As such, relative wealth is unproblematic and relatively uninteresting; skewed distributions of wealth favor the West and perpetuate exploitation. But everybody knows this, so that economic exploitation therefore can be taken as given. Whatever accomplishments the Third World has registered in the direction of emancipation have been made in spite of the prevailing unequal distribution of wealth and therefore must be explained by other factors.

Indeed, for Third World thinkers, ideas and ideologies are far more important. They drive world affairs. Dialectical processes push international history from intellectual synthesis to intellectual synthesis, and contemporary revolutionary visions become future social realities. Then again, for Third World thinkers, neither "war" nor "peace" are useful descriptions of international relational modes, and explaining the causes of war and the conditions of peace, which so much preoccupies Western theorists, becomes, for Third World thinkers, uninteresting. *Struggle* is the mode of International Relations; it is omnipresent, dynamic, incessant, and permanent. Explaining how struggle leads to emancipation is the intellectual challenge.

What Does It All Mean?

It is fair to say that most Western analysts are inclined to dismiss the work of the Third World thinkers discussed here, and many of their Western-oriented and Western-educated colleagues in the Third World are similarly inclined. This inclination to take the non-Western radicals less than seriously is founded more often than not in the belief that forces of modernization, Westernization, global cultural homogenization, global economic interdependence, cosmopolitanism, "Mcworldism," and science and technology are driving world affairs today and that these forces will constitute the future.[53] Romanticism never wins out in the face of progress; weakness never prevails in the face of power; conformity always smothers diversity; people are better at consuming than believing; and we have truly arrived at the "end of history."[54]

Some of the very few Western scholars who have taken Third World articulations at face value, have tended toward alarmist scenarios. Adda Bozeman, for example, fears a catastrophic confrontation between the West and the non-West. The end of the Cold War, she believes, has made way for a rerunning of deep-seated cultural algorithms—Islamic jihad, Persian Manichaeanism, African exclusivistic communalism, Chinese Middle Kingdom thinking, Kautilyan realpolitik—that will increasingly influence the international strategies of Third World actors after the universalism of Western liberalism has been thoroughly debunked.[55] The determined pursuit of any of these strategies, including Western liberal internationalism, could readily foment cold warfare of a twenty-first-century variety that Huntington calls "clashing civilizations."

Neither global homogenization nor intercultural helter-skelter is what Third World thinkers expect. They anticipate struggle, to be sure, but what they predict is emancipation, and, as noted already, along with it, justice and a new human civilization elevated in quality. History continues to look different through Third World eyes. It is a narrative of progress, albeit not a progression toward Francis Fukuyama's liberal utopia. Significant emancipation has occurred. Milestones have been posted. New ones—the economic success of the East Asians, the Chinese awakening, the massive migration of peoples moving today from South to North, successful black majority rule in South Africa, Palestinian autonomy, the 1993 UN Conference on Human Rights, the Chiapas uprising, Pakistan's nuclear bomb, Paz's poems and Said's books—are being posted.

There is, moreover, social turbulence everywhere within the Third World and within the West as well, and this turbulence, in the slums of Mexico City, the North African suburbs of Paris, the streets of Istanbul, the countrysides of Guatemala, Colombia, Peru, and Afghanistan, the Turkish neighborhoods of Berlin and the boroughs of New York, is significant because much of it represents the Third World confronting the West over questions of culture. "Come down from your swell co-ops, you general partners and merger lawyers!" Tom Wolfe has his mayor of New York admonish white, middle-class supporters in *The Bonfire of the Vanities,*

> It's the Third World down here! Puerto Ricans, West Indians, Haitians, Dominicans, Cubans, Colombians, Hondurans, Koreans, Chinese, Thais, Vietnamese, Ecuadorians, Panamanians, Filipinos, Albanians, Senegalese, and Afro-Americans! Go visit the frontiers, you gutless wonders! Morningside Heights, St. Nicholas Park, Washington Heights, Fort Tryon—*por qué pagar más!* The Bronx—the Bronx is finished for you! Riverdale is just a little freeport up there![56]

For the next several decades, the struggle between the Third World and the West is likely to be most intense, and consequential. It will happen *within* societies rather than between states, because power differentials will constrain confrontations between states. And it will happen both within societies where Third World thinking predominates and within societies where Western thinking predominates because the Third World and the West are juxtaposed everywhere. What is emerging is a new kind of International Relations, where interstate interactions of a national government-to-national government sort are receding in significance, and where both conflict and conflict resolution are increasingly appearing as intrastate and transsocietal phenomena. This emergent kind of intercultural, International Relations within and across societies might well favor the Third World, which, after all, is accustomed to protracted, irregular struggle. These peoples, moreover, are increasingly morally self-assured and prepared to press on indefinitely.

Notes

1. The research and writing of this chapter were supported by the Richard L. Walker Institute of International Studies at the University of South Carolina.

2. Timothy Brennan, *Salman Rushdie and the Third World* (NY: St. Martin's Press, 1989), p. 147.

3. Ali A. Mazrui, *Cultural Forces in World Politics* (London: James Currey; Nairobi: Heinemann Kenya; and Portsmouth, NH: Heinemann, 1990), p. 89.

4. Aziz Al-Azmeh, "The Satanic Flame," *New Statesman & Society,* 20 January 1989, p. 17; Ali A. Mazrui, *Cultural Forces in World Politics,* p. 84; Edward Said, *Culture and Imperialism* (NY: Alfred A. Knopf, 1993), p. 306.

5. Shabbir Akhtar, *Be Careful with Muhammad! The Salman Rushdie Affair* (London: Bellew Publishing, 1989), p. 64.

6. Ibid., p. 65.

7. Akhtar, *Be Careful with Muhammad!* p. 83.

8. Judith Miller, "Faces of Fundamentalism: Hassan al-Turabi and Muhammed Fadlallah," *Foreign Affairs,* vol. 73, no. 6 (November/December 1994), p. 132.

9. Said, *Culture and Imperialism,* p. 310.

10. Samuel Huntington, "The Clash of Civilizations," *Foreign Affairs,* vol. 72, no. 4 (Summer 1993), pps. 22–49; Samuel Huntington, "If Not Civilizations, What?" *Foreign Affairs,* vol. 72, no. 5 (November/December 1993), pps. 186–94. Since this chapter was originally written, Samuel Huntington has elaborated and defended his positions on clashing civilizations in *The Clash of Civilizations and the Remaking of World Order* (NY: Simon & Schuster, 1996).

11. In some writings the community of like-minded thinkers that I call the Third World is referred to as the non-West, and I occasionally insert this designation largely to avoid stylistic monotony. Non-West however is problematic because it confuses the cultural heritage of South and Central America, where a good deal of Third World thinking takes place in the context of otherwise Western culture.

12. Edward Said, *Orientalism: Western Conceptions of the Orient* (NY: Penguin Books, 1991), pps. 201–328. In this well-known study, Said shows how depictions and understandings of non-Western societies contained in Western scholarship have tended to be misleading due to inabilities to communicate across cultures, so that the "Orient" as we came to know it is largely a Western creation.

13. Adda B. Bozeman, "American Policy and the Illusion of Congruent Values," *Strategic Review,* vol. 15, no. 1 (Winter 1987), pps. 12–23.

14. Said, *Culture and Imperialism,* p. 258.

15. Miller, "Faces of Fundamentalism," p. 126.

16. Adda B. Bozeman, "Non-Western Orientations to Strategic Intelligence and Their Relevance for American National Interests," *Comparative Strategy,* vol. 10 (1991), p. 53.; see also, Adda B. Bozeman, "War and the Clash of Ideas," *Orbis,* vol. 20, no. 1 (Spring 1976), pps. 61–102.

17. C. L. R. James, *The Black Jacobins: Toussaint L'Ouverture and the Santo Domingo Revolution,* second edition (NY: Vintage Books, 1968), p. 391; Ngugi wa Thiong'o, *Decolonizing the Mind: The Politics of Language in African Literature* (London: James Currey, 1986), p. 2 ; Frantz Fanon, *The Wretched of the Earth* (NY: Grove Press, 1968), pps. 7 and 36; Muhammad Iqbal, *Poems From Iqbal* (London: Murray, 1955).

18. Rhoda E. Howard, "Occidentalism, Human Rights, and the Obligations of Western Scholars," *Canadian Journal of African Studies,* vol. 29, no. 1 (1995), p. 111.

19. Edward Said, *Culture and Imperialism,* p. 311.

20. Aimé Césaire, "Cahier d'un retour au pays natal," cited in C. L. R. James, *The Black Jacobins,* p. 399.

21. David Diop, "The Vultures," *The Penguin Book of Modern African Poetry,* second edition, eds., Gerald Moore and Ulli Beier (London: Penguin Books, 1984), p. 246.

22. Franke Wilmer, *The Indigenous Voice in World Politics* (Newbury Park, CA: Sage Publications, 1993).

23. William Pfaff, *Barbarian Sentiments: How the American Century Ends* (NY: Hill and Wang, 1989), pps. 167–68.

24. Bernard Lewis, "The Roots of Muslim Rage," *The Atlantic Monthly,* (September 1990), pps. 53–54.

25. Fareed Zakaria, "Culture is Destiny: A Conversation with Lee Kuan Yew," *Foreign Affairs,* vol. 73, no. 2 (March/April 1994), p. 111.

26. Josiah A. M. Cobbah, "African Values and the Human Rights Debate: An African Perspective," *Human Rights Quarterly,* vol. 9 (1987), p. 323.

27. Zakaria, "Culture is Destiny," p. 119; Kishore Mahbubani, "The West and the Rest," *The National Interest,* vol. 28 (Summer 1992), pps. 8–10; Miller, "Faces of Fundamentalism," pps. 133–37.

28. David C. Gordon, *Images of the West: Third World Perspectives* (Totowa, NJ: Rowen and Littlefield Publishers, 1989), p. 105.

29. James, *The Black Jacobins,* pp. 408–9.

30. Ngugi, *Decolonizing the Mind,* p. 2.

31. Pfaff, *Barbarian Sentiments,* p. 158.

32. Barbara Harlow, *Resistance Literature* (London: Methuen, 1987), pps. 3–30.

33. Fanon, *The Wretched of the Earth,* p. 7.

34. Said, *Culture and Imperialism,* p. 307.

35. Basil Davidson, "On Revolutionary Nationalism: The Legacy of Cabral," *Race and Class,* vol. 27, no. 3 (Winter 1986), pps. 43–44.

36. The *dependencia* literature is voluminous, and reached peak output in the 1970s. A fine overview, as well as an original contribution is to be found in Fernando Henrique Cardoso and Enzo Faletto, *Dependency and Development in*

Latin America (Berkeley, CA: University of California Press, 1978); informative reviews of the dependent development literature were written by Robert Cox, "Ideologies and the New International Order: Reflections on Some Recent Literature," *International Organization,* vol. 33, no. 2 (Spring 1979), pps. 257–302; and James A. Caporaso, "Dependency Theory: Continuities and Discontinuities in Development Studies," *International Organization,* vol. 34, no. 4 (Autumn 1980), pps. 605–28.

37. United Nations, General Assembly, Doc. A/PV.2096, December 4, 1972; see also, Paul E. Sigmund, *The Ideologies of the Developing Nations,* revised edition, (NY: Frederick A. Praeger, 1967), pps. 306–425.

38. Pfaff, *Barbarian Sentiments,* p. 169; Benjamin R. Barber, *Jihad vs. McWorld* (NY: Random House, 1994), pps. 157, 206, 207.

39. Ngugi, *Decolonizing the Mind,* p. 3.

40. Barber, *Jihad vs. McWorld,* p. 209.

41. Harlow, *Resistance Literature,* p. 14.

42. Ngugi, *Decolonizing the Mind,* p. 3.

43. Paul-Marie de la Gorce, "Le Recul des grandes esperances revolutionnaires," *Le Monde Diplomatique* (May 1984), pps. 16–17 ff.

44. David C. Gordon, *Images of the West,* p. 9.

45. Davidson, "On Revolutionary Nationalism," p. 36; See also, Amilcar Cabral, "Resistencia cultural," seminar paper at PAIGC conference of cadres, November 19–24, 1969, and Amilcar Cabral, *Unity and Struggle: Speeches and Writings* (NY: Monthly Review Press, 1979), pps. 29–45, 139–54.

46. Miller, "Faces of Fundamentalism," p. 127.

47. I am indebted to Naeem Inayatullah for bringing these notions of "justice" and "salvation" to my attention in his valuable critique of an earlier version of this chapter.

48. Nizar Qabbani, "Footnotes to the Book of Setback," *Modern Poetry of the Arab World,* ed., Abdullah al-Udhari (Hammondsworth, Middlesex, England: Penguin Books, 1986), pps. 100–1.

49. Cabral, *Unity and Struggle,* p. 31.

50. Fanon, *The Wretched of the Earth,* pps. 35, 37, and 100.

51. Harold D. Lasswell, *World Politics and Personal Insecurity* ([1935] NY: The Free Press, 1965); F. S. C. Northrop, *The Taming of Nations: A Study of the Cultural Bases of International Policy* (NY: Macmillan, 1954); F. S. C. Northrop, *The Meeting of East and West* (Woodbridge, CT: Ox Box Press, 1979); F. S. C. Northrop, ed., *Ideological Differences and World Order* (New Haven, CT: Yale University Press, 1949); Adda B. Bozeman, *Politics and Culture in International History* (Princeton, NJ: Princeton University Press, 1960); Paul E. Sigmund, *The Ideologies of the Developing Nations* (NY: Frederick A. Praeger, 1967).

52. Michael Barnett, "The Consolidation of Sovereignty and Order in the Arab State System," paper presented at the conference "Comprehending State Sovereignty," Brown University, February 26–28, 1993.

53. For a concise statement of this position, see Ronald Dore, "Unity and Diversity in Contemporary World Culture," in *The Expansion of International*

Society, eds., Hedley Bull and Adam Watson (NY: Oxford University Press, 1984), pps. 407–24.

54. Francis Fukuyama, The End of History and the Last Man (NY: The Free Press, 1992).

55. Adda Bozeman, "The International Order in a Multicultural World," in *The Expansion of International Studies*, eds., Hedley Bull and Adam Watson, pps. 387 ff.

56. Tom Wolfe, *The Bonfire of the Vanities* (NY: Bantam Books, 1988), p. 7.

Bibliography

Akhtar, Shabbir. *Be Careful with Muhammad! The Salman Rushdie Affair.* London: Bellew Publishing, 1989.

al-Udhari, Abdullah, ed. *Modern Poetry of the Arab World.* Hammondsworth, Middlesex, England: Penguin Books, 1986.

Barber, Benjamin. *Jihad vs. McWorld.* NY: Random House, 1994.

Bozeman, Adda B. "Non-Western Orientations to Strategic Intelligence and Their Relevance for American National Interests." *Comparative Strategy.* Vol. 10 (1991), pps. 53–72.

———. "American Policy and the Illusion of Congruent Values." *Strategic Review.* Vol. 15, no. 1 (Winter 1987), pps. 12–23.

———. *Politics and Culture in International History.* Princeton, NJ: Princeton University Press, 1960.

Brennan, Timothy. *Salman Rushdie and the Third World.* NY: St. Martin's Press, 1989.

Cabral, Amilcar. *Unity and Struggle: Speeches and Writings.* NY: Monthly Review Press, 1979.

Cardoso, Fernando Henrique and Enzo Faletto. *Dependency and Development in Latin America.* Berkeley, CA: University of California Press, 1978.

Carrier, James G., ed. *Occidentalism: Images of the West.* Oxford: Clarendon Press, 1995.

Cobbah, Josiah A. M. "African Values and the Human Rights Debate: An African Perspective." *Human Rights Quarterly.* Vol. 9 (1987), pps. 309–31.

Davidson, Basil. "On Revolutionary Nationalism: The Legacy of Cabral." *Race and Class.* Vol. 27, no. 3 (Winter 1986), pps. 21–46.

Fanon, Frantz. *The Wretched of the Earth.* NY: Grove Press, 1968.

Fukuyama, Francis. *The End of History and the Last Man.* NY: The Free Press, 1992.

Gordon, David C. *Images of the West: Third World Perspectives.* Totowa, NJ: Rowen and Littlefield Publishers, 1989.

Harlow, Barbara. *Resistance Literature.* London: Methuen, 1987.

Howard, Rhoda E. "Occidentalism, Human Rights, and the Obligations of Western Scholars." *Canadian Journal of African Studies.* Vol. 29, no. 1 (1995), pps. 110–26.

Huntington, Samuel. *The Clash of Civilizations and the Remaking of World Order.* NY: Simon & Schuster, 1996.

————. "The Clash of Civilizations." *Foreign Affairs.* Vol. 72, no. 4 (Summer 1993), pps. 22–49.

James, C. L. R. *The Black Jacobins: Toussaint L'Ouverture and the Santo Domingo Revolution,* second edition. NY: Vintage Books, 1968.

Lasswell, Harold D. *World Politics and Personal Insecurity.* [1935] NY: The Free Press, 1965.

Mahbubani, Kishore. "The West and the Rest." *The National Interest.* Vol. 28 (Summer 1992), pps. 3–12.

Mazrui, Ali A. *Cultural Forces in World Politics.* London: James Currey, 1990.

Miller, Judith. "Faces of Fundamentalism: Hassan al-Turabi and Muhammed Fadlallah." *Foreign Affairs.* Vol. 73, no. 6 (November/December 1994), pps. 123–42.

Moore, Gerald and Ulli Beier, eds. *The Penguin Book of Modern African Poetry,* second edition. London: Penguin Books, 1984.

Ngugi wa Thiong'o. *Decolonizing the Mind: The Politics of Language in African Literature.* London: James Currey, 1986.

Northrop, F. S. C. *The Meeting of East and West.* Woodbridge, CT: Ox Box Press, 1979.

————. *The Taming of Nations: A Study of the Cultural Bases of International Policy.* NY: Macmillan, 1954.

————, ed. *Ideological Differences and World Order.* New Haven, CT: Yale University Press, 1949.

Pfaff, William. *Barbarian Sentiments: How the American Century Ends.* NY: Hill and Wang, 1989.

Said, Edward. *Culture and Imperialism.* NY: Alfred A. Knopf, 1993.

————. *Orientalism: Western Conceptions of the Orient.* NY: Penguin Books, 1991.

Sigmund, Paul E. *The Ideologies of the Developing Nations,* revised edition. NY: Frederick A. Praeger, 1967.

Wilmer, Franke. *The Indigenous Voice in World Politics.* Newbury Park, CA: Sage Publications, 1993.

Zakaria, Frank. "Culture is Destiny: A Conversation with Lee Kuan Yew." *Foreign Affairs.* Vol. 73, no. 2 (March/April 1994), pps. 109–26.

SEVEN

Beyond Anarchy: Third World Instability and International Order after the Cold War

Amitav Acharya

Introduction

In recent literature on International Relations, there has been much debate on the consequences of the end of the Cold War for war and peace in the international system. A major contributor to this debate, John Mearsheimer, has argued emphatically that "a Europe without the superpowers . . . would probably be substantially more prone to violence than the past 45 years," despite the continent's growing economic interdependence, the role of political and functional institutions such as the European Union and the Organization of Security and Cooperation in Europe, and the pluralist domestic structure of European nations.[1] As he sees it, "with the end of the Cold War, Europe is reverting to a state system that created powerful incentives for aggression in the past." Because of this, he concludes, "we are likely soon to regret the passing of the Cold War."

Mearsheimer's controversial thesis[2] focuses on the European theater. Several commentators, although not necessarily sharing Mearsheimer's avowedly realist assumptions, have nonetheless reached a similar pessimistic conclusion about stability in the post–Cold War Third World. Thus, Jose Cintra argues that the Cold War had suppressed "many potential third-world conflicts"; their geopolitical retrenchment will ensure that "other conflicts will very probably arise from decompression and from a loosening of the controls and self-controls" exercised by the superpowers.[3] Stanley Hoffmann similarly envisages a New World Disorder in the Third World, "a situation far more chaotic than the world of the Cold War, when the superpowers, knowing that they could blow themselves up, restrained themselves and their allies."[4] Testifying before the Senate Armed Services Committee, the director of the U.S. Defense Intelligence Agency warns of "regional flashpoints" in the Middle East, East Asia, and South Asia, which could become serious threats to U.S. security because the end of bipolarity "has removed the tampering mechanism that often kept these situations under control."[5] In a more cautious vein, Robert Jervis argues that while the Cold War might have had a mixed impact on Third World conflicts, "in the net, however, it generally dampened conflict and we can therefore expect more rather than less of it in future."[6]

If such views are to hold, it will have major ramifications for theorists and practitioners of International Relations. The long-standing debate in International Relations Theory on the linkage between polarity and stability has remained unsettled; if the end of the Cold War is to engender greater instability in the greater part of the international system where the vast majority of the world's population lives, then the debate has to be settled decisively in favor of those who view bipolarity as a more "stable" international order than multipolarity. A more unstable Third World will also legitimize the rampant interventionism of the superpowers in the Third World during the Cold War period and silence critics of Great Power intervention as a tool of global order and maintenance. Academic analysts concerned with the future of war will need to pay more attention to systemic, as opposed to domestic or local, causes of international conflict.

This chapter addresses the issue of whether the Third World will be more or less conflict-prone in the aftermath of the Cold War. At the outset, it examines the theoretical assumptions behind the polarity-stability debate with a view to assess their relevance in the context of the Third World. Subsequent sections examine the empirical validity of the pessimists' claim (that the end of bipolarity may have a destabilizing impact on Third World stability) by focusing on three sets of questions: First, can we regard bipolarity and the Cold War as a period of "stability" in the Third World, especially when compared to the stability of Europe and the central strategic balance? Second, has the end of the Cold War contributed to greater instability in the Third World? Can conflicts in the post–Cold War Third World be *causally* linked to the end of bipolarity? Third, what is the capacity of, and constraints on, the emerging multipolar structure in so far as the regulation of conflict and intervention in the Third World is concerned, especially when viewed against the record of the bipolar system?

Polarity, Stability, and Anarchy:
The Third World and International Order

The relationship between polarity and stability has attracted much debate in International Relations Theory. An influential strand of realist theory holds that bipolar systems are more stable than multipolar systems, an argument made most forcefully by Kenneth Waltz (although, as John Lewis Gaddis points out, Morton Kaplan also made similar arguments).[7] Writing at the height of the Cold War, Waltz argued that bipolarity "encourage[s] the limitation of violence in the relations of states,"[8] primarily by reducing the scope for misunderstanding, misperception, and confusion. The fewer the number of actors, the greater the predictability of interaction between them. As Waltz put it, "in a bipolar world uncertainty lessens and calculations are easier to make."[9] Furthermore, bipolarity leads to an overall extension of the sphere of international stability because "with only two world powers, there are no peripheries." The intensity of superpower competition during the Cold War, which Waltz accepted as the chief empirical model of bipolarity, produced a reluctance on their part to accept even small territorial losses anywhere in the world. This reduced the possibility of international conflict by extending "the geographic scope of both powers' concern." Waltz contrasts these attributes of bipolarity with the dangers inherent in a multipolar system. In a "multipolar world, who is a danger to whom is often unclear; the incentive to regard all disequilibrating changes with concern and respond to them with whatever effort may be required is consequently weakened."[10] Mearsheimer carries this argument further by pointing out that while "a bipolar system has only one dyad across which war might break out," a "multipolar system is much more fluid and has many such dyads," thereby making war more likely.[11]

A specific virtue of the Cold War bipolarity emphasized by Waltz and Gaddis relates to the restrained and regulatory role of the superpowers in dealing with major international conflicts. According to Waltz, "the pressures of a bipolar world strongly encourage[d] them [the superpowers] to act internationally in ways better than their characters may lead one to expect."[12] Gaddis speaks of the tendency of "self-regulation" in the bipolar relationship. Referring to the willingness and ability of the two superpowers to manage major international crises during the Cold War period, Gaddis concludes that this functioned like "the automatic pilot on an airplane or the governor on a steam engine" in counteracting threats to international stability. The critical elements of these "self-regulating mechanisms" include, among other things, a "fundamental agreement among major states within the system on the objectives they are seeking to uphold by participating in it" as well as "agreed-upon procedures exist[ing] for resolving differences among them."[13] Moreover, a bipolar structure is more likely than a multipolar system to ensure the stability of alliances, thereby helping the ability of the leading actors to regulate international conflict.

Realists, Waltz in particular, point to historical evidence to support their claim regarding the positive correlation between bipolarity and international stability. Thus, the experience of the U.S.–Soviet rivalry attests to the ability of a bipolar system to manage crises and maintain alliances without resort to war. These attributes of bipolarity compare favorably to the relationship among the pre-1945 Great Powers interacting in a multipolar international environment.

Waltz's arguments concerning the positive linkage between bipolarity and international stability have not gone unchallenged in International Relations Theory. Gilpin, himself a realist, rejects Waltz's view that wars are caused by uncertainty and miscalculation that are characteristic features of multipolarity. Instead, "it is the perceived certainty of gain [associated with bipolarity] that most frequently causes nations to go to war."[14] Gilpin further argues that bipolarity creates the "conditions for relatively small causes to lead to disproportionately large effects."[15] Thus, under a bipolar order, minor crises in obscure countries could escalate into serious international confrontation as a result of superpower involvement. A similar argument concerning the conflict-escalating potential of bipolarity has been made by Richard Rosecrance. Referring to the zero-sum nature of bipolar competition, Rosecrance points to the risk that even a simple action by one principal actor is likely to provoke hostile countermeasures from the other side. Because a bipolar system ensures that antagonisms will be reciprocated, it "does not reduce motivations for expansion [in the geopolitical conduct of the two principal actors] and may even increase them."[16]

While these arguments cast doubt on the theoretical position concerning the stability of bipolar systems, other theorists have pointed to the positive effects of multipolarity on international stability. Karl W. Deutsch and J. David Singer argue that multipolarity, by increasing "the range and flexibility of interactions" among a larger number of powerful actors, inhibits recourse to war and facilitates cooperation. In their view, "as the number of possible exchanges increases, so does the probability that the 'invisible hand' of pluralistic interests will be effective."[17] Furthermore, in multipolarity, "the share of attention that any nation can devote to any other must of necessity diminish"; thus conflicts in peripheral areas will have a limited potential for escalation.[18] Multipolarity is also likely to have a "dampening effect upon arms races."[19]

The theoretical debate on the linkage between polarity and stability has produced no clear winner.[20] But in this chapter, I argue that the debate fails to capture key aspects of the security predicament of the Third World. It takes a virtually undifferentiated view of the international system, ignoring important dissimilarities between the North and the South. The fact that much of this debate took place before problems of conflict and security in the Third World became a subject of attention and serious scholarship among International Relations theorists further underscores this point. Similarly, the historical evidence used to support the arguments of both sides comes from the historical evolution of the European states system.[21] These generalizations miss out on the consequences of the decolonization process and the emergence of the Third World for the maintenance of international order.

Viewed from the perspective of the Third World, I note two major deficiencies of the polarity-stability debate. The first relates to an excessively narrow view of stability and a tendency to conflate stability and peace. Because of their tendency to generalize from Great Power behavior, the polarity-stability debate equates stability with absence of system-threatening war among the Great Powers. For Waltz, stability meant, first and foremost, the capacity of a system to maintain itself, and not necessarily the frequency or intensity of conflicts within or between its constituent units. In other words, the stability of the system does not depend on the stability of all its constituents. Even his critics, including those who view multipolar systems as being more stable, shared similar assumptions about the meaning of stability. Deutsch and Singer, for example, define stability as "the probability that the system retains all of its essential characteristics: that no single nation becomes dominant; that most of its members continue to survive; and that *large-scale war* does not occur" (emphasis added). For Gaddis, "the most convincing argument for 'stability' [of the bipolar world] is that so far at least, World War III has not occurred."[22]

If such a narrow view of "stability" is accepted, then a "stable" system should permit any number of limited or small-scale and internal wars, including conflicts in its peripheral areas, so long as such conflicts do not threaten the existence of the system structure. Thus, according to Waltz, the risk of miscalculation inherent in multipolarity is "more likely to permit the unfolding of a series of events that finally threatens a change in the balance and brings the [major] powers to war" while bipolarity "is the lesser evil because it costs only money and *the fighting of limited wars*" (emphasis added).[23] But the category of limited war can be very broad indeed. Under bipolarity, Rosecrance points out, "substantial territorial and/or political changes can take place in International Relations without impinging on the overarching stability."[24] Since the notion of system structure refers to the distribution of capabilities among the units, only those units who occupy the upper rungs of the power matrix could affect system structure by virtue of their conflictual or cooperative behavior. Systemic instability could only result from major power or hegemonic wars. The weaker members of the system, such as the Third World countries, simply do not possess the capabilities needed to affect the system structure. Thus, if one accepts Waltz's theoretical position, the high incidence of Cold War conflicts in the Third World did not challenge the essential stability of bipolar international systems, as long as the central balance and its European strategic core remained war-free.

A second problem with the polarity-stability debate should be noted. Because of their preoccupation with the major power relationships and a consequent tendency to rely on the European states system for evidence, the protagonists in the debate ignored actual trends regarding conflict and order in the Third World. Neither Waltz nor his critics looked at the Third World to seek evidence for their theoretical arguments. In a similar vein, the current pessimistic predictions about post–Cold War instability in the Third World are based on a considerable amount of false alarm and exaggeration. If one examines trends in the Third World carefully, as this chapter does, then a different picture of its stability will emerge.

Moreover, because both bipolarity and multipolarity are systemic attributes, to use them as central explanatory variables in assessing the likelihood of international conflict means ignoring the importance of domestic and regional factors in conflict formation. As this chapter argues, it is precisely these factors that are often central to an understanding of the security problematic of the Third World.[25] Furthermore, a system-centric view is likely to ignore the role of regionally based security institutions and regimes that may significantly affect the probability and scale of conflict in the Third World. Finally, by focusing on the relationship among the Great Powers as the central determinant of international stability and order, the polarity-stability debate has ignored another crucial systemic factor affecting order-maintenance: the relationship between the North and the South.

These reasons limit the relevance of the polarity-stability debate as a conceptual framework for assessing prospects for Third World stability in the post–Cold War era. To be useful for this purpose, the debate must go beyond its Eurocentric universe and its hitherto preoccupation with Great Power relationships. It must embrace a more differentiated view of the conditions of international order, one that reflects the distinctive security predicament of the Third World. To provide such a view is a key aim of this chapter. But an important point of clarification regarding my conceptual framework needs to be made here. While my assessment is intended to highlight the limitations of the hitherto narrow and somewhat ethnocentric conceptual terrain of both sides of the polarity-stability debate, my critique is directed specifically against the position of Waltz, Mearsheimer, and company who make grand claims about the essential stability of bipolar systems. My findings support the view that multipolarity may be more conducive to stability and peace, but I arrive at this conclusion by examining a broader and more complex range of determinants, with particular emphasis on the linkage between systemic structure and regional stability and the indigenous sources of conflict and order in the Third World.

Third World Instability and the Cold War "Order"

The Cold War period was marked by a large number of conflicts in the Third World. Third World conflicts, intrastate, interstate, and regional, vastly outnumbered those occurring in the developed segment of the international system.[26] Yet the view has prevailed that bipolarity and superpower rivalry contributed to order and stability. This view rests essentially on two features of the Cold War security relationship between the United States and the Soviet Union: first, the two superpowers' shared need to ensure that Third World regional conflicts did not escalate into a direct global confrontation between them; and second, their consequent willingness to control their Third World regional clients whenever conflicts involving them threatened to get out of hand.[27] Both claims are consistent with the structural realist perspective associated with Waltz and Gaddis. Robert Jervis agrees: "The superpowers offered security to their [Third World] clients as well as enforcing a degree of restraint on them."[28]

But such claims must be weighed against a number of other factors related to the dynamic of superpower rivalry and its impact in generating conflict and disorder throughout the Third World. At least five deserve attention.

First, an important feature of the Cold War order was the essential "permissibility" of Third World conflicts. This is in marked contrast to the situation in Europe, where fear of the catastrophic escalation potential of any East-West confrontation prevented even the most minor form of warfare between the two power blocs. In the Third World, on the other hand, the danger of nuclear escalation was considerably more remote (though the nuclear option was contemplated by one or both the superpowers in Korea, Vietnam, and the Middle East). In this context, Third World conflicts were not only more "permissible," but superpower intervention in them might have served as a necessary "safety valve" not available in the European context. As Ayoob has forcefully argued, systemic stability or stability of the central strategic balance rendered a great deal of Third World conflicts necessary, as the superpower viewed these conflicts "as a way of letting off steam which helps to cool the temperature around the core issues which are directly relevant and considered vital to the central balance and, therefore, to the international system."[29]

Second, the Cold War "order," instead of dampening conflicts in the Third World, actually contributed to their escalation. Although rarely a direct cause of Third World conflicts,[30] opportunism and influence-seeking by the superpowers contributed significantly to the ultimate severity of many cases of incipient and latent strife in the Third World. It led to the internationalization of civil war and internalization of superpower competition.[31] It also contributed to the prolongation of regional wars by preventing decisive results in at least some theaters, including the major regional conflicts of the 1970s and 1980s in Central America, Angola, Horn of Africa, Cambodia, Afghanistan, and the Iran–Iraq War.[32]

Third, the Cold War directly contributed to the ineffectiveness of global and regional institutions created after World War II to promote pacific resolution of international conflicts. As Stanley Hoffmann argues, superpower rivalry was the principal factor depriving the post–World War II international system of the necessary degree of "moderation,"[33] which the founding fathers of the UN had assumed as a basic precondition for collective security. Ernst Haas's study of the UN's peace and security role finds both bipolarity and the Cold War to be responsible for the organization's ineffectiveness. It shows that the poor conflict control record of the UN and macroregional bodies such as the Organization of American States, the Organization of African Unity, and the Arab League, was especially evident in the case of Cold War disputes, as opposed to disputes over decolonization. Moreover, the period of least effectiveness, between 1948 and 1955, was also the period of tight bipolarity.[34] Superpower rivalry also crippled the role of regional organizations in managing Third World conflict. While groups such as the OAS, OAU, and the Arab League were initially more effective in isolating Third World conflicts, an inability to avoid entanglement in superpower rivalry contributed significantly to their declining performance in subsequent periods.[35] Moreover, the limitations of conflict control through both global and regional frameworks both accounted for and were reinforced by the preference of the superpowers for regional security systems. These regional alliances, including the South East Asia Treaty Organization (SEATO), and the Central Treaty Organization (CENTO), were short-lived experiments whose credibility in deterring regional conflict suffered from the weak superpower commitment; neither did they provide mechanisms for the pacific settlement of disputes within a region.[36] Indeed, their very existence might have indicated and aggravated regional polarization and conflict in many parts of the Third World.

Fourth, the Cold War was a major, if not the only, factor in the North-South polarization, which in itself represented a formidable challenge to international order. The great majority of Third World states viewed the superpower competition and the entangling Cold War alliance systems as a major threat to international order in general and their own security in particular. This fear and the consequent rejection of superpower security guarantees was a principal motivating factor behind the emergence of Third World platforms such as the Nonaligned Movement. But the Third World's campaign for structural reforms to the global economic and political systems[37] was construed by the Northern powers as a key factor contributing to international disorder. Moreover, like the East-West rivalry, North-South conflict also contributed to the demise of hopes for a "moderate international system" conducive to the effectiveness of international institutions for conflict control, including the UN and regional groupings with First World members (such as the OAS).

Fifth, contrary to periodic expectations, the Cold War did not produce any long-term and substantive understanding between the superpowers to regulate Third World conflicts by devising explicit and implicit norms or "ground rules of conduct."[38] In Europe, for all their differences, the two power blocs recognized a common interest in reducing the prospect of war through mutually acceptable measures on crisis prevention and arms control. No comparable willingness existed on the part of the superpowers to forge mutual understanding on Third World security issues, or devise stable frameworks for conflict control.[39]

One may agree with Jerry Hough's assessment that the two Cold War classics, the Korean and Vietnam wars, were "fought by implicit rules that minimized the danger of Soviet-American confrontation."[40] In the Arab–Israeli wars, superpower action to diffuse escalation possibilities included steps to ensure avoidance of direct engagement of their armed forces, as well as to impose some degree of restraint on their own clients while urging the other side do the same.[41] The neutrality and neutralization of Laos and Cambodia under the Geneva Accords of 1954 and 1962 respectively were the result of the superpowers' willingness to regulate their competition when both perceived very high stakes in a given conflict.[42] Similarly, the superpowers showed a degree of restraint in conflicts "where truly important interests of the other was involved," as in the cases of the Iran and Afghanistan conflicts.[43]

Nonetheless, many of the superpowers' attempts to devise a code of conduct for Third World conflicts were ad hoc, prescriptive, and limited.[44] For example, the principles embodied in the June 1973 agreement on the prevention of nuclear war signed by Nixon and Brezhnev "were framed so generally that they never came close to a definition of where their interests actually clashed."[45] Those developed in relation to the Middle East conflict were so informal or tacit that they could not be applied effectively to other theaters.[46] Indeed, the record of superpower regional security cooperation in the Third World during the Cold War bears out Robert Jervis's argument that the so-called rules of conduct evident in the superpowers' behavior toward regional conflicts were "too directly linked to immediate self-interest," were "neither unambiguous nor binding," and tended to change with changes in the "power and interests" of the superpowers in relation to a particular conflict.[47]

Well-known differences between the superpowers over the meaning of detente[48] were also a key factor that accounted for their failure to build a durable code of conduct to manage Third World conflicts. The U.S. view of detente emphasized the principle of linkage, which posited a feedback relationship between U.S. interest in nuclear arms control and Soviet restraint on Third World regional security issues. But the Soviet Union vehemently resisted the inclusion of regional conflicts in the superpower arms control agenda; linkage to Moscow meant giving a "'guarantee' of the sociopolitical status quo in developing regions"—an obligation that "it could undertake neither on principle nor physically."[49] Moscow distinguished adamantly issues of regional conflict from those of the central strategic balance (until the Reagan administration succeeded in linking the two), thereby preventing any long-term understanding to promote mutual restraint in, and cooperative approaches to, management of Third World conflicts.[50]

An additional barrier to a superpower code of conduct governing Third World conflicts was opposition from their Third World clients, including states and revolutionary movements averse to "solutions imposed from outside."[51] To the extent that many Third World regimes sought superpower patronage to gain leverage against their domestic opponents,[52] they had a minimal interest in a general code of conduct that would facilitate a superpower-imposed solution. In this respect, while the superpowers might have had some degree of success in devising broad diplomatic formulas to govern their own "external" involvement, they were much less able to settle internal matters involving power-sharing. The recent experience of regional conflicts in Afghanistan, Cambodia, and El Salvador attests to this problem.

Two other closely related factors explain why efforts by the superpowers to regulate their competition in the Third World bore limited results, especially when compared with Europe. The first is the futile attempt by the superpowers to duplicate their Europe-style alliances in the Third World, which might have facilitated collaborative management of regional conflicts. The reference here is to regional security alliances, such as SEATO and CENTO. These alliances proved extraordinarily ineffective and short-lived.

The absence of an European-style security order in the Third World could also be ascribed to another factor. In Europe, the essential bipolarity of the post–World War II security structure in Europe remained relatively undiminished, despite the assertive role of France. The Third World, on the other hand, was a much more complex arena where several states were able to pursue their own independent geopolitical ambitions, sometimes with the explicit backing of the superpowers suffering geopolitical fatigue (as in the case of the Shah of Iran under the Nixon Doctrine), or by a clever maneuvering between superpower blocs (as in the case of India or China). This undermined the degree of superpower control over Third World regimes and their behavior in regional conflicts.

To sum up the argument made so far, if superpower rivalry created a framework of order in the Third World, it was very specific in its scope and objective. The purpose of this order was limited to avoiding direct super-power confrontation and preventing local conflicts among their clients from developing into global war. Such an order left considerable room for the escalation of local conflicts to regional war, actively aided and fueled by the superpowers. The Cold War order was neither interested in, nor capable of, addressing the indigenous roots of Third World conflicts. It might have contained certain Third World conflicts, especially the Arab–Israeli ones, but overall it did not provide an adequate framework for conflict resolution. It is therefore not surprising that the political settlement of the major regional conflicts of the Cold War period (such as Cambodia, Afghanistan, Namibia, and others) had to await, rather than precede, the end of the Cold War brought about by, among other things, domestic changes in the Soviet Union.

The arguments discussed concerning the effects of the Cold War on the Third World negate many of the arguments made by structural realists concerning the stabilizing effects of bipolarity. The stability supposed to accrue from the simplicity and predictability of bipolar interactions was more true of Europe than of the Third World. The superpowers' capacity for self-regulation was in limited display and did not prevent a high incidence of conflict and violence in the Third World. Finally, security regimes in the Third World were short-lived and largely ineffectual.

A "Decompression Effect"?

If the bipolar structure during the Cold War was hardly a period of stability in the Third World, will its end prove even more destabilizing? Surveying the vast literature on Third World security, one finds at least five ways in which the end of the Cold War could fuel greater instability and conflict in the Third World.[53] These factors are more or less a direct offshoot of the end of bipolarity, although none had been directly predicted by structural realist theory (suggesting a general neglect of Third World issues by the latter). A brief examination of each is necessary in order to assess the possibility and scope of the alleged "decompression effect."

Sources of Instability

The first of these is rooted in the effect of superpower withdrawal in altering regional balances of power in the Third World.[54] A common fear of Western strategists has been that superpower retrenchment might encourage locally dominant actors (which may include regional powers[55] such as India, Indonesia, Nigeria, Iran, and Iraq) to step into the resulting geopolitical "vacuum." This fear is compounded by what George Bush called "a dangerous combination . . . [of] regimes armed with old and unappeasable animosities and modern weapons of mass destruction."[56] Third World proliferation, as the pessimists see it, not only makes regional wars more likely, but also raises their destructive potential by a significant margin.

A second and closely related concern regarding Third World instability is that superpower disengagement, including cuts in military assistance programs to the Third World, would force their former clients to seek greater military self-reliance, thereby fueling new regional arms races.[57] In the words of one analyst, the withdrawal of the superpowers from Third World regions "entails merely that the Third World will do more of its own fighting."[58] Reinforcing the possibility of greater militarism in the Third World is the availability of large quantities of surplus military hardware from the vast arsenals of the major powers at bargain prices. Indonesia's recent acquisition of an entire East German fleet is a case in point. The same factor has helped Russia to establish itself as a major supplier to regional markets (such as in Southeast Asia), which had been previously closed to it for ideological reasons. Thus, the end of the Cold War has raised the possibility of a regional "arms race" in East Asia.[59]

A third source of disorder in the Third World that may be linked to the end of the Cold War concerns the possibility of greater regime instability. The end of the Cold War has been a blow to many authoritarian regimes (such as those in Cuba, El Salvador, Nicaragua, Somalia, Ethiopia, and North Korea), who had managed to remain in power thanks to massive amounts of superpower military and economic aid. The extent of their dependence is indicated by the fact that between the beginning of 1990 and mid-1992, as many as 11 African leaders fell from power.[60] That governments in Ethiopia, Liberia, Chad, and Somalia, all major recipients of superpower aid, were overthrown during this period cannot simply be a coincidence. This trend is in sharp contrast to the fact that between 1957 and 1990, Africa had seen only one successful insurgency (in Uganda in 1986). Regime instability caused by the loss of superpower aid is compounded by new restrictions on aid imposed by the major Western donor nations as well as international financial institutions controlled by them as part of the "New World Order." These restrictions have made economic assistance conditional on political reforms including the introduction of multiparty democracy.[61] As an African scholar put it, "a new spectre is now haunting Africa: Western gospel to Africa, with its uncompromising moralism about the multiparty system."[62]

Thus, the end of superpower rivalry and patronage has been a major contributing factor to democratic transitions in the Third World, transitions that have raised the possibility of heightened political turmoil. In Latin America, the loss of Soviet support for leftist regimes as well as the end of American backing for right-wing authoritarian regimes, both linked to the Cold War geopolitics, was a major factor behind democratic transitions.[63] In Southeast Asia, authoritarian regimes, such as the Association of Southeast Asian Nations (ASEAN) member-states, can no longer fend off demands for political liberalization by invoking external dangers (including Communist subversion) from prolonged regional conflicts in their neighborhood fueled by the intervention of the superpowers.

A fourth source of post–Cold War instability in the Third World identified by the pessimists relates to ethnic conflict. A recent survey of the world's conflicts found that of the 23 wars being fought in 1994, all but five are "based on communal rivalries and ethnic challenges to states." According to this study, ethnic conflict accounts for about three-quarters of the world's refugees (some 27 million people), while of the 13 peacekeeping operations recently undertaken by the UN, 8 involve situations of ethnopolitical conflict.[64] Such data has formed the basis of the view that ethnic conflicts are a major aspect of the so-called decompression effect (even if, as will be seen later, a closer look at the survey suggests less dramatic conclusions). The end of the Cold War has been linked to the outbreak of ethnic conflict, since in many parts of the Third World, it meant "the removal of ideological models that ha[d] offered uniting symbols of nation-building in countries that would otherwise be torn apart by ethnic, cultural, religious, or linguistic differences."[65]

Finally, the end of the Cold War has raised concerns about territorial conflicts in the Third World. In Europe and Central Asia, the collapse of the Soviet empire was accompanied by a proliferation of territorial claims, including an escalation of long-standing territorial disputes. This, some analysts fear, could have a "demonstration effect" in other parts of the Third World. As Barry Buzan argues, "if the territorial jigsaw can be extensively reshaped in the First and Second Worlds, it will become harder to resist the pressures to try to find more sensible and congenial territorial arrangements in the ex-Third World."[66] The separation of Eritrea from Ethiopia, the escalation of the Kashmir dispute between India and Pakistan, recent border skirmishes between Ecuador and Peru, and flashpoints in the South China Sea over the Spratlys Islands dispute, can be taken as a confirmation of this possibility. Of particular concern here is the fate of Africa's "successful boundary-maintenance regime," which had been the "great, though unheralded, accomplishment of African foreign policy."[67]

From the preceding discussion, certain aspects of the alleged decompression effect may be noted. An obvious point is that it involves domestic as well (or as much) as interstate or regional conflicts. Moreover, much of the fear about a decompression effect relates to the possible *reemergence and/or aggravation* of long-standing conflicts, rather than the emergence of new forms of conflict. Both these aspects lead to the question: to what extent can the *origins* of recent Third World conflicts be attributed entirely and directly to the end of the Cold War?

Exaggerating the Risks

In answering this question, I will make two arguments. First, the sources of Third World instability that are usually associated with the decompression effect are in reality part of a larger and long-term historical process that cannot be appreciated if viewed within the confines of the Cold War geopolitical space or time frame. Second, the seriousness of those causes, which may be somehow linked to the end of the Cold War, could be exaggerated.

Whether one includes the newly independent states of Europe and Central Asia in the Third World category or not, it is a reasonable assumption that the Third World is where the vast majority of the conflicts of the post–Cold War period will take place. A recent survey by the *Economist* shows that 28 out of 32 current wars (including insurgency, civil strife, and interstate wars), are taking place in the Third World.[68] But such data should be put in proper perspective, as the Third World is a much larger arena than Europe. What is more important is the fact that many of these conflicts emerged well before the end of the Cold War. These include many of the current or potential interstate conflict situations, including India–Pakistan, Arab–Israeli, and Korean conflicts. It is tempting to explain the Iraqi invasion of Kuwait, billed to be the first Third World conflict of the post–Cold War era, as an act of opportunism in the face of declining superpower involvement in the region, but its roots can only be explained in terms of the nature and position of the Saddam Hussein regime within the Iraqi polity. The Iraqi aggression was at least partly an attempt by the regime to ensure its survival in the face of a growing economic burden imposed by the Iran–Iraq War and the consequent political challenges to its legitimacy.

Another important source of instability in the Third World is also not directly linked or attributable to the end of bipolarity or the Cold War. This is the closely interrelated problems of overpopulation, resource scarcity, and environmental degradation, viewed by many as the chief source of what Kaplan has called the "coming anarchy."[69] Thomas Homer-Dixon, in a particularly sophisticated analysis of such conflicts, identifies three categories: "simple scarcity conflicts" (conflict over natural resources such as river, water, fish, and agriculturally productive land), "relative deprivation conflicts" (the impact of environmental degradation in limiting growth and thereby causing popular discontent and conflict), and "group-identity conflicts" (the problems of social assimilation of the migrant population) in the host countries.[70] These forms of conflict, Homer-Dixon's analysis suggests, are likely to be more acute in the Third World than in the developed states of the North. But even if such dire predictions are to prove accurate, the fact remains that the causes of such conflicts have little to do with changing polarity in the system structure.

Instead, it can be safely argued that the fundamental causative factors behind many Third World conflicts predate the end of the Cold War and remain unchanged in its wake. As argued by Mohammed Ayoob, Barry Buzan, Edward Azar and Chung-in Moon, Stephen David, and others,[71] the causes of Third World conflict during the Cold War were rooted in essentially domestic and regional factors, including a combination of weak postcolonial state structures and political threats to the legitimacy of the regimes that preside over these structures. Moreover, it is these local factors that often lead to the escalation of intrastate violence and strife into interstate and regional conflict. During the Cold War, these factors not only explained the higher incidence of intrastate conflict in the Third World, but also enjoyed a great deal of autonomy from external factors, including the bipolar system structure and the attendant superpower rivalry.[72] There is little reason to believe that the Third World's security problematic would be substantially different in the post–Cold War era.

Thus, it can be safely argued that in the post–Cold War era, essentially local factors related to weak national integration, economic underdevelopment, and competition for political legitimacy and control, rather than the changing structure of the international system from bipolarity to multipolarity, would remain the major sources of Third World instability. The polarity-stability debate in International Relations Theory, which is rooted in a narrower and more conventional notion of security, has simply ignored such conflicts (including the resource and environmental conflicts identified by Homer-Dixon). To quote Fred Halliday, "since the causes of third world upheaval [were] to a considerable extent independent of Soviet-US rivalry they will continue irrespective of relations between Washington and Moscow."[73] The best that can be said for the alleged "decompression" effect is that with the end of Cold War:

> Many of the regional problems and or conflicts that were essentially local expressions of the rivalry are now proving soluble. But there are many other conflicts rooted in other sources, among them historical, political, colonial, ethnic, religious, or socio-economic legacies, that continue to produce

international tensions. Cutting across these local issues are the major disparities of wealth and opportunity that separate the industrialized nations and the developing world. These have existed for decades. The failure to deal effectively with this gap is a source of additional tension, which itself frustrates long-term efforts to provide wider prosperity. The end of the Cold War has been irrelevant for many such conflicts.[74]

Apart from not being linked to the end of the Cold War, some of the sources of Third World instability are clearly exaggerated. Take for example, the phenomenon of ethnopolitical conflict, which is widely seen as a byproduct of the end of the Cold War. But data compiled by the Minorities at Risk Project suggests that "ethnopolitical conflicts were relatively common, and increased steadily, throughout the Cold War," with the greatest absolute and proportional increase in number of groups involved in ethnopolitical conflicts occurring between the 1960s and 1970s (from 36 groups to 55). This contrasts with a rate of increase of only 8 (from 62 to 70) from the 1980s to the early 1990s.[75] Thus, as the project's director, Ted Robert Gurr, concludes, "the 'explosion of' ethnopolitical conflicts since the end of the Cold War is, in fact, a continuation of a trend that began as early as the 1960s."[76] His project's findings also suggest that "ongoing ethnopolitical conflicts that began after 1987 are not appreciably more intense than those that began earlier," although they might "have caused greater dislocation of populations."[77] These empirical trends correspond to the theoretical explanation of the root causes of ethnic conflict, which focuses on the process of state-formation and economic development leading to an increased awareness of ethnic and cultural differences within Third World societies.[78] Moreover, these trends suggest that it was decolonization (which reached a peak in the 1960s and 1970s), rather than any shift from bipolarity, which should be regarded as the chief catalyst of ethnopolitical conflict in the post–World War II international system. The Third World's ethnic problems not only predate the end of the Cold War, they were also not necessarily suppressed by superpower rivalry.

While it is commonplace to characterize many recent outbreaks of violence in the Third World as ethnic conflicts, the reality may be more complex. Rwanda is a case in point. Although the media views it as an apocalyptic symbol of ethnic bloodletting in the post–Cold War era, on closer and sober reflection, the origins of the conflict can be found in "an intra-class power struggle among Rwandan elites who have manipulated and politicised ethnicity and/or regionalism, in order to divide the masses of Rwandan population into personal or group power constituencies." Moreover "there is nothing naturally innate or even historical about" the conflict; "the centuries-old history of pre-colonial Rwanda does not document a single ethnic war between the Hutu and the Tutsi."[79]

As with ethnic conflict, fears that postcolonial boundaries in the Third World are being undermined by the end of the Cold War are, to say the least, premature. The separation of Eritrea from Ethiopia after three decades of struggle makes it the first African state to be created through secession since decolonization. But in many respects, Eritrea is a special case.[80] As the *Economist* put it, while Eritrean independence breaks Africa's secession taboo, its claim for independence is "unusually strong" due to special historical circumstances in the sense that it never formed part of Ethiopia during the colonial era. Even if it encourages other movements, it "need not spell disaster for the continent."[81] Similarly, the likelihood of serious territorial conflicts elsewhere in the Third World could be overstated. Even at the height of the decolonization process during the Cold War, territorial conflicts were not a significant feature of the Third World's security dilemma. As research by Kal Holsti suggests, "the traditional national security problematic of most states in Europe was defined as protecting specific pieces of real estate. This is not the premier security problem for most states in the Third World."[82] There is as yet no concrete proof that we are about to see a major outbreak or escalation of territorial conflicts in the Third World. On the contrary, SIPRI data shows that the total number of major conflicts over territorial issues in the world remained constant at 16 from 1989 to 1992. In the Third World, territorial conflicts have actually declined from 15 in 1989 to 12 in 1992, while for Europe they increased from 1 to 4. In Africa, where the vast majority of conflicts continue to be intrastate, rather than interstate, the number of territorial conflicts has actually declined, from 3 in 1989 to 1.[83]

Similarly, it is an exaggeration to suggest that the end of the Cold War may be responsible for Africa's current political turmoil. Regime instability in Africa owes to a more fundamental process long predating the end of the Cold War: structural adjustment reforms carried out by African states "in the face of massive internal opposition from popular forces, the increasing delegitimization of the state and intensification of intra- and inter-class contradictions and conflicts." As a report issued by the Africa's main regional organization, the Organization of African Unity (OAU), put it, "in some African countries, the political consequences of . . . adjustment measures have been severe and have met with popular resistance in the form of riots on account of, for instance, the rising cost of food. Indeed, the social consequences of these programmes are threatening the very foundation and stability of the African social and cultural structures."[84] Furthermore, the link between democratization and conflict is a tenuous one. Contrary to the view of the pessimists, the process of democratization does not necessarily generate greater instability. Throughout the Third World, including Africa itself, many cases of democratization have been remarkably peaceful. Multiparty democratic elections led to the replacement of existing regimes in Zambia,

Madagascar, and Cape Verde. Internationally monitored elections saw the peaceful return of the governments of Seychelles, Guinea Bissau, and Kenya. In the Horn of Africa, the independent state of Eritrea embraced democracy, which led to the end of the revolutionary war in Ethiopia. These developments provide further confirmation that the appeal of violent methods of political change in the Third World may be diminishing. As Richard Falk points out: "The great struggles in the South during the 1980s, ranging from the overthrow of the Marcos regimes [*sic*] to the heroic challenges directed at oppressive rule in China and Burma, and on behalf of expanded democracy in South Korea, relied on non-violent mass mobilization, explicitly renouncing armed struggle." Even the intifada, Falk adds, conformed to this trend, resting "upon an inner logic of confronting the military violence of the occupiers with an essential vulnerability of unarmed civilians."[85]

Moreover, while the downfall of repressive regimes leading to democratic transitions may contribute to increased Third World instability in the short term, democratization should also create more favorable conditions of stability and order in the long term.[86] As Brad Roberts contends, democratization will "constrain" Third World anarchy by "compelling a search for common interests with erstwhile competitors."[87] Democratization addresses many causes of internal instability in the Third World. This is not just the view of Western liberals. A recent report by a panel sponsored by the OAU notes, "despite their apparently diverse causes, complex nature and manifold forms, internal conflicts in Africa were basically the result of denial of basic democratic rights and freedoms, broadly conceived; and that they tended to be triggered-off by acts of injustice, real or imagined, precisely in situations where recourse to democratic redress seemed hopeless."[88] At a time when "the romance seems to have gone out of Third World revolutions,"[89] democratization provides an alternative, and peaceful approach to desired political change. Whether democracies tend to live in peace with each other may be a debatable proposition in the West.[90] But in the Third World, the corelation (spillover effect) between internal strife and regional instability has always been strong, largely due to the tendency of weak states ruled by insecure regimes to "succumb to the temptation to consolidate their domestic position at the expense of their neighbours by cultivating external frictions or conflicts."[91] Thus, greater internal stability and regime legitimacy in Third World states enhances the prospects for regional security and lessen the scope for unwelcome external meddling in these countries.

Finally, fears that superpower retrenchment will lead to greater Third World militarization are proving to be somewhat unfounded. Recent data shows that the military buildup in the Third World has substantially declined with the end of the Cold War. The reasons for this trend may be found in the fact that "the end of the East-West divide has . . . heralded the demise of 'patron support,' 'militarization by invitation,' and soft financing terms. Only the richest countries are now able to buy weapons on a large scale."[92] In Africa, there has been a marked reduction in the volume of arms transfers. As Thomas and Mazrui argue, this is primarily due to the end of superpower competition and several of its related effects such as recent successes in settling African civil wars (which were escalated by the Cold War) and the rise of pro-democracy movements (other factors include the end of anticolonial armed struggles, economic crisis, and concerns expressed by the International Monetary Fund [IMF] and the World Bank regarding high levels of military spending in countries undergoing structural adjustment). In the rich nations of East Asia, defense expenditures and arms imports have risen since the end of the Cold War. This need not be viewed as an arms race signaling greater regional instability but rather could be a by-product of post–Cold War bargain-hunting and economic affluence.[93]

International stability in the post–Cold War world is, of course, threatened by the proliferation of weapons of mass destruction in the Third World. But this danger cannot be attributed to the end of the Cold War. If anything, the Cold War itself had aggravated the problem, especially in cases where the United States and the Soviet Union overlooked and tolerated proliferation efforts by their clients and allies in the Third World. For example, massive U.S. military and economic aid to Pakistan in the aftermath of the Soviet invasion of Afghanistan was meant to discourage the latter's nuclear program by providing it with a conventional alternative. But its net effect was to ease the pressure on Pakistan's nuclear program, which reached weapon capability during this very period. A number of Soviet allies acquired chemical and nuclear material, ostensibly with Moscow's knowledge and backing. On the other hand, the end of the Cold War has led to greater recognition of the danger posed by proliferation of weapons of mass destruction and international cooperation on counterproliferation efforts has intensified, culminating in the indefinite extension of the Nuclear Non-Proliferation Treaty.

Furthermore, while concerns about the proliferation of weapons of mass destruction have been central to fears of greater Third World anarchy, this view ignores some of its likely stabilizing consequences. Brad Roberts points out that, "states acquiring massively destructive military capabilities will be forced by the power inherent in those weapons to learn to possess them wisely . . . this requires of leaders in the developing world that they act like the rational actors assumed in all deterrence models."[94] Given the demonstrated effect of nuclear weapons in inducing caution in the European theater (as well as the central strategic balance in general) during the Cold War, there is no reason to believe, short of blind ethnocentrism, that the Third World leaders will behave like "madmen" once in possession of such weapons.

Sources of Stability

In addition to the list of false alarms about increased Third World conflict, one could cite certain effects of the end of the Cold War that have contributed to more favorable conditions for stability. First, the end of the U.S.–Soviet strategic rivalry means an end to the general tendency of the Northern Great Powers to view Third World conflicts as permissible. Second, the Great Powers have become far less interventionist. In a bipolar world, as Kenneth Waltz argued, "with two powers capable of acting on a world scale, anything that happen[ed] anywhere [was] potentially of concern to both of them."[95] In the emerging multipolar world not all Great Powers will wield a similar capacity, and the only power capable of global power projection—the United States—is likely to be quite selective in choosing its areas of engagement. One safe generalization from the recent academic debate over the relative importance of the Third World vis-à-vis Europe is that apart from Europe, the Gulf, the Arab–Israeli zone, and the Korean Peninsula would surely attract the bulk of U.S. strategic attention and resources in the post–Cold War era.[96] Of course, individual Great Powers may have special interests and concerns in other parts of the Third World, a major example being France's special ties with Africa and interests in the South Pacific, China's interests in Southeast Asia, and Russia's historic interests in its "near-abroad" and the Middle East. But these powers are no longer capable of acting on a global scale. (While China's capacity for global intervention may grow, its quest for ideological expansion has ended, even in its regional neighborhood). While selective global engagement by the Great Powers creates some potential risk that bloody conflicts in marginal areas of the Third World might go unnoticed by the international community (as happened in Liberia from 1990 to 1992 and initially in Somalia in 1991 and Rwanda in 1994), it will also prevent the internationalization of local wars and localization of systemic tensions resulting from Great Power intervention.

To be sure, Great Power intervention in the Third World is not likely to disappear entirely. Despite the trend toward military cutbacks, no major Western power has forsaken military intervention as a policy option for dealing with Third World conflicts. On the contrary, some of the force structures previously deployed in Europe are being earmarked for Third World contingency missions.[97] In addition, there are moves toward greater cooperation and coordination of military assets for deployment in Third World contingencies within the framework of major Western alliances such as NATO and the Western European Union.[98] But Great Power intervention in the Third World is likely to become a highly selective affair. The political and military constraints on such interventions are growing.

The dampening of the Great Power interventionist impulse is partly explained by the rising costs of such interventions. Without a global Soviet threat to provide it justification, the United States and other Western countries are increasingly constrained by the weight of public opinion against foreign military action. Furthermore, although the end of bipolarity removed what Hedley Bull called the "balance among the interveners which has worked to the advantage of the intervened against,"[99] the growing military capabilities of Third World states ensures that the costs of regional intervention by Great Powers are much higher today than in the early days of decolonization.[100] As Joseph Nye argues, the "forces that many Third World states will be able to deploy in the 1990s will make regional superpower intervention more costly than was the case in the 1950s."[101]

As with Great Power intervention, local intervention by Third World regional powers is also becoming more difficult. As noted earlier, the declining involvement of the Great Powers in the Third World theoretically creates a greater scope for hegemonism by regional actors. But this prospect is offset by the diminished opportunity for potential Third World hegemons to secure external backing (especially from the Northern powers) for their own power and security interests and ambitions. During the Cold War, regional powers derived a measure of autonomy from the superpower standoff while securing material assistance from them to further their regional ambitions. The end of the Cold War marks the end to the need for the superpowers to cultivate "regional policemen" (such as Iran under the Nixon Doctrine), or regional proxies (such as Vietnam and Cuba for the Soviet Union) as part of their competitive search for influence. For their part, the regional powers, as Chubin argues, can no longer "count on foreign patrons to support them reflexively, supply them with arms, or salvage for them an honourable peace."[102] Without massive superpower backing, even the most powerful among Third World states may find it more difficult to sustain military adventures,[103] and may be deterred from seeking to fulfill their external ambitions through military means. The Iraqi experience during the Gulf War is illustrative of the predicament of regional powers deprived of an opportunity to exploit the superpower rivalry.[104]

Arguably, these developments are conducive to greater stability and order in the Third World. They are also consistent with a recent survey of trends in international conflict that deny the existence of a decompression effect for the international system as a whole. As a recent SIPRI survey noted: "The data on major armed conflicts do not support the expectation that the end of the Cold War would result in increased global disorder but rather show a very gradual decrease in the annual total number of conflict locations since 1989."[105]

The following discussion suggests that just as some analysts have overstated the role of the Cold War in promoting order and stability in the Third World, those who fear a "decompression effect" seem to exaggerate the destabilizing consequences of the end of the Cold War. It also leads to another important point about the impact of the end of the Cold War, that it does not have a single or uniform effect on Third World instability. In some parts of the Third World, such as in sub-Saharan Africa, the end of the Cold War has led to greater domestic disorder, while in Southeast Asia it has led to increased domestic tranquility and regional order (with the end of Communist insurgencies and settlement of the Cambodia conflict)[106] and in the Middle East,[107] to greater interstate cooperation (especially after the Israeli–Palestinian accords). In Africa, the end of the Cold War has contributed to a sharp decline in arms imports, while in East Asia, it has created fears of an all-out arms race. Furthermore, the impact of the end of the Cold War varies according to the type of conflict. The rise of domestic conflicts in Africa contrasts sharply with the settlement of its long-standing regional conflicts (especially in Southern Africa).[108] In Eastern Asia, especially in the Korean Peninsula, the end of the Cold War has led to greater interstate conflict. Regional hegemonism is a marked trend in East Asia with China's emergence, but elsewhere, it is the regional powers, India, Nigeria, Vietnam, Iraq, and Brazil that have felt the squeeze by being denied privileged access to arms and aid from their superpower patrons. Thus, to talk of a uniform and Third World–wide "decompression" effect sparked by the end of bipolarity is misleading and not supported by the evidence. In general, the end of the Cold War is having a mixed and region specific impact on Third world stability.

Finally, it should be noted that a great deal of instability in the Third World took place at the height of the decolonization process and was directly associated with it. These include anticolonial wars (wars of national liberation), ethnic and nationalist conflicts resulting from the imposition of artificial national boundaries by the departing colonial powers, and threats to regime stability resulting from the implantation of alien political systems in relatively inhospitable local political and social settings. As the decolonization process fades into distant memory, many Third World states have been able to achieve greater sociopolitical cohesion and regime stability. They now have greater experience in state-making, managing political transitions, and reducing ethnic tensions through peaceful means. Thus, there is some basis to think that the widespread instability of the Third World was a historically specific phenomenon and that the passage of time and more favorable domestic and external conditions will allow at least some of these states to experience greater stability and order.

To sum up, risks of conflict under conditions of multipolarity can be exaggerated, and prospects for stability understated. The post–Cold War situation supports a number of theoretical arguments concerning the stabilizing effects of multipolarity. The end of bipolarity has reduced chances of conflict escalation, since, in multipolarity, the "share of attention" that the two superpowers devoted has significantly diminished, leading to a lesser probability of conflict escalation. Also there is evidence that multipolarity may be having a "dampening effect upon arms races" in much of the Third World.

Changing Conditions of Conflict-Management

In their discussion of polarity and stability, Deutsch and Singer imply that the "'invisible hand' of pluralistic interests" associated with multipolarity may be more conducive to international security cooperation than the zero-sum nature of bipolar interactions.[109] This argument has considerable relevance to prospects for conflict management in the post–Cold War Third World. A world with several Great Powers sharing leadership in international security affairs is naturally different in its capacity for, and approach to, conflict management.[110] The bipolar international security order, despite the claims of Waltz and Gaddis regarding its capacity for self-regulation, permitted an abundance of conflicts in the Third World and had limited success in ensuring conflict management. Now the question arises: how different will things be under conditions of multipolarity?

The first consequence of the demise of superpower rivalry is what I. William Zartman has called a "regime change" brought about by the changing "structures of world power."[111] What Zartman referred to was a shift from East–West competition to East–West collaboration in resolving Third World conflicts.[112] To be sure, Moscow's subsequent relegation from superpower status, its drastic disengagement from Third World theaters,[113] and the emerging signs of discord in the U.S. and Russian perspectives on regional security, means that the idea of such a Great Power condominium in resolving Third World conflicts is no longer relevant. But East–West cooperation produced a renewed commitment to multilateralism and collective security. Unlike the Cold War order, which permitted only ad hoc and informal rules of the game[114] as the basis for superpower conflict management, the post–Cold War has been more conducive to collective and common security mechanisms.[115] The end of the Cold War also raises hopes for more effective regional security arrangements.[116]

It is worth noting that the peacemaking role of the UN was more central in ending Cold War regional conflicts in the Third World, such as those in Southeast Asia (Cambodia), the Persian Gulf (the Iran–Iraq War), and in Southern Africa (Namibia and Angola)[117] than in Europe, where indigenous regional security regimes like the CSCE (now OSCE) have had a major role in the easing of East–West tensions. In addition to the peacemaking role, the role of the UN in handling the first major conflict of the post–Cold War era outside Europe—the Iraqi invasion of Kuwait—attested to a revival of its collective security function for the first time since the Korean War.[118] While the initial euphoria surrounding the "rebirth" of the UN has been considerably dampened by its recent setbacks in Somalia and Bosnia, this should not detract from the significant role the UN has already played in facilitating the settlement of a number of conflicts.

The shortcomings of the UN in dealing with regional conflict has rekindled the realist critique of the role of international institutions in promoting peace.[119] Such scepticism about institutions has been even more pronounced in the case of regional security institutions in the Third World.[120] Thomas G. Weiss and S. Neil McFarlane question the ability of regional organizations to remain impartial and play an effective role in mediating and managing regional conflicts.[121] In examining the prospects for order in the post–Cold War era, James M. Goldgeier and Michael McFaul contrast the "periphery" sector of Third World states, marked by fragile regional security systems and displaying a high degree of conflict and disorder with the "core" sector of stable major powers within which interdependence and shared norms minimize the risk of armed conflict.[122] Yet such pessimism about Third World regional institutions may be unwarranted. At least three reasons for this view deserve notice.

First, the Cold War was marked by a competition between global and regional security frameworks.[123] Many Third World states accused the superpowers of ignoring, bypassing, and manipulating indigenous security arrangements in the Third World geared to pacific settlement of disputes, and encouraging balance-of-power arrangements that often aggravated ideological polarizations within Third World regions. With the diminished engagement of the Great Powers in the Third World and the strain on the UN's resources caused by a dramatic expansion of peacekeeping operations, regional security organizations now have an opportunity to assume a greater role in the security management in their respective areas. Here, existing regional security organizations, such as the Gulf Cooperation Council and the Association of Southeast Asian Nations, which reflected regional competition and ideological polarization during the Cold War, are under pressure to accommodate former adversaries and promote regional reconciliation and order.[124]

Second, not all Third World regional security arrangements have been ineffective in managing conflict. Three examples stand out. The Central American peace agreement was regionally led. The contribution of the Contadora and Esquipulus groups in ending the bloody and prolonged Nicaragua-El Salvador conflict is a good example of the potential of regional common security arrangements to foster regional order and stability.[125] Second, the

Gulf Cooperation Council, while failing to deter a violent military threat from Iraq against a member state, Kuwait, was nonetheless successful in dealing with threats of internal subversion backed by Iran. Third, in the Asia Pacific region, ASEAN not only played an instrumental role in facilitating the resolution of the Cambodia conflict, but has been exceptionally active in developing a regional security structure for the Asia Pacific region.[126]

There are other examples of relative success of regional arrangements in conflict management. The role of the ECOWAS in the Liberian conflict, though far more controversial than ASEAN's record in Cambodia, has nonetheless resulted in a government of national unity. The South Pacific Forum has not been entirely ineffective either. Its role in creating a nuclear weapons free zone has received international support and raised the level of international condemnation of French nuclear testing in the South Pacific.

Third, one should not use unrealistic criteria in judging the effectiveness of Third World regional organizations. The latter cannot be expected to perform collective security or alliance functions because of the military weakness of their members. But they can develop norms, principles, and habits of cooperation and reduce sources of tension through functional interaction. Thus, while regional security arrangements in the Third World may fall short of a full-fledged collective security apparatus with enforcement capacity, they can complement the preventive diplomacy, peacemaking, and peacebuilding roles of the UN.[127]

There are indications that the end of the Cold War has led to a revival of interest in such regional approaches to peace and security. The ECOWAS has created a Standing Mediation Committee to facilitate pacific settlement of disputes among its members.[128] Another notable African regional initiative is the 1991 Kampala Declaration for the Creation of a Conference on Security, Stability, Development and Cooperation in Africa (CSSDCA), jointly sponsored by the OAU, the UN Economic Commission for Africa, and the African Leadership Forum.[129] In June 1993, an OAU summit in Cairo agreed to create a mechanism for preventing, managing, and resolving African conflicts.[130] Among other things, this mechanism is intended to organize African peacekeeping operations in close cooperation with the UN. In Latin America, the efforts of the OAS in promoting respect for human rights and democracy, as evident in the "Santiago Commitment to Democracy and the Renewal of the Inter-American System," are aimed at preventing future domestic and regional instability.[131] Among other things, the OAS and the UN organized a joint effort to send a special envoy and an international human rights commission to Haiti. In Southeast Asia, ASEAN has taken the lead in creating a forum for dialogue on regional security issues among the principal Asia Pacific nations.

To be sure, the continued interventionism of the Western powers in selected Third World theaters to protect their "vital interests" could constrain the role of multilateral institutions in conflict management. Conflicts in those areas deemed to be vitally important to the Western powers are especially susceptible for their unilateral action. As the columnist Steven S. Rosenfeld notes, "by definition, vital interests are those that cannot be left to the discretion of others and which justify Washington in deciding how to assert them in its own way."[132] Thus, global as well as regional security arrangements in the post–Cold War era are likely to have limited autonomy in managing conflicts in areas of the Third World that lie within the strategic perimeters of the Western Great Powers. In these areas, the dependence of Third World states on Great Power security guarantees will continue.[133] In the Gulf, for example, Kuwaiti security agreements with the United States have conflicted with postwar regional security arrangements involving the GCC. Similarly, many countries of the Asia-Pacific prefer to see security arrangements with the United States as a more realistic security option in countering the influence of regional powers than common security arrangements. It is only in areas of marginal strategic significance to the Great Powers that the UN and regional groupings could manage greater autonomy in providing mechanisms for conflict resolution.

But there still remains considerable scope for Great Power security cooperation in managing Third World conflicts. While both the UN and regional arrangements face major constraints in their peace and security roles, most of these relate to a paucity of resources rather than to the kind of Great Power disagreement that was so common during the Cold War period. The post–Cold War relationship among the Great Powers points to greater cooperation, if not an outright concert system, and is a far cry from the balance-of-power model envisaged in realist thought.[134] Both realist and liberal institutionalist theory agree that institutions matter when they serve the interests of the Great Powers. Without the framework of conflict regulation provided by superpower rivalry, the Great Powers have no real alternative to global and regional institutions in facilitating conflict resolution in the post–Cold War era.

Perhaps a more serious problem for international security cooperation in the post–Cold War era is the persistence of the North–South disagreements over global "order-building" mechanisms. Michael Klare has predicted a heightened period of North–South (or rather West–South) tensions to follow the end of East–West rivalry.[135] It is arguable that this North–South divide is a more serious threat to international order than Samuel Huntington's thesis about a "clash of civilizations"[136] (which itself does have a North-South dimension, although it theoretically allows for intra-North [for example, Japan versus the United States] and intra-South [for example,

Hindu versus Muslim] conflicts). At least three areas of North–South disagreement deserve notice. The first concerns the North's commitment to genuine cooperative action. Bush's vision of a New World Order promised a return to multilateralism and the revival of the UN's collective security framework. But the first major test of this New World Order, the U.S.-led response to the Iraqi invasion of Kuwait, prompted widespread misgivings in the South. Although the UN resolutions against Iraq were supported by most Third World states, this was accompanied by considerable resentment of the U.S. domination of the UN decision-making process. The U.S.'s military actions against Iraq were seen as having exceeded the mandate of UN resolutions,[137] and the U.S. claims about collective security were greeted with scepticism. Many in the South would perhaps agree with Zbigniew Brzezinski's remark that "once the symbolism of collective action was stripped away [the war against Iraq] was largely an American decision and relied primarily on American military power."[138] The Gulf War fed Southern apprehension that notwithstanding their protestations about collective action,[139] the United States and other Western powers (such as France in Africa) would surely retain their option for unilateral managerial and interventionist action in Third World conflicts in the post–Cold War era. A similar scepticism marks Southern attitudes toward armed intervention in support of humanitarian objectives. The concept of "humanitarian intervention" professes to be free of crude calculations of geopolitics and national interest, but the delayed response to humanitarian disasters in Somalia and Rwanda suggests a reluctance to intervene unless national interests are clearly threatened. The West's approach to humanitarian intervention is constrained by the principles of "doability" as well as domestic public opinion trends, which are ultimately judged unilaterally by national decision makers.

A second area of North–South tension concerns the Northern approach to arms control and nonproliferation as the Nuclear Non-Proliferation Treaty (NPT), the Missile Technology Control Regime (MTCR), and the Australia group on chemical weapons. These are essentially supplier clubs that seek to control proliferation through restrictions on export of military or dual-use technology. Southern objections to these regimes focus on their selective application and discriminatory nature. As Shahram Chubin argues, in the case of nuclear weapons, the North's antiproliferation campaign "frankly discriminates between friendly and unfriendly states, focussing on signatories (and potential cheats) like Iran but ignoring actual proliferators like Israel. It is perforce more intelligible in the North than in the South."[140] In a more blunt tone, the Indian scholar K. Subrahmanyam charges that nonproliferation regimes based on export controls "project a racist bias," because they "embody a fundamental double standard whereby nuclear weapons and missiles are deemed essential for the security of industrialized countries but dangerous in the hands of developing nations."[141] While such views might reflect the special interest of countries like India, they are also widely shared in the Third World. Moreover, the handful of proliferators are also the most critical players in any multilateral approach to peace and security in their respective regions. Hence, their dissenting views cannot be ignored if the West is to devise a genuinely collective approach to conflict management.

A third area of North–South tension in the post–Cold War era relates to the West's advocacy of human rights and democracy as the basis for a new global political order. The leaders of the West see the "enlargement" of democracy as a logical corollary to the successful "containment" and defeat of communism. The Western agenda on human rights is being promoted through a variety of means, including aid conditionality (linking development assistance with human rights records of aid recipients), support for self-determination of persecuted minorities and, as in the case of Haiti, direct military intervention. All these instruments affect the political and economic interests of Third World states, many of whom see these conditions as a threat to their sovereignty and economic well-being.[142] Thus, Malaysian Prime Minister Mahathir Mohammed sees the West's human rights campaign as a device to perpetuate the condition of dependency of the South. Citing the example of the former Communist states of Eastern Europe, Mahathir contends that the campaign of human rights and democracy is a prescription for disruption and chaos in weaker countries, a campaign that makes the target ever more dependent on the donor nations of the West. Other critics of the South accuse the West of hypocrisy and selectivism in applying its human rights standards. The Foreign Minister of Singapore finds that "concern for human rights [in the West] has always been balanced against other national interests."[143] To support this argument, Singapore's policymakers contrast the U.S. support for absolutist regimes in the oil-rich Arabian Peninsula with its response to the recent crisis in Algeria in which Western governments acquiesced to a military coup that overthrew a duly elected government with a strongly Islamic orientation. There are a number of general areas in which the views of many Southern governments seem to converge. These include a belief that the issue of human rights must be related to the specific historical, political, and cultural circumstances of each nation. Governments in East Asia have added their voice to this "cultural relativist" position by rejecting the individualist conception of human rights in the West, arguing instead for a "communitarian" perspective that recognizes the priority of the "society over the self."[144] The developing countries in general have stressed that economic rights, especially the right to development, be given precedence over purely political ones in the global human rights agenda.[145]

But the position of the South on the issue of human rights is marked by significant regional variations; the attitude of the Latin American nations contrasts sharply with those in East Asia, and even within the latter, differences exist between South Korea and Taiwan on the one hand and the ASEAN countries and China on the other. Moreover, the projection of a North–South divide on human rights is a statecentric understanding, as there is little disagreement between Northern and Southern nongovernmental organizations over the issue of human rights.

Thus, while there is a risk that the positive impact of the end of East–West rivalry on the working of the UN and regional security arrangements could be offset by prevailing suspicions and problems arising in the North–South security relationship, the scope of the latter can be overstated. While the issues of contention discussed earlier undermine the prospects for international cooperation in developing effective conflict-management mechanisms, they need not be crippling. This is not only because the Third World is less united today in articulating its political and security concerns, but because bipolarity and the Cold War are no longer serving as cementing factors for an otherwise diverse and unwieldy grouping.[146] The Third World's major political security platform, the Nonaligned Movement, is of diminishing relevance in a multipolar international system. Despite a growing membership (now at 108), the NAM's post–Cold War direction remains unclear. Some members, such as Malaysia, would like to use NAM to counter "this so-called New World Order propagated by a big power [the United States]."[147] But others, perhaps the majority led by Indonesia (the current chair of NAM), seek to shift the priorities of NAM from the political to the economic arena[148] and to strike a moderate and pragmatic tone for NAM in global North-South negotiations.[149] Such a shift is likely to engender greater cooperation between the North and the South in international security affairs, especially if such cooperation is facilitated by a greater reliance of both on multilateral organizations. This trend is reinforced by growing economic interdependence between the North and the South.[150] Faster growth rates in Third World are already providing Northern countries with greater market opportunities. Moreover, greater productivity in the Third World is having beneficial effects on the North's standard of living, as for the latter, "cheaper imports mean lower prices and, hence, higher real incomes."[151] At the same time, market-oriented economic reforms (including IMF-induced structural adjustment) are lessening the earlier distrust among Third World elites of Western multinationals and investments flow. The end of the Cold War has already ended the economic isolation of many former Socialist economies, such as Vietnam and India. Their progressive integration into the global economy will have a moderating effect on the prospects for North–South economic cooperation in the post–Cold War era and help prevent the escalation of political, cultural, and civilizational differences that would otherwise constrain conflict management.

To sum up, while the post–Cold War period is marked by greater East–West collaboration on regional conflicts, it is the state of North–South security relations that is likely to prove more decisive in prospects for conflict regulation in the Third World. But here there are grounds for some optimism. The end of the Cold War has reduced the relevance of the South's radical platforms, such as the Nonaligned Movement, although the more interventionist aspects of the North's current approach to nonproliferation and human rights are creating new tensions between the North and the South. While failure to manage and overcome these tensions will undermine the prospects for cooperation and collective action, the end of superpower rivalry has created favorable conditions for a more "adaptive" role by Third World states in the making of a new international security order. In the Cold War era, Third World states generally distrusted the security framework of the superpowers, even while they had to rely on it for protection. In their present condition of vulnerability, as well as due to the mitigation of their fears of superpower rivalry, the majority of Third World states are likely to settle for a less confrontational role, and participate in collective and common security frameworks. While the end of the East–West conflict facilitates the working of global conflict-management mechanisms such as the UN, the North–South security relations will be important to the working of regional security arrangements that are needed to compensate for deficiencies in the global collective security framework.

To this end, greater reliance on regional organizations will serve to decentralize the global collective security mechanism and address demands voiced in many parts of the Third World for a greater democratization of the UN's peace and security function. Many regional security organizations have failed not because of any inherent weakness, but because the larger powers of the international system, which control most of the resources required for peacemaking and collective security, have chosen to act through the UN Security Council system (where they can exercise greater control) rather than to allow a devolution of authority to regional institutions where developing coutnries may weild greater influence. A genuine willingness on the part of the Great Powers to empower regional bodies (it should be noted that where Great Powers have willingly devoted resources to regional security arrangements, such as NATO, the latter have been quite effective) will go a long way in ensuring more effective conflict control mechanisms in the Third World.

With these caveats in mind, one can argue that there now exists a much improved condition for international cooperation, both East–West and North–South, to promote order and stability in the Third World. Moreover, considering the dismal record of the Cold War order in preventing Third

World violence, a multipolar order may prove more successful in dampening Third World crises than the balance-of-power mechanisms devised by the superpowers.

Conclusion

The main conclusion of this chapter is that for the Third World in general, multipolarity is likely to be less conflict-prone than the bipolar Cold War period. I arrive at this conclusion by looking at the conflict-escalating tendency of the Cold War, the sources and trends in Third World conflicts in the post–Cold War period, and the effectiveness of conflict-control mechanisms in the post–Cold War period. The impact of the end of the Cold War on the long-term outlook for Third World stability is positive, although it might have created short-term negative consequences. Thus it is important that pessimism about a "decompression effect" should not obscure or detract from the opportunities created by the end of superpower rivalry for a new global regime for conflict prevention and regulation. Along with the benefits accruing from East-West reconciliation, improving the climate for North-South security relations should negate claims that the end of the Cold War might exacerbate instability and disorder in the Third World.

While bipolarity might have been an era of structural stability, it was also a period of heightened regional instability in the Third World. Unless one takes a very narrow definition of stability to include system structure and interactions among the major powers only, as the polarity-stability debate has tended to, bipolarity cannot be considered as having been more conducive to international stability. The theoretical arguments concerning the simplicity, predictability, and self-regulatory capacity of bipolar systems do not hold when seen in the context of the actual extent of violence in the Third World during the Cold War period.

In looking at the post–Cold War period, I find that many arguments concerning the sources of conflicts in the Third World have been exaggerated, while the effects of the end of the Cold War in reducing the probability of conflict escalation have been understated. Moreover, prospects for conflict and disorder in the post–Cold War period may have less to do with changes to the system structure than to developments at the local and regional levels. In this respect, a major weakness of the polarity-stability debate is its failure to account for domestic and intraregional sources of Third World conflict, as well as important variations in the pattern of conflict and order between regions, variations that are likely to be accentuated by the end of the Cold War.

While Waltz, Gaddis, and Mearsheimer have stressed the superior capacity of bipolar systems to regulate international conflict, the preceding discussion suggests that multipolar systems may be no less effective in controlling Third World conflict. On balance, the end of the Cold War might have enhanced the prospects for pacific settlement of Third World conflicts with a greater use of cooperative multilateral approaches. Although these approaches have their own limitations, these relate primarily to North-South tensions, which appear to be easing, rather than the relationship among the Great Powers, as the polarity-stability debate holds. An analysis of the prospects for international order that focus on Great Power relationships and ignore the North–South conflict is likely to be of limited value in addressing security problems of the post–Cold War period.

The overall findings of this chapter suggest the need to rethink the relevance of the polarity-stability debate as a framework for analyzing Third World conflict. But I single out structural realism for criticism because its claims about stability during the Cold War period are particularly tenuous when judged against the security experience of Third World states. The findings of this chapter support those, such as Deutsch and Singer, who claim that multipolar systems are likely to be more stable than bipolar ones. But unlike the latter, I arrive at this conclusion by taking into account the specific security experience of the Third World and going beyond the authors' essentially structuralist logic and Eurocentric evidence, which does not relate to the complexities of the Third World security predicament.[152]

My conclusion that multipolarity may prove to be substantially more peaceful for the Third World than the era of U.S.–Soviet rivalry has two major implications for international security studies. It was not until the 1980s that the latter begun to appreciate the distinctive security predicament of Third World countries. Until then, problems of regional conflict in the Third World had received only secondary attention relative to the salience of the central strategic balance and European regional security issues.[153] Incorporation of the Third World experience can only enrich major theoretical debates in security studies, such as that concerning the linkage between stability and polarity. Secondly, although the primary aim of this chapter is to highlight the *relative* stability of the Third World after the end of the Cold War, its conclusions do have some relevance for more general studies of war and peace. In his recent work, *Retreat From Doomsday*, John Mueller has argued that war among the industrialized nations is becoming "obsolescent." The end of the Cold War, according to Mueller, will accelerate this trend. But he is less certain about the fate of war in the Third World (although he sees some positive signs here as well[154]). Francis Fukuyama clearly excuses the Third World from the era of tranquility that he expects to result from "the end of history."[155] In this chapter, I have sought to demonstrate that the Third World, or at least many parts of it, can expect to see a decline of conflict and violence as a result of the end of the Cold War.

To be sure, peace will not become universal, but conflict will be rarer and more localized. The overarching geopolitical rivalry between the United States and the Soviet Union magnified local conflicts in the remotest part of the Third World. The end of the Cold War will spare many parts of the Third World from this unhappy predicament.

Notes

1. John Mearsheimer, "Back to the Future: Instability in Europe After the Cold War," *International Security,* vol. 15, no. 1 (Summer 1990), pps. 5–55.

2. Critical responses to Mearsheimer can be found in two subsequent issues of *International Security* (vol. 15, no. 2 [Fall 1990] and vol. 15, no. 3 [Winter 1990/91].) Although no forceful and predictive commentary about Third World security has yet been made, Mearsheimer's thesis appears to have found an echo in a number of recent scholarly writings on the subject.

3. Jose Thiago Cintra, "Regional Conflicts: Trends in a Period of Transition," in *The Changing Strategic Landscape,* Adelphi paper no. 237 (London: International Institute for Strategic Studies, 1989), pps. 96–97.

4. Stanley Hoffmann, "Watch Out for a New World Disorder," *International Herald Tribune,* February 26, 1991, p. 6.

5. Testimony by Lieutenant General James Clapper to the Senate Armed Services Committee, January 22, 1992, in "Regional Flashpoints Potential for Military Conflict" (Washington, DC: United States Information Service, December 24, 1992), p. 6.

6. Robert Jervis, "The Future of World Politics: Will it Resemble the Past?" *International Security,* vol. 16, no. 3 (Winter 1991/92), p. 59.

7. John Lewis Gaddis, "International Relations Theory and the End of the Cold War," *International Security,* vol.17, no. 3 (Winter 1992/93), p. 30.

8. Kenneth N. Waltz, "The Stability of a Bipolar World," *Daedalus,* vol. 93, no. 3 (1964), p. 882. In this article, Waltz identified four factors: absence of peripheries, the range and intensity of competition, the persistence of pressure and crisis, and the preponderant power of the two leading actors as the reasons for the stability of bipolar systems.

9. Kenneth N. Waltz, *Theory of International Politics* (Reading, MA: Addison-Wesley, 1979), p. 168.

10. Ibid., p. 171.

11. John Mearsheimer, "Why We Will Soon Miss the Cold War," in *Crosscurrents: International Relations in the Post–Cold War Era,* eds., Mark Charlton and Elizabeth Ridell-Dixon (Toronto: Nelson Canada, 1993), p. 16.

12. Waltz, "The Stability of a Bipolar World," p. 907.

13. John Lewis Gaddis, "The Long Peace: Elements of Stability in the Post-War International System," *International Security,* vol. 10, no. 4 (Spring 1986), pps. 103–4.

14. Robert Gilpin, *War and Change in World Politics* (Cambridge: Cambridge University Press, 1981), p. 92.

15. Ibid., p. 91.

16. Richard N. Rosecrance, "Bipolarity, Multipolarity, and the Future," in *International Politics and Foreign Policy*, eds., James N. Rosenau (NY: The Free Press, 1969), pps. 326–27.

17. Karl W. Deutsch and J. David Singer, "Multipolar Power Systems and International Stability," in *International Politics and Foreign Policy*, eds., James N. Rosenau (NY: The Free Press, 1969), p. 318.

18. Ibid., p. 320.

19. Rosecrance, "Bipolarity, Multipolarity, and the Future," p. 328.

20. John Lewis Gaddis, "International Relations Theory and the End of the Cold War," *International Security*, vol.17, no. 3 (Winter 1992/93), pps. 5–58; Jack S. Levy, "The Causes of Wars: A Review of Theories and Evidence," in *Behaviour, Society and Nuclear War*, eds., Philip E. Tetlock et al, vol.1 (NY: Oxford University Press, 1989), p. 235.

21. This applies especially to Mearsheimer, whose arguments to the effect that bipolarity is more stable are specifically derived from the European experience.

22. Gaddis, "The Long Peace," p. 104.

23. Waltz, *Theory of International Politics*, p. 172.

24. Rosecrance, "Bipolarity, Multipolarity, and the Future," p. 327.

25. Major theoretical attempts to develop an understanding of Third World regional conflict and security issues in terms of their local, rather than systemic or structural, determinants during the Cold War period include Ayoob's work on regional security in the Third World, and Buzan's work on "regional security complexes." Contending that "issues of regional security in the developed world are defined primarily in Cold War terms (NATO versus Warsaw Pact, etc.) and are, therefore, largely indivisible from issues of systemic security," Ayoob demonstrated convincingly that "the salient regional security issues in the Third World have a life of their own independent of superpower rivalry." Buzan similarly urged greater attention to the "set of security dynamics at the regional level" in order to "develop the concepts and language for systematic comparative studies, still an area of conspicuous weakness in Third World studies." His notion of "security complex," defined as "local sets of states . . . whose major security perceptions and concerns link together sufficiently closely that their national security perceptions cannot realistically be considered apart from one another," was designed to understand "how the regional level mediates the interplay between states and the international system as a whole." It should be noted, however, that while both Ayoob and Buzan called for greater attention to the regional and local sources of conflict and cooperation, Ayoob's was specifically focused on the Third World. Buzan's approach is also more structuralist, emphasizing the role of systemic determinants such as colonialism and superpower rivalry (which he calls "overlays") in shaping regional security trends. This seems to undercut his earlier call for "the relative autonomy of regional security relations." See Mohammed Ayoob, "Regional Security and the Third World," in *Regional Security in the Third World*, ed. Mohammed Ayoob (London:

Croom Helm, 1986); Barry Buzan, *People, States and Fear* (Brighton: Wheat-sheaf Books, 1983), p. 186, and Barry Buzan, "Third World Regional Security in Structural and Historical perspective," in *The Insecurity Dilemma: National Security of Third World States,* ed., Brian L. Job (Boulder, CO: Lynne Rienner Publishers, 1992), pps. 167–89.

26. One study by Evan Luard estimates that between 1945 and 1986, there were some 127 "significant wars." Out of these, only two occurred in Europe, while Latin America accounted for 26, Africa 31, the Middle East, 24, and Asia 44. According to this estimate, the Third World was the scene of more than 98 percent of all international conflicts. Evan Luard, *War in International Society,* (London: I. B. Taurus, 1986), appendix 5.

27. Both of these positions conforms to arguments made by Waltz regarding the "stability" of bipolar systems; see note 8.

28. Jervis, "The Future of World Politics," p. 31.

29. Ayoob, "Regional Security and the Third World," p. 14. A similar view had been offered by another Third World scholar, Sisir Gupta, who argued that for the superpowers "to fight out their battles in the Third World is one way of en-suring that their own worlds are not touched by their conflicts and that they retain a greater measure of option to escalate and de-escalate their conflicts ac-cording to the needs of their relationships." Cited in Mohammed Ayoob, ed., *Conflict and Intervention in the Third World* (Canberra, Australian National University Press, 1980), p. 242. According to another Indian scholar, K. Sub-rahmanyam, the tendency of the superpowers to play out their rivalry in the Third World was accentuated by detente: "Once detente came about, nuclear weapons could not be used as the stock currency of international transactions in Europe. The only way they could still be used was to test the efficiency of the deterrent effect of the nuclear arsenal in confrontations in the Third World." K. Subrahmanyam, "Regional Conflicts and their Linkage to Strate-gic Confrontation," in *Nuclear Strategy and World Security,* eds., Joseph Rotblat and Sven Hellman (London: Macmillan, 1985), p. 325

30. Edward A. Kolodziej and Robert Harkavy, "Developing States and the Inter-national Security System," in *Journal of International Affairs,* vol. 34, no. 1 (Spring/Summer 1980), p. 63.

31. Shahram Chubin, "The Super-powers, Regional Conflicts and World Order," in *The Changing Strategic Landscape,* Adelphi papers, no. 237 (London: Inter-national Institute for Strategic Studies, 1989), p. 78.

32. In a comprehensive survey of 107 wars in the Third World between 1945 and 1990, Guy Arnold found that "many would almost certainly have been far shorter in duration and less devastating in their effects had the big powers not intervened." See Guy Arnold, *Wars in the Third World since 1945* (London: Cassell Publishers, 1991), p. xvi.

33. Stanley Hoffmann, "International Organization and the International Sys-tem," in *International Organization: Politics and Process,* eds., Leland M. Goodrich and David A. Kay (Madison: University of Wisconsin Press), pps. 49–73.

34. Ernst B. Haas, "Collective Security and the Future International System," in *The Future of the International Legal Order,* eds., Richard A. Falk and Cyril E. Black, (Princeton, NJ: Princeton University Press, 1969), pps. 226–316.

35. Ernst B. Haas, *Why We Still Need the United Nations* (Berkeley, University of California, Institute of International Relations, 1986); Leslie H. Brown, "Regional Collaboration in Resolving Third World Conflicts," *Survival,* vol. 28, no. 3 (May-June 1986), pps. 208–20.

36. Lynn H. Miller, "The Prospects for Order Through Regional Security"; Amitav Acharya, "Regional Military-Security Cooperation in the Third World: A Conceptual Analysis of the Relevance and Limitations of ASEAN," *Journal of Peace Research,* vol. 29, no. 1 (January 1991), pps. 7–21.

37. Fen Osler Hampson and Brian S. Mandell, "Managing Regional Conflict," *International Journal,* vol. xlv, no. 2 (Spring 1990), p. 194.

38. Chubin has identified several rules relating to conflict-avoidance: one, refraining from intervening unilaterally in the other's sphere; two, seeking to avoid the confrontation of armed forces; three, seeking to restrain allies and associates; four, urging each other to restrain respective allies; five, refraining from direct intervention in a number of conflicts outside the established sphere of influence of either, where clear intervention by one would only spark intervention by the other (for example, Congo in 1960; Nigeria from 1967 to 1970; India-Pakistan in 1971). Chubin "The Super-powers, Regional Conflicts and World Order," p. 79. See also Joanne Gowa and Nils Wessell, *Ground Rules: Soviet and American Involvement in Regional Conflicts* (Philadelphia: Foreign Policy Research Institute, 1982); Neil Matheson, *The 'Rules of the Game' of the Superpower Military Intervention in the Third World* (Washington, DC: University Press of America, 1982); Alexander George, "Factors Influencing Security Co-operation," in *U.S.-Soviet Security Cooperation: Achievements, Failures and Lessons,* eds., Alexander George, Philip J. Farley and Alexander Dallin (NY: Oxford University Press, 1988), pps. 655–78.

39. The major exception to this is their cooperation to control nuclear proliferation in the Third World. See Joseph S. Nye, "U.S.-Soviet Cooperation in a Nonproliferation Regime," in *U.S.-Soviet Security Cooperation: Achievements, Failures and Lessons,* eds., Alexander George, Philip J. Farley and Alexander Dallin (NY: Oxford University Press, 1988), pps. 336–52.

40. Jerry Hough, *The Struggle for the Third World: Soviet Debates and American Options* (Washington, DC: Brookings Institution, 1986), p. 227.

41. Harold Saunders found that although the superpowers "sensed some tacit rules for regulating their competition" in the Arab-Israeli conflict, it did not reduce "their level of competition to the point of moving to cooperation as the norm in their interaction." Harold H. Saunders, "Regulating Soviet-U.S. Competition and Cooperation in the Arab-Israeli Arena, 1967–1986," in *U.S.-Soviet Security Cooperation: Achievements, Failures and Lessons,* eds., Alexander George, Phillip J. Farley and Alexander Dallin, (NY: Oxford University Press, 1988), p. 574.

42. David K. Hall, "The Laos Neutralization Agreement, 1962," in *U.S.-Soviet Security Cooperation: Achievements, Failures and Lessons,* eds., Alexander George, Philip J. Farley and Alexander Dallin (NY: Oxford University Press, 1988), pps. 435–65.

43. Hough, *The Struggle for the Third World,* p. 276.

44. In analyzing U.S.–Soviet security understanding, Alex George distinguishes between "norms of restraint" and "rules of engagement." Norms of restraint are tacit and general understandings "regarding competitive behaviours that are and are not permissible in particular areas and under various conditions." Rules of engagement, on the other hand, are much more specific and explicit guidelines indicating "the various types of involvement and intervention that would be "permissible" to each superpower," and provide a common understanding of the conditions under which each type of intervention could be legitimately and safely resorted to." According to George, the latter provided a stronger basis for superpower cooperation. But both are prescriptive, rather than reflective of the actual situation. Alex George acknowledges that neither the Basic Principles Agreement nor the Agreement on Prevention of Nuclear War fell into the category of rules of engagement. Alexander George, et al., *Managing the U.S.-Soviet Rivalry: Problems of Crisis Prevention* (Boulder, CO: Westview Press, 1983), pps. 367–79.

45. Richard Ullman, "Ending the Cold War," *Foreign Policy,* no. 72 (Fall 1988), p. 143.

46. According to Shullman, "any across-the-board agreements in principle do not take into account the many kinds of problems that arise in particular cases—the differences in intensity of interest in one or another area, the kind of opportunities that may arise in unexpected ways, the particularities of local politics." Marshall D. Shullman, "Overview," in *East-West Tensions in the Third World,* ed., Marshall D. Shullman, (NY: W.W. Norton, 1986), p. 16.

47. Robert Jervis, "Security Regimes," *International Organization,* vol. 36, no. 2 (Spring 1982), pps. 371–73.

48. In the particular case of the 1972 U.S.–Soviet Basic Principles agreement, Jervis notes that the reason why it failed to regulate U.S.–Soviet competition in the Third World could be due to the fact that "the two sides brought very different expectations to the agreement. While the United States considered it relatively unimportant, the Soviets apparently saw it as ratifying their right as an equal superpower to engage in what the United States considered illegitimate adventures in the Third World." Thus, while "stylized and artificial restraints [were] deployed . . . there [was] a disproportion between the strength of the animal to be secured and the strength of the cage." Robert Jervis, "Conclusion," in *Soviet-American Relations after the Cold War,* eds., Robert Jervis and Seweryn Bialer, (Durham, NC: Duke University Press, 1991), pps. 304–5. For an analysis of the various theories as to U.S. and Soviet views of detente as it affected their policies toward regional conflicts, see George W. Braslauer, "Why Detente Failed: An Interpretation," in *Managing the U.S.-Soviet Rivalry,* ed., Alexander George et al., pps. 319–40.

49. Henry Trofimenko, "The Third World and the U.S.-Soviet Competition: A Soviet View," *Foreign Affairs,* vol. 59. no. 4 (Spring 1981), p. 1025.

50. Although Soviet policy has been blamed for the failure of the "linkage" principle, it should be noted that the United States's own commitment to linkage was also doubtful, given the uncertainly whether the Nixon-Kissinger duo would have risked confrontation with the Soviets over regional disputes.

51. Fred Halliday, *Cold War, Third World* (London: Hutchinson Radius, 1989), pps. 154–55.

52. Steven R. David brings out this aspect clearly in his study *Choosing Sides: Alignment and Realignment in the Third World* (Baltimore, MD: Johns Hopkins University Press, 1991).

53. Before concluding the assessment of whether a decompression is actually taking place, an important observation must be made about the physical extent of Third World or South. Traditionally, the term *Third World* included the countries of Latin America, Africa, Middle East, South Asia, Southeast Asia, South Pacific (excluding Australia and New Zealand) and Northeast Asia (excluding Japan). But after the collapse of the Soviet bloc and emergence of new states in Europe and Central Asia, it is important to ask whether these countries should be considered Third World. There is good reason to view these states as part of the Third World, since their security predicament closely resembles that of the original Third World. The insecurity of the Central Asian republics of the former Soviet Union is likely to center on problems of internal stability, low levels of sociopolitical cohesion, and regime legitimation.

   If such an expanded definition of the Third World is accepted, then the decompression effect may seem to have lot of validity. The outbreak of serious ethnic strife, secessionism, and territorial conflicts in the Balkans and Central Asia attest to this. But if one looks at the situation in the old Third World, the picture is very much mixed. Indeed, the following discussion will focus more specifically on the old Third World. The decompression effect in the new Third World is more pronounced, since it was this area which escaped the violence that was inflicted upon the old Third World. A more appropriate test of decompression is whether the old Third World is experiencing greater instability after the Cold War.

   For an argument concerning the definition of the Third World and the need to include the latter states in it, see Mohammed Ayoob, "State Making, State Breaking and State Failure: Explaining the Roots of Third World Instability," paper prepared for the seminar "Conflict and Development: Causes, Effects and Remedies," The Hague, The Netherlands Institute of International Relations, March 22–24, 1994, pps. 2–3.

54. Geoffrey Kemp, "Regional Security, Arms Control, and the End of the Cold War," *Washington Quarterly,* vol. 13, no. 4 (Autumn 1990), p. 33.

55. The definition of what constitutes a Third World regional power has not been precise, despite the growing literature on the subject. A rough picture of the attributes of regional power would include: first, a relative lead in most indicators of political military and economic power among all actors within the region;

second, a supportive as well as coercive power projection capability within the region; and third, a capacity, whether exercised or not, to deny outside powers direct or indirect control over regional security arrangements. Ayoob argues that the aspirations by Third World regional powers to play a "managerial" role in the post–Cold War world must be subject to approval by the United States, the sole remaining superpower. But the converse could be true as well; outside powers may not be able to impose regional security arrangements without the approval of regional powers. Mohammed Ayoob, "India as a Regional Hegemon: External Capabilities and Internal Constraints," in "Regional Powers," special issue of *International Journal*, vol. xlvi, no. 3 (Summer 1991), p. 420.

On the rise and role of Third World regional powers, see Raimo Vayrynen, "Economic and Military Position of Regional Power Centers," *Journal of Peace Research*, vol. 16, no. 4 (1979), pps. 349–69; Thomas Perry Thornton, "The Regional Influentials: Perception and Reality," *SAIS Review*, vol. 9, no. 2 (Summer\Fall 1989), pps. 246–60; Rodney W. Jones and Steven A. Hildreth, eds., *Emerging Powers: Defense and Security in the Third World* (NY: Praeger, 1986).

56. Cited in Paul Wolfowitz, "Regional Conflicts: New Thinking, Old Policy," *Parameters*, vol. 20, no. 1 (March 1990), p. 2.

57. "When Cold Warriors Quit," *The Economist*, February 8, 1992, p. 15; Gary Milholin and Jennifer Weeks, "Better to Block Nuclear and Chemical Weapons at the Source," *International Herald Tribune*, March 29, 1990, p. 6.

58. Christopher Carle, "The Third World Will Do More of Its Own Fighting," *International Herald Tribune*, March 15, 1989.

59. Ali E. Hillal Dessouki, "Globalization and Two Spheres of Security," *The Washington Quarterly*, vol. 16, no. 4 (1993), p.111.

60. Keith Somerville, "Africa After the Cold War: Frozen Out or Frozen in Time?" paper prepared for the workshop on "Developing States and the End of the Cold War," Oxford University, 30 September–1 October 1994, p. 6.

61. Julius O. Ihonvbere, "Political Conditionality and Prospects for Recovery in Sub-Saharan Africa," in *The South at the End of the Twentieth Century*, eds., Larry A. Swatuk and Timothy M. Shaw (Macmillan, 1994), p. 116.

62. Ibrahim S. R. Msabaha, "The Implications of International Boundary Changes for African States," in *Conflict Resolution in Africa*, eds., Francis M. Deng and I. William Zartman, (Washington, DC: The Brookings Institution, 1991), p. 83.

63. "When Cold Warriors Quit," p. 15; Jorge G. Castaneda, "Latin America Still Awaits the New Peace," *International Herald Tribune*, November 24, 1989, p. 4.

64. Ted Robert Gurr, "Peoples Against States: Ethnopolitical Conflict," Presidential Address to the International Studies Association Annual Meeting, April 1, 1994, Washington, DC, pps. 3 and 13.

65. Francis M. Deng and I. William Zartman, "Introduction," in *Conflict Resolution in Africa*, eds., Frances M. Deng and I. William Zartman, p. 13.

66. Barry Buzan, "New Patterns of Global Security in the Twenty-First Century," *International Affairs*, vol. 67, no. 3 (1991), p. 441.

67. Jeffrey Herbst, "Challenges to Africa's Boundaries in the New World Order," *Journal of International Affairs,* vol. 46, no. 1 (Summer 1992), p. 18. See also Ali Mazrui, "The Bondage of Boundaries," *The Economist,* September 11, 1993, pps. 28–29 (special edition on "150 Economist Years"). On the norms of territorial status in Africa see Robert H. Jackson and Carl G. Roseberg, "Why Africa's Weak States Persist: The Empirical and the Juridical in State-hood," *World Politics,* vol. 35, no. 1 (October 1982), pps. 194–208.

68. "The World's Wars: Tribalism Revisited," *The Economist,* December 21, 1991 through 31 January 1992, pps. 23–24.

69. Robert D. Kaplan, "The Coming Anarchy," *The Atlantic Monthly,* vol. 273, no. 2 (1994), pps. 44–76.

70. Thomas F. Homer-Dixon, "On the Threshold: Environmental Change as Causes of Acute Conflict," *International Security,* vol. 16, no. 2 (Fall 1991), pps. 76–116.

71. On the sources of Third World conflict and insecurity, see Mohammed Ayoob, "Security in the Third World: The Worm About to Turn," *International Affairs,* vol. 60, no. 1 (1984), pps. 41–51; Udo Steinbach, "Sources of Third World Conflict," in *Third World Conflict and International Security,* Adelphi papers no. 166 (London: International Institute for Strategic Studies, 1981), pps. 21–28; Soedjatmoko, "Patterns of Armed Conflict in the Third World," *Alternatives,* vol. 10, no. 4 (1985), pps. 477–93; Edward Azar and Chung-in Moon, "Third World National Security: Towards a New Conceptual Framework," *International Interactions,* vol. 11, no. 2 (1984), pps. 103–35; Barry Buzan, "People, States and Fear: The National Security Problem in the Third World," in *National Security in the Third World,* eds., Edward Azar and Chung-in Moon, (Aldershot: Edward Elgar, 1988), pps. 14–43; Yezid Sayigh, *Confronting the 1990s: Security in the Developing Countries,* Adelphi papers no. 251 (London: International Institute for Strategic Studies, 1990); Mohammed Ayoob, "The Security Predicament of the Third World State," in *The (In)Security Dilemma: The National Security of Third World States,* ed., Brian Job, (Boulder, CO: Lynne Rienner Publishers, 1992); Steven R. David, "Explaining Third World Alignment," *World Politics,* vol. 43, no. 2 (January 1991), pps. 232–56.

72. This point is made forcefully by Mohammed Ayoob who argued that "most of the salient regional security issues in the Third World have a life of their own independent of superpower rivalry, although . . . the latter . . . more often than not, exacerbates regional problems." This is as true of interstate as of intrastate disputes and conflicts. Mohammed Ayoob, "Regional Security and the Third World," in *Regional Security in the Third World,* ed., Mohammed Ayoob, (London: Croom Helm, 1986), p. 15.

73. Fred Halliday, *Cold War, Third World,* p. 162.

74. Roberto Garcia Moritan, "The Developing World and the New World Order," *The Washington Quarterly,* vol. 15, no. 4 (Autumn 1992), p.151.

75. Gurr, "Peoples Against States," p. 4.

76. Ted Robert Gurr and Barbara Harff, *Ethnic Conflict in World Politics* (Boulder, CO: Westview, 1994), p. 13.

77. Ibid., pps. 3–4.

78. For analysis of sources of ethnic conflict, see David Brown, "Ethnic Revival: Perspectives on State and Society," *Third World Quarterly,* vol. 11, no. 4 (October 1989), pps.1–17; Walker Connor, "Nation-Building or Nation-Destroying," *World Politics,* vol. 24 (1972), p. 319–55.

79. Charles P. Gasarasi, "The Rwanda Conflict: Sources, Evolution and Implications for Refugee Repatriation, National Reconciliation and Reconstruction," paper presented at the Workshop "In Pursuit of Lasting Resolutions: Post-Conflict Peace-building and Societal Reconstruction," Dalhousie University and the Pearson Peacekeeping Centre, March 3–5, 1995, pps. 1–2.

80. "Next Test for Eritrea," *International Herald Tribune,* April 29, 1993, p. 8.

81. "Another Country," *The Economist,* April 24, 1993, p. 20.

82. Holsti significantly adds that "there have been remarkably few militarized boundary disputes between states in the Third World. And where they have arisen, (e.g., India and China, Libya and Chad) values other than territory drove the conflicts. . . . Control of territory (excluding certain strategic areas such as the Bekka Valley) . . . is declining in importance as a major object of competitive claims and military actions. . . . Protection of territory is less the main task of national security policy than is protection of the state apparatus from various domestic challenges." K. J. Holsti, "International Theory and War in the Third World," in *The InSecurity Dilemma: National Security of Third World States,* ed., Brian L. Job, (Boulder, CO: Lynne Rienner Publishers, 1992), pps. 55–57. As Buzan himself concedes, no direct and clear link can be established between the Cold War and adherence to norms regarding territorial status quo, such as those adopted by the Organization of African Unity relating to the inviolability of colonial boundaries. In this respect, the situation in Europe is rather different. In Europe, the Cold War did play a part in freezing the territorial status quo once it was formally or tacitly agreed upon by the superpowers prior to the unravelling of their wartime alliance. But in the Third World, the only credible attempt to devise norms regarding territorial status quo—the OAU—was an indigenous attempt, rather than superpower influenced. Finally, the major sources of territorial disputes today are not necessarily the legacies of colonial rule but the relatively recent Law of the Sea, which has contributed to a host of maritime boundary disputes. These disputes were not caused by end of superpower rivalry but by disagreements regarding the Law of the Sea. Thus, fears that end of bipolarity could lead to the unravelling of territorial consensus could be overstated.

83. Ramses Amer, et al., "Major Armed Conflicts," in *SIPRI Yearbook 1993: World Armaments and Disarmament* (Oxford: Oxford University Press, 1993), p. 87.

84. Cited in Julius O. Ihonvbere, "Political Conditionality and Prospects for Recovery in Sub-Saharan Africa," in *The South at the End of the Twentieth Century,* eds., Larry Swatuk and Timothy Shaw, (London: Macmillan, 1994), p. 115.

85. Richard Falk, "Recycling Interventionism," *Journal of Peace Research,* vol. 29, no. 2 (1992), p. 133.

86. I am grateful to Sean M. Lynn Jones for raising and discussing this point.

87. Brad Roberts, "Human Rights and International Security," *The Washington Quarterly* (Spring 1990), pps. 72–73.

88. Cited in Francis M. Deng, "Anatomy of Conflicts in Africa," paper presented to the seminar "Conflict and Development: Causes, Effects and Remedies," Netherlands Institute of International Relations, The Hague, March 22–24, 1994, p. 7.

89. John Mueller, *Retreat From Doomsday: The Obsolescence of Major War* (NY: Basic Books, 1989), pps. 254–56.

90. For an interesting debate on the link between war and democracy in the context of the post–Cold War era, see the response published in two subsequent issues of *International Security* to John Mearsheimer's article on "Back to the Future: Instability in Europe After the Cold War," *International Security*, vol. 15, no. 1 (Summer 1990), pps. 5–55.

91. Buzan, "People, States and Fear," p. 32. See also Mohammed Ayoob, *Conflict and Intervention in the Third World;* Ayoob, "Regional Security and the Third World," pps. 3–32.

92. L. L. P. van de Goor, "Conflict and Development: The Causes of Conflict in Developing Countries," paper presented to the conference "Conflict and Development: Causes, Effects and Remedies," The Netherlands Institute of International Relations, The Hague, March 22–24, 1994, p. 46.

93. Amitav Acharya, *An Arms Race in Post–Cold War Southeast Asia? Prospects for Control,* Pacific Strategic Papers no. 8 (Singapore: Institute of Southeast Asian Studies, 1994); Desmond J. Ball, "Arms and Affluence: Military Acquisitions in the Asia-Pacific Region," *International Security*, vol. 18, no. 3 (Winter 1993/94), pps. 78–112.

94. Roberts, "Human Rights and International Security," pps. 72–73.

95. Kenneth N. Waltz, *Theory of International Politics* (Reading, MA: Addison-Wesley, 1979), p. 171.

96. Robert Art argues that "the United States should confine its war-prevention efforts to the Middle East, Europe and the Far East in a highly selective fashion." Robert Art, "A Defensible Defense: America's Grand Strategy after the Cold War," *International Security*, vol. 15, no. 4 (Spring 1991), p. 44. For a debate on the relative importance of the Third World to U.S. strategy in the post–Cold War era, see Stephen R. David, "Why The Third World Matters," *International Security*, vol. 14, no. 1 (Summer 1989), pps. 50–85; Michael C. Desch, "The Keys that Lock Up the World: Identifying America's Interests in the Periphery," *International Security*, vol. 14, no. 1 (Summer 1989), pps. 86–121; Stephen Van Evera, "Why Europe Matters, Why the Third World Doesn't: American Grand Strategy After the Cold War," *Journal of Strategic Studies,* vol. 13, no. 2 (June 1990), pps. 1–51; Valerie M. Hudson, et al., "Why the Third World Matters, Why Europe Probably Won't: The Geoeconomics of Circumscribed Engagement," *Journal of Strategic Studies,* vol. 14, no. 3 (September 1991), pps. 255–98; see also Zbigniew Brzezinski, "Selective Global Commitment," *Foreign Affairs,* vol. 70, no. 4 (Fall 1991), pps. 1–20.

97. Don Oberdorfer, "U.S. Military Strategy Shifts to Large-Scale Mobile Forces: Plan Emphasizes Regional Threats," *International Herald Tribune,* May 20, 1991, p. 1. For the origin and evolution of U.S. rapid deployment forces see Amitav Acharya, *U.S. Military Strategy in the Gulf: Origin and Evolution under the Carter and Reagan Administrations* (NY: Routledge, 1989).

98. Admittedly, the record of such cooperation has been modest to date. On debates over possible Third World contingency role for NATO, see Amitav Acharya, "NATO and 'Out of Area' Contingencies: The Persian Gulf Experience," *International Defense Review,* vol. 20, no. 5 (May 1985), pps. 569–81; Marc Bentinck, *NATO's Out-of-Area Problem,* Adelphi paper no. 211 (London: International Institute for Strategic Studies, 1986); Jonathan T. Howe, "NATO and the Gulf Crisis," *Survival,* vol. 33, no. 3 (May/June 1991), pps. 246–59. On West European cooperation on Third World conflicts, see Ian Gambles, *Prospects for West European Security Cooperation,* Adelphi paper no. 244 (London: International Institute for Strategic Studies, 1989), pps. 35–41. For an assessment of the WEU's role during the recent Gulf War, see Willem Van Eekelen, "WEU and the Gulf Crisis," *Survival,* vol. 32, no. 6 (November/ December 1990), pps. 519–32.

99. Hedley Bull identified four major constraints on Western intervention in the Third World: first, "a remarkable growth in Third World countries of the will and capacity to resist intervention"; second, "a weakening in the Western world of the will to intervene, by comparison with earlier periods, or at least of the will to do so forcibly, directly and openly"; third, the growing Soviet capacity to project power, which "facilitated Third World resistance to Western intervention"; and fourth, "the emergence of a global equilibrium of power unfavourable to intervention" in the sense that "there has emerged a balance among the interveners which has worked to the advantage of the intervened against." Hedley Bull, "Intervention in the Third World," in *Intervention in World Politics,* ed., Hedley Bull, (Oxford: Clarendon Press, 1984), pps. 135–56.

100. Joseph S. Nye, "Arms Control after the Cold War," *Foreign Affairs,* vol. 68, no. 5 (Winter 1989/90), p. 52.

101. Nye, "Arms Control after the Cold War," p. 52.

102. Shahram Chubin, "Third World Conflicts: Trends and Prospects," *International Social Science Journal,* no. 127 (February 1991), p. 157.

103. Yezid Sayigh, *Confronting the 1990s, Security in the Developing Countries,* Adelphi papers no. 251 (London: International Institute for Strategic Studies, 1990), p. 64.

104. Lawrence Freedman argues that the U.S. victory over Iraq would discourage Third World regional powers from mounting a frontal assault on Western interests. Lawrence Freedman, "The Gulf War and the New World Order," *Survival,* vol. 33, no. 3 (May/June 1991), p. 203.

105. Ramses Amer, et al., "Major Armed Conflicts," in *SIPRI Yearbook 1993: World Armaments and Disarmament* (Oxford: Oxford University Press, 1993), p. 81.

106. For an optimistic assessment of Southeast Asia's security in the post–Cold War era, see Muthiah Alagappa, "The Dynamics of International Security in

Southeast Asia: Change and Continuity," *Australian Journal of International Affairs,* vol. 45, no. 1 (May 1991), pps. 1–37.

107. As one observer notes, regional conflicts in the Middle East have declined while cooperation has increased compared to the situation during the Cold War. Abdul-Monem Al-Mashat, "The Regional Dimension of the Causes of Conflict: the Middle East," paper presented at the seminar "Conflict and Development: Causes, Effects and Remedies. An Agenda for Research." Netherlands Institute of International Relations, The Hague, The Netherlands, March 22–24, 1994, p. 5.

108. In Southern Africa, the end of apartheid in South Africa and the settlement of regional conflicts involving Mozambique, Zaire, and Namibia are particularly noteworthy as a direct offshoot of the end of the Cold War. See Colin Legum, letter to *The Times* (London), July 7, 1993, cited in Francis Deng, "Anatomy of Conflict in Africa," paper presented to the "Clingendael Institute" seminar "Conflict and Development: Causes, Effects and Remedies. An Agenda for Research," The Hague, The Netherlands, March 22–24, 1994, p. 10.

109. Deutsch and Singer, "Multipolar Power Systems and International Stability," p. 318.

110. A major assumption of this chapter is that the post–Cold era will be multipolar although scholars are not in agreement over the structure of the post–Cold War international system. Kenneth Waltz has argued that "the emerging world will be one of three or four great powers whether the European one is called Germany or the United States of Europe." See Kenneth Waltz, "The Emerging Structure of International Politics," testimony before the Committee on Foreign Relations, U.S. Senate, hearings on *Relations in a Multipolar World,* Part 1, November 26–30, 1990 (Washington, DC: U.S. Government Printing Office, 1991), p. 221. A similar view has been taken by Buzan and Rosecrance. See Barry Buzan, "North-South Balance of Power," *International Affairs,* vol. 67, no. 3 (1991), pps. 431–51; Richard Rosecrance, "Regionalism and the Post–Cold War Era," *International Journal,* vol. xlvi, no. 3 (Summer 1991), pps. 373–93; On the other hand, Charles Krauthammer argued that the international system in the wake of the U.S. victory in the Gulf War had entered an "unipolar" phase. Charles Krauthammer, "The Unipolar Moment," *Foreign Affairs;* vol. 70, no. 1 (1991), pps. 23–33. But Krauthammer himself concedes that unipolarity would not last more than a few decades. For a counter to Krauthammer, see William Pffaf, "Redefining World Power," *Foreign Affairs,* vol. 70, no. 1 (1991), pps. 34–48.

111. I. William Zartman, "Conflict and Resolution: Contest, Cost and Change," in *Resolving Regional Conflicts: International Perspectives,* special issue of *The Annals of the American Academy of Political and Social Science,* no. 518 (November 1991), p. 19.

112. See the articles in I. William Zartman, ed., *Resolving Regional Conflicts: International Perspectives,* special issue of *The Annals of the American Academy of Political and Social Science,* no. 518 (November 1991); For a background see Jiri Valenta and Frank Cibulka, eds. *Gorbachev's New Thinking and Third World*

Conflicts (New Brunswick, NH: Transaction Books, 1990); Roger E. Kanet and Edward A. Kolodziej, *The Cold War as Cooperation: Superpower Cooperation in Regional Conflict Management* (London: Macmillan, 1991).

113. It should be noted that mere East-West collaboration is neither an adequate nor durable basis for a more effective regime on Third World conflict management. During the Gulf War, U.S.–Soviet collaboration proved fragile, especially the Soviet attempt to secure a last-minute reprieve for Satem, which invoked images of old superpower horse-trading. Thomas L. Friedman, "U.S.–Soviet Horse Trading," *International Herald Tribune,* February 1, 1991, p. 4; Leslie H. Gelb, "The Soviet-American Honeymoon May be Ending," *International Herald Tribune,* January 10, 1991, p. 4. Similar disagreements between Russia and the United States over future Third World conflicts cannot be ruled out. Also the East-West agreement leaves out prospects for a durable North-South consensus within the Security Council, with China remaining a major uncertain player. During the Gulf War, China, while going along with the UN consensus forged by the United States, criticized Western countries "for using the current dramatically changing world situation to peddle their value concepts within the UN . . . [and] trying to interfere in other countries' internal affairs." "Beijing Seeks Stronger Voice in New World Order," *The Straits Times,* January 8, 1991, p. 4.

114. In the post–Cold War era, balance of power mechanisms will not disappear, although their impact should be felt mostly at a regional, rather than a global level. Balance of power mechanisms will be especially relevant to conflict management in regional theaters such as in South Asia involving the India-Pakistan nuclear rivalry, in the Korean Peninsula, in the Middle East in conflicts involving Iran, Iraq, and Saudi Arabia, as well as that between Syria and Israel. For the relative merits of collective security and balance of power approaches to international order see Inis L. Claude, *Power and International Relations* (NY: Random House, 1962).

115. Common security arrangements are based on the principle of "security with," as opposed to "security against" (as in the case of an alliance), one's opponents. On common security see Olof Palme, *Common Security: A Blueprint for Survival* (NY: Simon and Schuster, 1982); The Palme Commission on Disarmament and Security Issues, *A World at Peace: Common Security in the Twenty-first Century* (Stockholm: The Palme Commission, 1989); SIPRI, *Policies for Common Security,* (London: Taylor and Francis, 1985).

116. A regional security arrangement may refer to a variety of things, including collective security systems, alliances, or common security forums. Collective security systems should not be confused with alliance-type regional security arrangements such as the Bush administration's idea of a "regional security structure" in the wake of the Iraq's expulsion from Kuwait. Collective security refers to the role of a global or regional system in protecting any member state from aggression by another member state. The inward-looking security role of a collective security system is to be contrasted with the outer-directed nature of an alliance that is geared to protect its members from a common external

threat. See Ernst B. Haas, *Tangle of Hopes* (Englewood-Cliffs, NJ: Prentice Hall), p. 94.

117. Roger A. Coate and Donald J. Puchala, "Global Policies and the United Nations System: A Current Assessment," *Journal of Peace Research,* vol. 27 (1990), pps. 127–40; Harvey Feldman, "The United Nations and Conflict-Resolution," paper presented to the symposium "The Changing Role of the United Nations in Conflict-Resolution and Peacekeeping," Singapore, March 13–15, 1991. For an earlier study of the UN's performance in international conflict resolution see: Ernst B. Haas, *Why We Still Need the United Nations* (Berkeley: University of California, Institute of International Relations, 1986).

118. Analysts are divided on the real significance of the Gulf crisis for the future role of the UN. Russett and Sutterlin take an optimistic view, arguing that the Gulf episode demonstrated the Security Council's "capacity to initiate collective measures essential for the maintenance of peace in a new world order." On the other hand, Robert Art warns that the UN action against Iraq took place under distinctive circumstances that are unlikely to be present in future crises. Bruce Russett and James S. Sutterlin, "The U.N. in a New World Order," *Foreign Affairs,* vol. 70, no. 2 (Spring 1990), pps. 69–83; Robert J. Art, "A Defensible Defense," p. 44.

119. John J. Mearsheimer, "The False Promise of International Institutions," *International Security,* vol. 19, no. 3 (Winter 1994/95), pps. 5–49.

120. Ibid.

121. S. Neil MacFarlane and Thomas G. Weiss, "Regional Organizations and Regional Security," *Security Studies,* vol. 2, no. 1 (Autumn 1992), pps. 6–37.

122. James M. Goldgeier and Michael McFaul, "Core and Periphery in the Post–Cold War Era," *International Organization,* vol. 46, no. 2 (Spring 1992), pps. 467–92.

123. On the competition between global and regional security frameworks, see Lynn H. Miller, "The Prospects of Order through Regional Security," in *Regional Politics and World Order,* eds., Richard A. Falk and Saul H. Mendlovitz, (San Francisco: W.H. Freeman, 1973), pps. 50–74; Francis Wilcox, "Regionalism and the United Nations," *International Organization,* vol. 10 (1965), pps. 789–811; Ernst B. Haas, "Regionalism, Functionalism and Universal Organization," *World Politics,* vol. 8 (January 1956), pps. 238–36; Inis L. Claude, *Swords into Plowshares* (NY: Random House, 1964); Norman J. Padelford, "Regional Organizations and the United Nations," *International Organization,* vol. 8 (1954), pps. 203–16.

124. Barry James, "De Michelis Urges 'Helsinki' Talks on War's Aftermath," *International Herald Tribune,* February 18, 1991, p. 3; "Australia Proposes Security Forum for Asia-Pacific Area," *The Straits Times,* July 28, 1990; "Secretary of State For External Affairs Outlines Security Initiative," *Canada-ASEAN,* vol. 10, no. 3 (September-October 1990), pps. 1–2.

125. Esperanza Duran, "Pacification, Security and Democracy: Contadora's Role in Central America," in *The Central American Security System: North-South or East-West,* ed., Peter Calvert (Cambridge: Cambridge University Press, 1988),

pps. 155–76; Kenneth Roberts, "Bullying and Bargaining: The United States, Nicaragua, and Conflict-Resolution in Central America," *International Security,* vol. 15 (Fall 1990), pps. 67–102.

126. Amitav Acharya, *A New Regional Order in Southeast Asia: ASEAN in the Post–Cold War Era,* Adelphi paper no. 279 (London: International Institute for Strategic Studies, 1993).

127. Thomas Perry Thornton, "Regional Organizations in Conflict-Management," *Annals of the American Academy of Political and Social Science,* no. 518 (November 1991), pps. 132–42; Fen Osler Hampson, "Building a Stable Peace: Opportunities and Limits to Security Cooperation in Third World Regional Conflicts," *International Journal,* vol. xlv, no. 2 (Spring 1990), pps. 454–59; Tom J. Farer, "The Role of Regional Collective Security Arrangements," in *Collective Security in a Changing World,* ed., Thomas G. Weiss (Boulder, CO: Lynne Rienner Publishers, 1993), pps. 153–86; Amitav Acharya, "Regional Approaches to Security in the Third World: Lessons and Prospects," in *The South at the End of the Twentieth Century,* eds., Larry A. Swatuk and Timothy M. Shaw (London: Macmillan, 1994), pps. 79–94; Paul F. Diehl, "Institutional Alternatives to Traditional U.N. Peacekeeping: An Assessment of Regional and Multinational Options," *Armed Forces and Society,* vol. 19, no. 2 (Winter 1993); Benjamin Rivlin, "Regional Arrangements and the UN System for Collective Security and Conflict Resolution: A New Road Ahead," *International Relations,* vol. 11 (1992), pps. 95–110.

128. See Igezundia Abutudu, "Regime Change, Political Instability and Economic Integration in West Africa: The Experience of ECOWAS," *Nigerian Journal of International Affairs,* vol. 16, no. 1 (1990), pps. 90–107; See also the series of articles under the section on "Conflict Resolution, Crisis Prevention and Management and Confidence-Building in West Africa," *Disarmament: A Periodic Review by the United Nations,* vol. 12, no. 1 (Winter 1988/1989), pps. 43–109.

129. O. Adeniji, "Regionalism in Africa," *Security Dialogue,* vol. 24, no. 2 (June 1993), pps. 211–20.

130. Gareth Evans, *Cooperating for Peace* (Sydney: Allen and Unwin, 1993), p. 31.

131. The OAS foreign ministers in a joint declaration at Santiago in June 1991 stressed their "uncompromising commitment to the defense of democracy" and their intention to renew the OAS as "the political forum for dialogue, understanding, and cooperation among all countries in the hemisphere." Robert B. Andersen, "Inter-IGO Dynamics in the Post–Cold War Era: The O.A.S. and the U.N.," paper prepared for the 1994 Annual Convention of the International Studies Association, Washington, DC, March 28 through April 1, 1994, p. 2.

132. Steven S. Rosenfeld, "America's Bigger Load Frees its Hands," *International Herald Tribune,* December 24–25, 1990, p. 6.

133. See Amitav Acharya, "Regional Military-Security Cooperation in the Third World: A Conceptual Analysis of the Relevance and Limitations of ASEAN," *Journal of Peace Research,* vol. 29, no. 1 (February 1992), pps. 7–21; Amitav Acharya, "The Gulf Cooperation Council and Security: Dilemmas of

Dependence," *Middle East Strategic Studies Quarterly,* vol. 1, no. 3 (1990), pps. 88–136.

134. While regional balances are possible at the systemic level, balance of power is unlikely to be the chief framework of relations among the major powers, with the possible exception of the United States and China. It is noteworthy that the arguments of leading realist scholars about the structure of the post–Cold War system appear to support this view. Rosecrance believes that a concert of powers (an extended concert of Europe) is the most likely pattern; while Buzan envisages a "security community among the leading capitalist powers." Either outcome favors the functioning of collective security, as opposed to balance of power, mechanisms. Rosecrance, "Regionalism and the Post–Cold War Era," pps. 379–85; Buzan, "New Patterns of Global Security," pps. 436–37.

135. Michael T. Klare, "Peace Studies in the 1990s: Assessing Change in the Global War/Peace System," in *Peace and World Order Studies,* eds., Michael T. Klare and Daniel C. Thomas (Boulder, CO: Westview Press, 1989), p. 67.

136. Samuel P. Huntington, "The Clash of Civilizations?" *Foreign Affairs,* vol. 72, no. 3 (1993), pps. 22–49. For critical responses to Huntington, see the series of articles "Clash of Civilizations: Responses to Huntington," *Foreign Affairs,* vol. 72, no. 4 (September/October 1993), pps. 1–26.

137. During the Gulf War, the U.S. pressure on the UN gave the impression that the world body was being manipulated for the narrow strategic purpose of a superpower. Although the United States sought to inject a degree of legitimacy to its actions by seeking UN endorsement, in the final analysis, the United States would have pursued its strategic options irrespective of the UN mandate. Richard Falk observed that "behind this formal mandate from the United Nations [to the U.S. approach to the Gulf crisis] lie extremely serious questions about whether the UN has been true to its own Charter, and to the larger purposes of peace and justice that it was established to serve. And beyond these concerns is the disturbing impression that the United Nations has been converted into a virtual tool of U.S. foreign policy, thus compromising its future credibility, regardless of how the Gulf crisis turns out." Richard Falk, "UN being made a tool of U.S. foreign policy," *Guardian Weekly,* January 27, 1991, p. 12. See also "The Use and Abuse of the UN in the Gulf Crisis," *Middle East Report,* no. 169 (March-April 1991). For a more positive assessment of the UN's role see: Sir Anthony Parsons, "The United Nations After the Gulf War," *The Round Table,* no. 319 (July 1991), pps. 265–74.

138. "New World Order: An Interview with Zbigniew Brzezinski," *SAIS Review,* vol. 11, no. 2 (Summer-Fall 1991), p. 2.

139. It is noteworthy that the Bush administration's concept of a New World Order envisions "An era in which the nations of the world, East and West, North and South, can prosper and live in harmony," cited in Lawrence Freedman, "The Gulf War and the New World Order," *Survival,* vol. 33, no. 3 (May/June 1991), p. 195.

140. Shahram Chubin, "The South and the New World Disorder," *Washington Quarterly* (Autumn 1993), p. 98.

141. K. Subrahmanyam, "Export Controls and the North-South Controversy," *The Washington Quarterly* (Spring 1993), p. 135.

142. "NAM Warns West to Stop Exploiting Human-Rights Issue," *The Straits Times* (Singapore), August 13, 1992, p. 16.

143. "Take Pragmatic Line on Human Rights: Kan Seng," *The Straits Times* (Singapore), June 17, 1993, p. 1.

144. Christopher Tremewan, "Human Rights in Asia," *Pacific Review,* vol. 6, no. 1 (1993), pps. 17–30; "Cultural Divide," *Far Eastern Economic Review,* June 17, 1993, pps. 20–21.

145. See Adamantia Pollis, "Liberal, Socialist and Third World Perspectives of Human Rights," *Towards a Human Rights Framework,* eds., in Peter Schwab and Adamantia Pollis, (NY: Praeger, 1982). The updated version of this article can be found in Richard P. Claude and Burns Weston, eds., *Human Rights in the World Community,* second edition (Philadelphia: University of Pennsylvania Press, 1992).

146. See Barry Buzan, "New Patterns of Global Security in the Twenty-First Century"; John Ravenhill, "The North-South Balance of Power," *International Affairs,* vol. 66, no. 4 (October 1990), pps.731–66; Peter Lyon, "Marginalization of the Third World?" *Jerusalem Journal of International Relations,* vol. 11, no. 3 (September 1989), pps. 64–73; Richard E. Bissell, "Who Killed the Third World?" *The Washington Quarterly,* vol. 13, no. 4 (Autumn 1990), pps. 23–32.

147. "NAM Must Stay United Against Developed States," *The Straits Times* (Singapore), August 7, 1992, p. 23; "NAM Needed to Balance North Bloc," *The Straits Times* (Singapore), August 4, 1992, p. 21.

148. "Jakarta Wants NAM to Focus on Pressing Economic and Human Problems," *The Straits Times* (Singapore), August 4, 1992, p. 17.

149. "Goodbye Nehru, Hello Suharto," *The Economist,* September 19, 1992, p. 32.

150. A recent survey by *The Economist* reveals the extent of North-South economic interdependence. The Third World and the countries of the former Soviet bloc are the destination of 42 percent of America's, 20 percent of Western Europe's (47 percent if intra-European Union trade is excluded) and 48 percent of Japan's exports. On the import side, the magazine reports that American imports of manufactured goods from the Third World rose from 5 percent of the value of its manufacturing output in 1978 to 11 percent in 1990. "A Survey of the Global Economy," *The Economist,* September 1, 1994, pps. 13 and 16.

151. "Rich North, Hungry South," *The Economist,* October 1, 1994, p. 18.

152. Karl W. Deutsch and J. David Singer, "Multipolar Power Systems and International Stability," *International Politics and Foreign Policy,* ed., James N. Rosenan (NY: The Free Press, 1969).

153. Joseph S. Nye and Sean M. Lynn-Jones, "International Security Studies: Report of a Conference on the State of the Field," *International Security,* vol. 12, no. 4 (1988), p. 27. See also Amitav Acharya, "The Periphery as the Core: The Third World and Security Studies," in *Critical Security Studies,* eds., Keith Krause and Michael Williams (Minneapolis: University of Minnesota Press, 1997).

154. John Mueller, *Retreat From Doomsday: The Obsolescence of Major War* (NY: Basic Books, 1989), pps. 251–57.
155. Francis Fukuyama, "The End of History," *The National Interest*, vol. 16 (Summer 1989), p. 18.

Bibliography

Acharya, Amitav. *An Arms Race in Post–Cold War Southeast Asia? Prospects for Control*, Pacific Strategic Papers no. 8. Singapore: Institute of Southeast Asian Studies, 1994.

———. "Regional Military-Security Cooperation in the Third World: A Conceptual Analysis of the Relevance and Limitations of ASEAN." *Journal of Peace Research*. Vol. 29, no. 1 (January 1991), pps. 7–21.

Arnold, Guy. *Wars in the Third World since 1945*. London: Cassell Publishers, 1991.

Ayoob, Mohammed. "State Making, State Breaking and State Failure: Explaining the Roots of Third World Instability." Paper prepared for the seminar "Conflict and Development: Causes, Effects and Remedies." The Hague: The Netherlands Institute of International Relations, March 22–24, 1994.

———. "The Security Predicament of the Third World States." In *The (In)Security Dilemma: The National Security of Third World States*. Ed. Brian Job. Boulder, CO: Lynne Rienner Publishers, 1992.

———. "India as a Regional Hegemon: External Capabilities and Internal Constraints." In *Regional Powers*, special issue of *International Journal*. Vol. xlvi, no. 3 (Summer 1991), pps. 420–48.

———. *Regional Security in the Third World*. London: Croom Helm, 1986.

———. "Security in the Third World: The Worm About to Turn." *International Affairs*. Vol. 60, no. 1 (1984), pps. 41–51.

———, ed. *Conflict and Intervention in the Third World*. Canberra: Australian National University Press, 1980.

Azar, Edward and Chung-in Moon. "Third World National Security: Towards a New Conceptual Framework." *International Interactions*. Vol. 11, no. 2 (1984), pps. 103–35.

Brown, David. "Ethnic Revival: Perspectives on State and Society." *Third World Quarterly*. Vol. 11, no. 4 (October 1989), pps. 1–17.

Buzan, Barry. "Third World Regional Security in Structural and Historical Perspective." In *The Insecurity Dilemma: National Security of Third World States*. Ed. Brian L. Job. Boulder, CO: Lynne Rienner Publishers, 1992.

———. "New Patterns of Global Security in the Twenty-First Century." *International Affairs*. Vol. 67, no. 3 (1991), pps. 431–52.

———. "People, States and Fear: The National Security Problem in the Third World." in *National Security in the Third World*. Eds. Edward Azar and Chung-in Moon. Aldershot: Edward Elgar, 1988.

———. *People, States and Fear*. Brighton: Wheatsheaf Books, 1983.

Carle, Christopher. "The Third World Will Do More of Its Own Fighting." In *International Herald Tribune*. March 15, 1989.

Chubin, Shahram. "Third World Conflicts: Trends and Prospects." *International Social Science Journal.* No. 127 (February 1991), pps. 147–61.

———. "The Super-powers, Regional Conflict and World Order." In *The Changing Strategic Landscape.* Adelphi paper no. 237. London: International Institute for Strategic Studies, 1989.

David, Stephen R. *Choosing Sides: Alignment and Realignment in the Third World.* Baltimore, MD: Johns Hopkins University Press, 1991.

———. "Why the Third World Matters." *International Security.* Vol. 14, no. 1 (Summer 1989), pps. 50–85.

Dessouki, Ali E. Hillal. "Globalization and Two Spheres of Security." *The Washington Quarterly.* Vol. 16, no. 4 (1993), pps. 109–17.

Deutsch, Karl W. and J. David Singer. "Multipolar Power Systems and International Stability." In *International Politics and Foreign Policy.* Ed. James N. Rosenau. New York: The Free Press, 1969.

Duran, Esperanza. "Pacification, Security and Democracy: Contadora's Role in Central America." In *The Central American Security System: North-South or East-West.* Ed. Peter Calvert. Cambridge: Cambridge University Press, 1988.

Gaddis, John Lewis. "International Relations Theory and the End of the Cold War." *International Security.* Vol. 17, no. 3 (Winter 1992–93), pps. 5–58.

———. "The Long Peace: Elements of Stability in the Post-War International System." *International Security.* Vol. 10, no. 4 (Spring 1986), pps. 99–142.

Garcia Moritan, Robertó. "The Developing World and the New World Order." *The Washington Quarterly.* Vol. 15, no. 4 (Autumn 1992), pps. 149–56.

Gasarasi, Charles P. "The Rwanda Conflict: Sources, Evolution and Implications for Refugee Repatriation, National Reconciliation and Reconstruction." Paper presented at the workshop "In Pursuit of Lasting Resolutions: Post-Conflict Peacebuilding and Societal Reconstruction." Dalhousie University and the Pearson Peacekeeping Centre, March 3–5, 1995.

George, Alexander. "Factors Influencing Security Co-operation." In *U.S.-Soviet Security Cooperation: Achievements, Failures and Lessons.* Eds. Alexander George, Philip J. Farley and Alexander Dallin. NY: Oxford University Press, 1988.

Gilpin, Robert. *War and Change in World Politics.* Cambridge: Cambridge University Press, 1981.

van de Goor, L. L. P. "Conflict and Development: The Causes of Conflict in Developing Countries." Paper presented at the conference "Conflict and Development: Causes, Effects and Remedies." The Netherlands Institute of International Relations. The Hague, March 22–24, 1994.

Gowa, Joanne, and Nils Wessell. *Ground Rules: Soviet and American Involvement in Regional Conflicts.* Philadelphia: Foreign Policy Research Institute, 1982.

Gurr, Ted Robert. "People Against States: Ethnopolitical Conflict." Presidential Address to the International Studies Association Annual Meeting. Washington, DC, April 1, 1994.

———, and Barbara Harff. *Ethnic Conflict in World Politics.* Boulder, CO: Westview, 1994.

Halliday, Fred. *Cold War, Third World.* London: Hutchinson Radius, 1989.

Hampson, Fen Osler and Brian S. Mandell. "Managing Regional Conflict." *International Journal*. Vol. xlv, no. 2 (Spring 1990), pps. 191–201.

Herbst, Jeffrey. "Challenges to Africa's Boundaries in the New World Order." *Journal of International Affairs*. Vol. 46, no. 1 (Summer 1992), pps. 17–30.

Hough, Jerry. *The Struggle for the Third World: Soviet Debates and American Options*. Washington, DC: Brookings Institution, 1986.

Hudson, Valerie M., et al. "Why the Third World Matters, Why Europe Probably Won't: The Geoeconomics of Circumscribed Engagement." *Journal of Strategic Studies*. Vol. 14. no. 3 (September 1991), pps. 255–98.

Ihonvbere, Julius O. "Political Conditionality and Prospects for Recovery in Sub-Saharan Africa." In *The South at the End of the Twentieth Century*. Eds. Larry A. Swatuk and Timothy M. Shaw. Macmillan, 1994.

Jackson, Robert H. and Carl G. Rosberg. "Why Africa's Weak States Persist: The Empirical and the Juridical in Statehood." *World Politics*. Vol. 35, no. 1 (October 1982), pps. 1–24.

Jervis, Robert. "The Future of World Politics: Will it Resemble the Past?" *International Security*. Vol. 16, no. 3 (Winter 1991–92), pps. 39–73.

———. "Security Regimes." *International Organization*. Vol. 36, no. 2 (Spring 1982), pps. 357–78.

Jones, Rodney W. and Steven A. Hildreth, eds. *Emerging Powers: Defense and Security in the Third World*. NY: Praeger, 1986.

Kolodziej, Edward A. and Robert Harkavy. "Developing States and the International Security System." *Journal of International Affairs*. Vol. 34, no. 1 (Spring/Summer 1980).

Evan Luard. *War in International Society*. London: I. B. Tauris, 1986.

MacFarlane, S. Neil and Thomas G. Weiss. "Regional Organizations and Regional Security." *Security Studies*. Vol. 2, no. 1 (Autumn 1992), pps. 6–37.

Matheson, Neil. *The "Rules of the Game" of the Superpower Military Intervention in the Third World*. Washington, DC: University Press of America, 1982.

Mearsheimer, John. "Why We Will Soon Miss the Cold War." In *Crosscurrents: International Relations in the Post–Cold War Era*. Eds., Mark Charlton and Elizabeth Ridell-Dixon. Toronto: Nelson Canada, 1993.

Miller, Lynn H. "The Prospects for Order Through Regional Security." In *Regional Politics and World Order*. Eds., Richard A. Falk and Saul H. Mendlovitz. San Francisco, CA: W. H. Freeman and Co., 1973), pps. 50–77.

Msabaha, Ibrahim S. R. "The Implications of International Boundary Changes for African States." In *Conflict Resolution in Africa*. Eds. Francis M. Deng and I. William Zartman. Washington, DC: The Brookings Institution, 1991.

Rosecrance, Richard N. "Bipolarity, Multipolarity, and the Future." In *International Politics and Foreign Policy*. Ed. James N. Rosenau. NY: The Free Press, 1969.

Shullman, Marshall D., ed. *East-West Tensions in the Third World*. NY: W.W. Norton, 1986.

Somerville, Keith. "Africa After the Cold War: Frozen Out or Frozen in Time?" Paper prepared for workshop on Developing States and the End of the Cold War. Oxford University, September 30–October 1, 1994.

Soedjatmoko. "Patterns of Armed Conflict in the Third World." *Alternatives*. Vol. 10, no. 4 (1985), pps. 477–93.

Steinbach, Udo. "Sources of Third World Conflict." In *Third World Conflict and International Security*. Adelphi paper no. 166. London: International Institute for Strategic Studies, 1981.

Subrahmanyam, K. "Regional Conflicts and the Linkage to Strategic Confrontation." In *Nuclear Strategy and World Security*. Eds. Joseph Rotblat and Sven Hellman. London: Macmillan, 1985.

Thiago Cintra, Jose. "Regional Conflicts: Trends in a Period of Transition." In *The Changing Strategic Landscape*, Adelphi paper no. 237. London: International Institute for Strategic Studies, 1989.

Thornton, Thomas Perry. "The Regional Influentials: Perception and Reality." *SAIS Review*. Vol. 9, no. 2 (Summer/Fall 1989), pps. 247–60.

Vayrynen, Raimo. "Economic and Military Position of Regional Power Centers." *Journal of Peace Research*. Vol. 16, no. 4 (1979), pps. 349–69.

Waltz, Kenneth N. *Theory of International Politics*. Reading, MA: Addison-Wesley, 1979.

———. "The Stability of a Bipolar World." *Daedalus*. Vol. 93, no. 3 (1964), pps. 881–909.

EIGHT

Conclusions:
System versus Units in
Theorizing about the Third World

Barry Buzan

The task of this chapter is to look for common threads in the preceding seven chapters. It tries to follow these threads in an attempt to (at least partially) unravel the knotty question of how, if at all, International Relations Theory and the Third World do, and might, relate to each other. Much the easiest way into this task is via levels of analysis, for whether consciously or not, nearly all of the authors in this volume have constructed their arguments in terms of levels. By levels of analysis I mean locations, or units of analysis where both outcomes and sources of explanation can be found. In International Relations (IR), levels are normally organized on a spatial scale with individuals as the smallest or lowest, collective units such as states in the middle, and the system as a whole as the largest or highest.[1] Thinking in terms of levels has been a feature of mainstream IR theory since the 1950s,[2] and is particularly associated with neorealism.[3] The attraction of levels was that they offered a sharper way of focusing debates about cause-effect relations. In particular, they offered a way of differentiating the system level from the unit (usually state) one, and thus of constructing system (especially structural) theories about International Relations. This was the key that unlocked the dominance of neorealist theory in IR during the 1980s.

Not surprisingly, it also unlocked an enduring confrontation between purveyors of system theories on the one hand, and advocates of unit-level explanations on the other. The attraction of system theories was that they provided relatively simple, and seemingly powerful, ways of thinking about the international system as a whole. The price paid for this parsimonious universalism was that they painted with a very broad brush, in the process obscuring, or pushing into the background, the multitude of factors and details that those with more local knowledge thought important in explaining their own patch. For many foreign policy analysts and area specialists the triumph of system theories was a disaster. Neorealism imposed an overarching, homogenizing framework on IR whose very oversimplification was one major source of its attractiveness and influence. The other main source of neorealism's influence was the good fit of its central idea of polarity, especially bipolarity, with both the Cold War in general, and U.S. superpower policy in particular. But this feature also worked to marginalize, and in a sense subordinate, the bulk of international actors who were not amongst the ranks of the Great Powers. Being essentially a theory of Great Power politics, neorealism did not have much time for the weaker players in the system.

Not surprisingly, this conflict still echoes strongly throughout the chapters in this book. There is virtual consensus among the authors about the numerous and large shortcomings of mainstream system-level theories of International Relations when it come to thinking about the Third World. There is an almost equally strong matching consensus that in order to understand what is (and will be) happening in the Third World, one needs to pay much more attention to the Third World state, a subject that almost (but as we shall see not quite) falls outside the purview of neorealism.

The next section reviews the critique of system level theory (mostly neorealism) in these chapters, while section 2 looks at their proposals on the unit level. Section 3 follows through the logic of these positions, arguing that they point toward a differentiated view of the international system into two (or more) "worlds," each of which, in principle, requires a different type of theorizing. Section 4 examines the limits of this view, arguing that it points back toward some interesting, and as yet not fully resolved, aspects of neorealism's understanding of system structure, and that these aspects offer one way of fruitfully reuniting system- and unit-level theory in thinking about the Third World.

1. The Critique of Neorealism as an Approach to the Third World

The authors in this book level many charges against neorealism, but two of them seem particularly central. The first is that neorealism is wrong to assume that the international system is populated by "like units." The supporting argument is that most Third World states fail in a multiplicity of ways to meet the criteria for being Westphalian states on the European/Western model. The second main charge, in part related to the first, is that neorealism's assumption of a sharp differentiation between the political world inside the state (hierarchy, that is, a central governing authority), and the political universe between states (anarchy, that is, no central governing authority) is also wrong. There are two supporting arguments for this view. One is that many Third World states are too weakly developed to qualify for hierarchy, and that de facto much of their domestic politics has anarchic qualities. The other is that there are significant elements of hierarchy in relations between states, and that these elements are particularly strong in relations between the more developed core and the less developed periphery. Taken together, these two points support a case for saying that the general model of the international system posited by neorealism misleads more than it informs. The model is insufficiently representative of actual conditions in so much of the international system, that using it is positively harmful to both understanding and policy-making, especially in relation to the Third World. It is worth examining both of these points, and possible replies to them, a little more closely.

The neorealist understanding of "like units" is based on the idea that there is no functional differentiation among them (or at least not among the major units in the system). Functional differentiation is quite frequently misunderstood to refer to the various roles that states can play in the international system: Great Powers, neutrals, leaders, followers, and so on. But in neorealism, structural differentiation quite clearly refers to the functions that states perform in order to constitute themselves as political units. Waltz's argument that there is no functional differentiation in anarchic international systems rests on the fact that all (or at least the vast majority, and all of the significant powers) claim sovereignty, which is to say that they claim the right to perform all of the functions of self-government. For neorealists, whether individual states *perform* these functions well or badly is not the point. The point is that they claim them, and that these claims are in nearly all cases formally accepted by the other members of the system. Although some states quite evidently fail to establish functional autonomy, Kenneth Waltz is confident that this empirical evidence does not undermine his argument that states represent like units. What turns states into like units, he insists, is not their ability to maintain autonomy, but the fact that they are faced with the same tasks to perform. He readily acknowledges that there are huge variations in their capacity to perform these tasks: "States are alike in the tasks that they face though not in their ability to perform them."[4] This does not matter, because so long as the major states "are the major actors, the structure of international politics is defined in terms of them."[5] It is this logic that excludes much of the Third World from neorealist theory.

This understanding of functional differentiation is based on a sharp distinction between power relations (usually very unequal) and politico-legal ones (formally equal), which enables Westphalian systems to be distinguished from a variety of other political systems such as the suzerainty-based empires of classical times, the medieval system in Europe, and possibly the emergent political union in contemporary Europe. In all of these, sovereignty is formally recognized as being *unequally* distributed, being either broken up, with different units holding different aspects of government (as in the medieval and EU systems), or with a clear hierarchy of suzerain and vassal (as in most classical empires).[6] In this rather narrow and formal, but important, politico-legal sense, neorealists are, on the face of it, quite right to claim that the international system lacks functional differentiation among its units. The neorealist formulation is biased toward the major states in the system, and works more clearly for them than it does for some of the minor states in the Third World. Nevertheless, the politico-legal principle of state sovereignty is strongly embedded in the system, and neorealists argue (rightly in my view) that this formal principle of legal equality needs to be kept distinct from the operation of power in the system, where huge differences make for very unequal relations. Neorealists, in other words, argue that although both anarchic and suzerain systems manifest big differences in power, there is a significant difference between their politico-legal structures. This difference is illustrated by the change in relations that took place with decolonization, where power differentials remained much the same, but politico-legal ones changed dramatically.

But while the neorealist position is defensible in this technical sense, it can still be criticized for taking too narrow a view of the nature of units. There is more to be said about differentiation of units than is contained in Waltz's formulation, and I will return to this point in section 4.

The neorealist distinction between anarchy among states and hierarchy within them clearly relates to concerns about the non-Westphalian character of many Third World states. Because many Third World states are weakly constituted as states, they fail to conform to a homogenous view of the units in the system, and also fail to maintain the sharp "inside/outside" distinction that the model demands.[7] The anarchy-hierarchy distinction is not just troubling to those interested in the third world. It is also one of the main bones of contention between neorealists and several other schools of thought in IR. Liberals, with their ideas of international institutions (whether organizations or regimes), and some proponents of the English school, with their idea of "international society," both see an international system in which there are elements of governance outside the state. So also do constructivists, whose more sociological view of International Relations focuses on shared intersubjective understandings about norms and rules.[8]

Waltz's answer to this critique is a bit slippery. He does not deny that it is possible to find evidence of functional differentiation and hierarchy within the international system—"flecked with particles of government," as he puts it—just as it is possible to identify elements of anarchy within many domestic political systems.[9] He is thus aware that his strong "either/or" position on anarchy/hierarchy can be challenged on empirical grounds: in the real world it is easy to find evidence of anarchy and hierarchy both within states and in relations between them. In such situations Waltz insists that expectation about the fate of such a system will differ depending upon whether hierarchy or anarchy is *seen to be the prevailing structure*. It is necessary for the analyst to form a judgement about whether the system should be identified as predominantly anarchic or hierarchical, and to make assessment and/or predictions about it on the basis of that judgement. As far as Waltz is concerned, there is no doubt that although NATO, the UN, and the EU provide evidence of hierarchy, these elements exist firmly within an anarchic international system. He is quite sure that there is insufficient evidence from current world politics to identify a transformation from an anarchic to a hierarchic international system. He concludes that "hierarchic elements within international structures limit and restrain the exercise of sovereignty but only in ways strongly conditioned by the anarchy of the larger system."[10]

In sum, Waltz's argument is that structural effects derive from the dominant character of first tier structure (that is, the political ordering principle of the system: anarchy or hierarchy), and that this does not require anarchy or hierarchy to be present in pure and exclusive form. Again, this is an effective technical defense of neorealist system theory, but not one that deals with (other than by marginalizing) the concerns of those trying to understand developments in the Third World. To the extent that Waltz is correct (and as most clearly articulated by Mohammed Ayoob, and in a different way by Amitav Acharya, in this volume) system theories cannot be excluded from thinking about the Third World no matter what their shortcomings in providing a full explanation for its conditions may be.

2. The Unit-Level Alternative

The authors in this volume are virtually unanimous in thinking that the high politics questions about the Third World (those of war and peace, both internal and external) can only be understood by giving more weight to the nature of the states that are found there. Their views vary somewhat, but they cluster around an image of the Third World state as a distorted, or incomplete, or weak, or badly transplanted copy of the original Westphalian model. All of them accept that the Third World state is a transplant. Such states are a product of the last two centuries during which European/Western power has been globally dominant. Most of them were laid down by patterns of European colonization that usually overrode indigenous political geography. Adopting the European political form was the price of independence for those that had been directly occupied, and the price for escaping colonization for the few such as Japan, Thailand, the Ottoman Empire, and Ethiopia that remained independent during the height of European world power.[11]

Beyond that common starting point, however, positions begin to diverge. Some of the authors (call them pragmatists) proceed from the view that what is done is done, whether desirable or not. They therefore define the problem as how to make the best of it. From this perspective, the central issue is how to bring the Third World state up to the Westphalian standard, by correcting its distortions, weaknesses, and lack of completeness. In other words, it is how to make Third World states into strong states, a line I have elsewhere argued myself.[12] In this view, Third World states are not fundamentally different from Western ones. Rather, they are of the same basic type, but at a different stage or level of development, an argument that is clearly set out by Ayoob and Steven R. David. The problem is to find ways of moving their development along so as to close the gap between them and the leading states in the system. There are differences about how to do this (for example, is democracy more help or more hindrance in the early and middle stages of state-making?), but the nature of the project overall is the same: finding ways of building properly hierarchical states with solid foundations of sociopolitical cohesion able to sustain modern economies. This understanding offers seemingly attractive possibilities for comparing Third World states with various stages in the evolution of the European state from medieval through early modern, to modern and postmodern. The one snag with such a comparison (and it is not clear how big a snag it is) is that the European development took place largely free from outside intervention. The Third World, by contrast, has to make its way in a highly developed, intense, and intrusive international system. It has the advantage of role models and outside help, but the disadvantages of a thousand strong constraints and influences that do not allow it to work out its own political forms as the Europeans did.

Other authors in this volume, most notably Donald J. Puchala and in some ways K. J. Holsti, take a more radical stance. They are not prepared simply to accept the transplanted European state system as a fait accompli. Rather than getting on with trying to make it work, they want to problematize the act of transplantation itself, and at least hold open the possibility of rejecting it. The difficulty with this position is that such a rejection is much more easily said than done—or even visualized in any coherent fashion. The pragmatic "make the best of it" school can at least formulate a clear set of aspirations, no matter how difficult it might be to realize them in practice. But the radicals have no obvious template. They can try to look back or try to look forward, but the view is seriously hazy in both directions. It is far from clear how useful it is to dig in the arcadian mine of the social and political constructions that existed before the European imposition. Some of these have been destroyed or corrupted beyond recovery, and even where they can be recovered it is not obvious that such constructions would be effective, efficient, or even possible in the modern world system. Some Western notions, such as nationalism (the idea that the ultimate source of political legitimacy and right to self-government lies in groups that share a common identity, and usually a common language and history), are now so deeply rooted in the Third World as to count as indigenous. Looking in the other direction—beyond the state—there is a stunning lack of anything concrete. The few scraps that are available, such as nearly stateless liberal utopias or EU-style political unions, are so far removed from Third World possibilities as to be more or less irrelevant. They are visions that seek to move beyond where the most advanced states now are, and they require the economic and cultural foundations of a well-consolidated late modern development. Such visions have little to offer those still trying to come to terms with modernism, and not yet possessing the economic and cultural requisites to get even that far.

So the radical position is a powerful critique, but until it can come equipped with a convincing vision of political forms other than the state, it is a weak alternative. Even more than the pragmatists, the radicals face the question of whether the fruits of modern science, technology and economics can be had without adopting the same sociopolitical forms that generated them (and were generated by them) in the West. In other words, can modernization be achieved separately from Westernization? Puchala's Third World radicals seem to believe that modernization can be separated from Westernization, and their project makes no sense without such a belief. But such evidence as we have from the evolution of successful modernizing states in East Asia suggests that over two or three generations, the price of modernization is a very substantial dose of Westernization. At the very least it remains to be argued, and even more so demonstrated, that economic development can be achieved within sociopolitical frameworks radically different from those in the West. And it is not clear whether such political alternatives would be allowed even if they could be imagined. All of the authors are conscious of the power differentials in the international system, and of the fact that part of what defines the Third World is its lack of power. The power of the system is strong. Its politico-legal foundation is the Westphalian state, and the risks of challenging that standard are formidable. Carlos Escudé notes the costs of rebellion, and it is no accident that even (or perhaps particularly) the most revolutionary states in the system (the former USSR, China, Iran) are tremendous sticklers about their sovereign rights.

For those wishing to pursue distinctive development projects that go against the political-economic mainstream, the politico-legal niceties of sovereignty are one of their main lines of defense.

But whatever their differences, both the pragmatists and the radicals are essentially saying (neorealist claims about lack of functional differentiation of units notwithstanding), that there are major differences between the states in the Third World and those in the West. And these differences are not just of population size, power, ideology, and geography, but in the fundamentals of the way in which they are constituted as states. On this basis, both perspectives point to a two (or possibly three) "worlds" perspective in which constitutive and/or developmental differences among the units in the international system are so great as to justify thinking about significantly different subsystems of International Relations.

3. The "Two-Worlds" View and Its Limits

The idea that the international system is composed of "like units" is very powerful in International Relations Theory, but quite recent, and probably quite temporary, in world history. In ancient and classical times, most international systems (the Middle East, the Mediterranean, South Asia, East Asia) were a mixture of city-states, empires, and barbarian tribes. The medieval system in Europe contained many different types of units, and Charles Tilly tells the medieval to modern story in Europe in terms of an interplay among empires, city-state federations, and national states.[13] Until decolonization required a more circumspect use of language, it was perfectly common for Europeans to classify the world in terms of "civilized," "barbarian," and "savage," and to make unequal treaties with the "lesser" political entities in the latter two categories. The ancient Greeks and Chinese, and no doubt many other "civilized" peoples also divided the world into "civilized" and "barbarian." These differentiations were partly matters of culture and degrees of economic development. But they could also be about different types of development, either in terms of different political forms, or different types of economy (nomadic herdsmen, settled agriculturalists, industrial). The tradition of thinking in terms of two worlds almost always carries a strong element of inequality, and thus some of the implications for the Third World of thinking about international politics in this way are not very pleasant. It should not be forgotten that Third World states are among the most vocal claimants of rights to sovereign equality, and can be expected to offer strong resistance to any attempt at formal (re)classification as unequal. Though sovereignty may be only a formal politico-legal standing, making little difference to huge inequalities of power, it should not be forgotten that it still represents a big political improvement over the formal inequality (plus huge inequalities of power) of colonial times.

Decolonization created a myth, and up to a point a reality, of "like units," though even during the Cold War it was common to talk of the "first," "second," and "third" worlds on the basis of the different types of states therein. But a generation after the global redistribution of formal sovereign equality, and with the Cold War (and the Second World) out of the way, the constitutive differences among the political units in the international system stand out pretty clearly, even though we still call them all states. At some risk of oversimplification the contemporary universe of states can be divided into three types: postmodern, modern, and premodern.[14]

The modern state can be seen in terms of the standard Westphalian model, defined by strong government control over society and restrictive attitudes towards openness. In many parts of the Third World, the states are still essentially modern (for instance, Iran, Iraq, China, the two Koreas). Until quite recently modern states dominated the whole international political landscape. They took their governments and their territory seriously, and saw themselves as independent, self-reliant, and culturally distinctive entities. They often had distinctive national development policies, and tried to keep control over a broad industrial base and an independent set of armed forces. They cultivated dominant identities, often, but not always, nationalist ones, as a means of unifying their populations. Their citizens enjoyed some individual and collective rights against the state, but strong internal sovereignty, and the ever-present threat of war gave priority to individual and collective responsibilities to the state, particularly in terms of military service. Their borders marked real lines of closure against outside economic, political, and cultural influences, and their sovereignty was sacrosanct. Modern states typically define a wide range of military, political, economic, and cultural factors as threats to national security. Such states shaped our understanding of what it meant to be a Great Power. The Soviet Union was a modern Great Power, and China is evidently trying to become one. Iran, Iraq, and India are all modern states aspiring to be Great Powers in their regions, and many of the states in the Middle East, Asia, and Latin America are still essentially modern in form. Most of the state-making projects in the former Soviet empire are also modernist.

But following a logic of liberalization, the leading states, and all of the great capitalist powers, have now evolved beyond the modernist model. In pursuit of wealth, democracy, and individual rights they have taken on a postmodern form. They still retain the trappings of modernity such as borders and sovereignty and national identity, but don't take them nearly so seriously as before. Postmodern states have a much more open and tolerant attitude toward cultural, economic, and political interaction, and define a much narrower range of things as threats to national security. They have substantially abandoned the autarchic tendencies of modernism, and opened up and hollowed out their economies by linking themselves together in a transnational global economy. In postmodern states civil society has as much or more influence than government. Postmodern states are democratic, but that may matter less than their relentless pluralism and individualism. Citizens focus much more on their individual and collective rights against the state than they do on their individual and collective responsibilities to it. The social cohesion of a single overriding national identity has given way to multiculturalism and multiple identities of all sorts, whether to do with gender, culture, sport, work, or style. Postmodern societies are prosperous and educated, and civil society no longer wants to be contained by the state either economically or socially, though it does still look to the state for some forms of security.

Postmodern societies are in many ways not compatible with many of the traditional roles and behaviors of the Great Powers. The weakening of shared identity means that individuals are no longer so prepared to die for their country. Smaller families and fewer children also make the sacrifices of war less acceptable to society as a whole. Social Darwinist ideas about "top nation" clash with multiculturalism and democracy, and cannot so easily be used to support aggressive foreign policies. Postmodern states have largely disengaged their armed forces from society by making them professional rather than conscript, capital rather than labor intensive, and therefore small rather than large. This should have made them easier to use, but has not. Postmodern citizens trust their governments less, and are much more critical about state actions that might require heavy costs or sacrifices. The emphasis on individual and human rights means that all foreign policy actions easily get bogged down in moral and legal debates. Because there is a whole group of powerful postmodern states the sense of threat from abroad has declined. Because postmodern societies are culturally and economically open, the attraction of distinctive national development projects has weakened.

The resources of power are still present in postmodern states, but they are either not under government command, or not available for use because of public attitudes hostile to the ways of *machtpolitik*. Postmodern states still have the technology, the weapons, and the money that are the classical ingredients of such power, but they can no longer use them in the familiar way. They can be thought of as "lite powers."[15] In the United States, elections have been lost by presidents seen as too concerned with foreign policy and won by candidates banging the domestic drum. In Europe, most energy is absorbed in the half-finished and still shaky attempt to build institutions for the whole continent. As yet, there are no real machineries for making collective foreign and security policies, and when there are, like those in the

United States they will be dominated by domestic concerns. Japan also lacks serious foreign policymaking institutions, not least because most of its citizens still reject the idea that their country is a Great Power.

At the opposite end of the spectrum, scattered throughout the Third World, but most notably in Africa and Central Asia, is a set of states that can loosely be described as premodern. Defining what this comprises is not easy. In part it is defined by low levels of sociopolitical cohesion and poorly developed structures of government (for example, Afghanistan, Tadjikistan, Somalia, Nigeria, Sudan, Zaire). Some of these are premodern in the sense that they aspire to modernity, and are headed in that direction, but have yet to consolidate themselves sufficiently to qualify. In many there are serious tensions between the framework of modernity and the traditional political and societal patterns that underlie it. Most are heavily penetrated by international institutions that represent and promote the modernist objective. Some are failed states, where the colonial transplant has broken down, and there is little other than external recognition to sustain the myth of statehood. Inside failed states there is much more anarchy than hierarchy, and the national government may be little more than the faction or warlord that currently occupies the principal city.

Perhaps nowhere is the sense of contrast amongst these three types clearer than in Europe, where they sit cheek by jowl. The EU project with its dissolving states, layered identities and polities, and single market is the essence of postmodernist development. Next door to it are the nineteenth-century style, modernist nation-state building projects of Central and Eastern Europe, with Poland, the Czech Republic, Hungary, and Slovenia caught awkwardly between the two. In the Balkans, Yugoslavia failed to the point of disintegration, and Albania and Bosnia look precariously close to being failed states. Even within the postmodern area there are patches of earlier forms that sustain political violence, such as Northern Ireland, the Basque country, and Corsica.

It is this differentiation of units that provides the basis for the "two worlds" view of the contemporary international system.[16] Contrary to neorealism, the two worlds view rests on the assumption that the overall character of International Relations is generated more by the internal character of the units comprising the system than by the system structure.[17] The two worlds view supposes that a partial transformation of the international system has taken place. Rather than being a single politico-strategic space, with a single set of rules of the game, the international system has divided into two worlds. One world (call it the zone of peace) is defined by a postmodern security community of powerful advanced industrial democracies, and International Relations within this world no longer operate according to old realist rules. In the zone of peace, states do not expect or prepare for war against each other, and since this zone contains most of the Great Powers this is a very significant development for the whole of the international system. Reflecting the character of postmodern states, economies and societies are highly open and interdependent, transnational players are numerous and strong, and international relations is heavily institutionalized.

The other world (call it the zone of conflict) is comprised of a mixture of modern and premodern states. In relations among (and within) these states classical realist rules still obtain, and war is a usable and used instrument of policy. In this zone, International Relations operate by the traditional rules of power politics that prevailed all over the world up to 1945. States expect and prepare for the possibility of serious tension with their neighbors. Some restraint is provided by deterrence (in a few places nuclear deterrence) but economic interdependence between neighbors is generally low, and populations can often be easily mobilized for war. Especially within premodern, but also within some modern states, political power is frequently contested by force. Even in the prospering states of East Asia where economic interdependence between neighbors is growing, the states are still often fragile and highly protective of sovereignty, and use of force among some of them cannot be ruled out.

To divide the world in this way of course oversimplifies. Some places close to the core of the zone of peace behave like the zone of conflict (ex-Yugoslavia, Albania, Northern Ireland), and some ostensibly in the zone of conflict have managed to build substantial regional barriers against local wars (the Association of South-East Asian Nations [ASEAN], the Southern African Development Community [SADC], and possibly the Mercosur in the Latin American southern cone). An alternative view is that these two worlds exist not as distinct and separate territorial spaces, but as interleaved modes of living. Thus parts of some cities in the West contain their own zones of conflict. Nevertheless the general distinction seems valid, and the claim for two parallel modes of International Relations seems plausible. There are fundamental qualitative differences in the way in which the states and societies of Europe, North America, and Japan relate both to one another and to their populations on the one hand, and the way in which states in the Middle East, South Asia, and many other places do so. These differences are rooted deeply in the form and character, and therefore also the history, of the states and societies within the two zones.

This line of reasoning has substantial implications for the whole issue of IR Theory and the Third World. It can be construed as an attack on the attempts of system theorists, especially neorealists, to impose a single, global theory on the study of International Relations. If unit-level thinking is given priority, then we are faced with at least a need for two theories, one for each zone. But as quickly becomes apparent, posing the choice as an either/or one, of system dominant or unit dominant, is not a fruitful way to proceed. Choosing the global level, system-dominant approach means marginalizing a huge chunk of the system. But choosing the unit dominant one risks assuming that the two zones operate largely disconnected from each other. Any such assumption would be quite implausible, as the authors in this volume all recognize. A central issue in the two worlds formulation is how the zone of peace and the zone of conflict relate to each other, for that they do relate in many and significant ways is beyond question. While there may well be a case for having two theories to explain how the different domestic structures in the two zones generate their distinctive forms of International Relations, there also needs to be an overarching theory that ties the two together.

In the past, the relationship between different zones of political economy was often the mainspring of history. Before the rise of Europe, the relationship between the barbarian and civilized zones was crucial. Sometimes the barbarians were vital intermediaries in the long-distance trading networks, and at other times they were fearsome invaders. Again, during the European expansion, the relationship between the modernizing European core and the premodern periphery was the defining feature of world history. As a rule, the nature and shape of zones in the international system changes over time, but the fact of them does not. At whatever point in history one looks at the international system, some strong pattern of uneven development and different forms of political economy will be present. The diffusion of goods, ideas, and peoples works continuously to erode uneven development, but never (yet) succeeds in doing so. Some cultures have great difficulty absorbing new goods and ideas without self-destructing. And the game is not static. The leading edge cultures are themselves continuously evolving (or in some cases declining), so are opening up new space and new zones to maintain the pattern of unevenness.

In recent times, some attention has focused on the relationship between center and periphery, and with the Cold War out of the way we can expect this to intensify. How the two zones will relate to each other is one of the great unanswered questions for the twenty-first century. Will the weaker, but perhaps more aggressive, zone of conflict begin to penetrate and impinge upon the zone of peace through threats of terrorism, long-range weapons of mass destruction, migration, disease, debt repudiation, and so on? Will the unquestionably more powerful zone of peace seek to penetrate and influences the zone of conflict, using the levers of geoeconomics, and occasionally more robust forms of intervention, to manipulate state-making in the zone of conflict? Will the postmodern world try to insulate itself by constructing buffer zones in Mexico, Central Europe, Turkey, and North Africa, and trying to stay out of the more chaotic parts of the zone of conflict? Or will it try to engage with the whole, pushing toward a new world order in its own image? We can only guess at the answers to these questions, but what is clear is that complete, or even substantial, separation of the two zones is highly unlikely.

If the interplay between them is significant, then we need both system-level and unit-level theories in order to comprehend what is going on. What seems absolutely clear is that the actors (states, multinationals, NGOs) in the zone of peace are largely responsible for creating and maintaining the international system and international society within which the actors in the zone of conflict have to operate. Everything from norms, rules, and laws, through capital and information flows, to the structure of power is shaped by the zone of peace, and *strongly* shaped. The international system and society in which the zone of conflict is embedded is arguably the most powerful, comprehensive, and pervasive ever seen on the planet. So great is its impact that it is possible to ask whether (or to theorize that) the core in the zone of peace is in some ways responsible for the social, political, and economic weakness in the periphery. Does economic, cultural, political, and military pressure from the core actually destabilize the periphery and inhibit its development, or does it provide role models, resources, and capital that should help the periphery to overcome obstacles to development that are rooted in its own cultures and history? The answer to that question is hotly contested and far from empirically clear, but it is not unreasonable to ask it. Neither is it unreasonable to ask whether the power differential between core and periphery is so great that it is only a matter of time before the core assimilates much of the periphery. The vast modernization process underway in much of East Asia, and possibly beginning in South Asia, will forever change the balance between wealth and poverty, and core and periphery, in the international system. If it succeeds, the core will no longer be rooted in just one civilization (the West), but will span several continents in a global network of power and prosperity.

There *are* two worlds whose political life is defined by differences in their level and type of political, social, and economic development. But while these worlds may well be different, they are not separate. There is a strong, if lopsided, interaction between them. In order to understand this configuration we need both unit-level and system-level theories.

4. Conclusions: What IR Theories Can One Use or Develop to Think about the Third World?

Up to this point, my argument has been that one needs both unit- and system-level theories to understand the Third World. Several of the chapters in this book make suggestions about unit-level theories so I will not dwell further on that level. But most of the discussion about system-level theories in the chapters focuses on criticism and rejection. Neorealism and (to a lesser extent) neoliberalism, are paraded, trashed, and thrown out. Yet while there is little dissent among the authors that the system level is important, it is far from clear what kind of theory they would like to see to cover this aspect of the Third World problematique. If my argument is correct, then it would clearly be a mistake to drop system-level theory and focus only on the unit level. This would simply repeat in reverse the original error of putting too much weight on system-level theory. To bring things back into balance it is this theory void at the system level that needs to be addressed, and that will be the task of this final section.

If one accepts that neorealism and neoliberalism have little useful to say about the Third World, where does one turn for appropriate system-level theory? One obvious place, almost entirely ignored in the preceding chapters, is the mostly Marxian-derived theories that already accept the two worlds view in the form of center and periphery. *Dependencia* theory is probably now too discredited and too old-fashioned to be a candidate, for much of both its analysis and its prescription have been undermined by events. But its analysis of political and economic weakness in the periphery as caused by the center should still hold some attractions to those studying the Third World—unless they accept the unpalatable view that the Third World's problems are entirely rooted within its own history and culture. Perhaps more attractive is the world system theory school of thought that developed out of the work of Immanuel Wallerstein, and which is still vigorous, even if somewhat isolated from the IR mainstream. With its focus on capitalism as the system structure, and on causal links between power in the center and weakness in the periphery, it would be surprising if this body of work did not have some useful ideas to offer to those thinking about a Third World whose own process of development is ensnared in a strong international political economy that is generated and controlled from outside it.

Another possibility is to reconsider the by now ritualistic rejection of neorealism, and look at the work of those who have been trying to develop a more open, "structural realist" form of the theory. Since most of the authors in this work are sympathetic to realism, while rejecting neorealism, this path may offer fewer normative problems than the Marxian-derived one (as well as being more congenial to my own expertise). The key to this path lies in the second tier of Waltz's conception of system structure: differentiation of units. Waltz closed the second tier of his theory, arguing by definition that in anarchic systems units must be sovereign and therefore be "like units" lacking functional differentiation. As a consequence he did not give all that much thought to the nature of functional differentiation, and even less to other ways of differentiating units. The whole idea of differentiation of units thus remains an underdeveloped area of neorealist theory. This is despite strong arguments that the closure of the second tier is a major error that distorts both neorealism's whole conception of international system structure, and its ability to identify significant change in international systems.[18] Differentiation of units, as argued earlier, is exactly what most of the authors in this volume are trying in some way to get at.

The pathway from the structural to the unit level in structural realism leads through the theory of the state that is hidden in neorealism. As Richard Little has pointed out, there is a quite strong theory of the state built into Waltz's account, even though few others, including Waltz, seem to be aware of it.[19] Waltz's theory of the state rather vaguely assumes that states form in isolation prior to the existence of an international system. This clearly does not apply to Third World states, most of which were created by the system. That does not matter much for the argument I want to make here, though it opens up an interesting area for development of the theory: for instance, what happens when the system creates states? But the most interesting part of the theory concerns what happens when states begin to interact. Then an anarchic system forms, and Waltz argues that the anarchic structure generates processes of socialization and competition that steadily pressure the states into becoming more alike. The driving logic here is the survival imperative within a balance of power. As some states find ways of increasing their power (new technologies, better organization) others have either to follow suit or lose power relative to those that do. Too much loss of power eventually threatens survival, eliminating those states that fail to respond adequately to the structural pressure. As Little argues, a careful reading of Waltz reveals that this logic applies not only to *functional differentiation,* that is, whether the units all claim full right of self-government (sovereignty), or only partial rights (for example, vassals, protectorates or dominions within suzerain relationships); but also to *structural differentiation,* that is, how units are internally organized and constructed. Waltz's expectation is that the system-level pressure of socialization and competition will produce homogenization at the unit level: "like units" both in functional terms (all sovereign) and in structural ones (on the current model, all having roughly similar organizational forms in terms of armies, navies, air forces, foreign ministries, education systems, health and welfare systems, and so on).

It is this theory that those Third World theorists rebelling against neorealism need to take as their target. On the face of it the target is no pushover. The states in the contemporary international system do display a remarkable degree of functional and structural similarity, even though it is not exactly clear what Waltz's expectation are in this regard. As noted earlier, he sees his theory as being mostly about the Great Powers, and is not bothered by discrepancies among the lesser actors. Yet it is not entirely obvious how one should place the claims for differentiation made by some of the authors in this volume. Unless they can distinguish their unit-level claims from mere differences in power (which neorealism easily contains), they do not have a good line of attack. One possible route would be to show that Third World states are not fully sovereign (as Escudé asserts, applying it as well to many non-Third World states), and that the system therefore is functionally differentiated. This is difficult to do without adopting a definition of sovereignty that seriously confuses the claim to self-government on the one hand, and the possession of autonomy of action on the other. In my view blurring the distinction between power and sovereignty in this way is not helpful to theory construction, though it has to be acknowledged that there is no consensus on the meaning of sovereignty in IR.

A more promising alternative would be to show that the differences between postmodern, modern, and premodern states count as structural differentiation (as might be inferred from Ayoob's and Holsti's positions). Taking this approach would also offer the opportunity to integrate system- and unit-level theory within a single set of concepts. The task may seem daunting, but history offers a lot of support for the idea that Waltz's homogenizing mechanisms at the very least don't work smoothly, and that structural differentiation of units is a normal and important feature of international systems. Consider the following:

- For the entire ancient and classical period (from 3000 BC to 1500 AD) international systems were composed of structurally differentiated units: city-states, empires, and barbarian tribes. Even where there was strong (that is, military) interaction, barbarian tribes and classical empires did not become structurally similar.
- From the perspective of world historians, the key turning points in world history (and thus the key transformations of the international system) are defined by structural changes in the character of the dominant units. The first change, circa 3000 BC, is the rise of civilization itself, when city-states, empires, and nomadic barbarians evolved from simpler hunter-gatherer and village agriculture. The second change is the rise of the national state in Europe circa 1500 AD, which quickly marginalized or eliminated all of the older political forms. These changes are more in structure than in function, for it might be argued that most of the political units in world history claimed self-government, albeit not explicitly in terms of the Westphalian idea of sovereignty.
- Waltz's theory assumes that system-level effects work evenly throughout the international system, but history suggests that they do not. No clearer illustration of this could be desired than the rise of Europe that

created the Third World. The socialization and competition among the European powers developed locally, and gave them an advantage over the rest of the world. The resulting European takeover created a global system that was sharply differentiated in functional terms, with a handful of metropolitan powers commanding a vast array of dominions, protectorates, and colonies. Mouritzen provides a useful theoretical explanation for this by noting the difference between systems in which the units are mobile (that is, not territorially fixed, as was true of many barbarian tribes in classical times) and those in which they are fixed (such as modern territorial states).[20] Systems with fixed units will tend to develop strong regional features because units will be more influenced by local than by global structural effects. Most states will be able to project power into those adjacent to them, but only a few will have global reach. If the units are mobile, then each is in principle a neighbor to all the others, and structural effects will be evenly distributed throughout the system. As in classical times, you might wake up one morning to find a Great Power such as the Golden Horde on your doorstep, where nothing had been before.

- Waltz's theory assumes that units are internally flexible enough to adapt to the pressures of socialization and competition fast enough so that catch-up is possible between innovators and followers. Ayoob's "subaltern realism" also seems to depend on this assumption. But while there is little doubt that units do respond to structural pressure (otherwise how do we come to be living in a system of states?), there is room for doubt about the prospects for catch-up. It could be argued that the postmodern core is currently accelerating away from much of the rest of the international system. It is massively restructuring its whole political economy, in the process seeming to move towards a much more complex, layered, and large-scale organization in terms of identity, governance, and markets. In Western Europe, the birthplace of the Westphalian state, a process of integration is unfolding (albeit haltingly) that is creating a new form of political economy in many ways transcending the state. While this is happening, much of the Third World is still trying to come to terms with modernism, and some of it is failing to do even that. What is one to make of the gulf between societies that are linking themselves together electronically on a global scale, and societies that cannot even keep their local railway system in operation? On Ayoob's model of parallel developmental stages between the Third World and the West, that suggests a gap of nearly 200 years. Uneven development is deeply embedded in the whole of human history, and Waltz's strong theoretical logic notwithstanding, seems unlikely to disappear soon.

- Waltz's theory assumes that the driving force behind system-level pressure for "like units" is the pursuit of survival (that is, security) against external threats. But as Robert Jackson[21] and others (some in this volume) have pointed out, in the contemporary international system many Third World states do not face survival threats from outside—at least not of the type that Waltz had in mind that did so much to shape the development of the state in Europe. By a curious irony, the sovereignty-based international society generated by the core now promotes a set of rules, norms, and practices that shield weaker states from the pressures that might otherwise have eliminated them. At a push, it could almost be argued that rather than promoting homogenization of units, the system is now providing conditions that stabilize certain types of differentiation.

If it is accepted that differentiation of units is a significant and durable feature of the international system, then a major theoretical task opens up in trying to assess and hypothesize both the behavioral consequences of differentiated systems, and the type and extent of change on the second tier that would suffice to count as a change in the structure of the system.[22] If structural effects are, for whatever reason, unevenly distributed in the international system, then regional approaches might well be warranted. There are good reasons for thinking that regionalization will be a strong feature of International Relations in the coming decades,[23] and if this is so, then there may well be a case for examining the interplay between system and units at the regional level.

Notes

1. Barry Buzan, "The Level of Analysis Problem in International Relations Reconsidered" in *International Political Theory Today*, eds., Ken Booth and Steve Smith (London: Polity Press, 1995), pps. 198–216.
2. Kenneth Waltz, *Man, the State and War* (NY: Columbia University Press, 1959); David J. Singer, "International Conflict: Three Levels of Analysis," *World Politics*, vol. 12, no. 3, pps. 453–61; David J. Singer, "The Level of Analysis Problem in International Relations," in *The International System: Theoretical Essays*, eds. Klaus Knorr and Sydney Verba (Princeton, NJ: Princeton University Press, 1961), pps. 77–92.
3. Kenneth Waltz, *Theory of International Politics* (Reading, MA: Addison-Wesley, 1979).
4. Ibid., p. 96.
5. Ibid., p. 94.
6. Barry Buzan and Richard Little, "Reconceptualizing Anarchy: Structural Realism Meets World History," *European Journal of International Relations*, vol. 2,

no. 4 (1996), pps. 403–38; John G. Ruggie, "Continuity and Transformation in the World Polity: Towards a Neorealist Synthesis," *World Politics,* vol. 35, no. 2 (1983), pps. 261–85, reprinted in Robert O Keohane, ed., *Neorealism and Its Critics* (NY: Columbia University Press, 1986), pps. 131–57; John G. Ruggie, "Territoriality and Beyond: Problematizing Modernity in International Relations," *International Organization* vol. 47, no. 1, (1993), pps. 139–74.

7. R. B. J. Walker, *Inside/Outside: International Relations as Political Theory* (Cambridge: Cambridge University Press, 1993).

8. John G. Ruggie, *International Transformations: Essays in Continuity and Change* (London: Routledge, 1998).

9. Waltz, *Theory of International Politics,* p. 114.

10. Ibid., pps. 115–16.

11. Gerrit W. Gong, *The Standard of "Civilisation" in International Society* Oxford: Clarendon Press, 1984).

12. Barry Buzan, *People, States and Fear,* second edition (London: Harvester Wheatsheaf, 1991), pps. 175–81.

13. Charles Tilly, *Coercion, Capital and European States AD 990–1990* (Oxford: Basil Blackwell, 1990).

14. Barry Buzan and Gerald Segal, "The Rise of the 'Lite' Powers: A Strategy for Postmodern States," *World Policy Journal,* vol. 13, no. 3 (1996), pps. 1–10; Barry Buzan and Gerald Segal, *Anticipating the Future* (London: Simon and Schuster, 1998), ch. 6.

15. Buzan and Segal, "The Rise of the 'Lite' Powers."

16. Barry Buzan, "New Patterns of Global Security in the Twenty-first Century," *International Affairs,* vol. 67, no. 3 (1991), p. 432; James M. Goldgeier and Michael McFaul, "A Tale of Two Worlds: Core and Periphery in the Post–Cold War Era," *International Organization,* vol. 46, no. 2 (1992), pps. 467–91; Max Singer and Aaron Wildavsky, *The Real World Order: Zones of Peace/Zones of Turmoil* (Chatham: Chatham House Publishers, 1993); and implicitly in an earlier version, Robert O. Keohane and Joseph S. Nye, *Power and Interdependence* (Boston: Little Brown, 1977).

17. For a different angle, see Alexander Wendt, "Anarchy Is What States Make of It: The Social Construction of Power Politics," *International Organization,* vol. 46, no. 2 (1992), pps. 391–425.

18. Ruggie, "Continuity and Transformation" and "Territoriality and Beyond"; Barry Buzan, Charles Jones, and Richard Little, *The Logic of Anarchy: Neorealism to Structural Realism* (NY: Columbia University Press, 1993); Buzan and Little, "Reconceptualizing Anarchy."

19. Buzan, Jones and Little, *The Logic of Anarchy,* pps. 116–19; Buzan and Little, "Reconceptualizing Anarchy," pps. 409–13.

20. Hans Mouritzen, "A Fallacy of IR Theory: Reflections on a Collective Repression," unpublished ms (Copenhagen, Centre for Peace and Conflict Research, 1995); Hans Mouritzen, "Kenneth Waltz: With Karl Popper Between International Politics and Foreign Policy," in *The Future of International Relations:*

Masters in the Making, eds. Iver Neumann and Ole Waever (London: Routledge, 1996) pps. 66–89.

21. Robert Jackson, *Quasi-States: Sovereignty, International Relations and the Third World* (Cambridge: Cambridge University Press, 1990).

22. Buzan and Little, "Reconceptualizing Anarchy."

23. Barry Buzan, Ole Wæver, and Jaap de Wilde, *Security: A New Framework for Analysis* (Boulder CO: Lynne Rienner Publishers, 1997); Andrew Hurrell, "Explaining the Resurgence of Regionalism in World Politics," *Review of International Studies,* vol. 21, no. 3 (1995), pps. 331–58.

Bibliography

Buzan, Barry and Gerald Segal. *Anticipating the Future.* London: Simon and Schuster, 1998.

———, Ole Waever, and Jaap de Wilde. *Security: A New Framework for Analysis.* Boulder, CO: Lynne Rienner Publishers, 1997.

——— and Richard Little. "Reconceptualizing Anarchy: Structural Realism Meets World History." *European Journal of International Relations.* Vol. 2, no. 4 (1996), pps. 403–38.

——— and Gerald Segal. "The Rise of the 'Lite' Powers: A Strategy for Postmodern States." *World Policy Journal.* Vol. 13, no. 3 (1996), pps. 1–10.

———. "The Level of Analysis Problem in International Relations Reconsidered." In *International Political Theory Today.* Eds., Ken Booth and Steve Smith. London: Polity Press, 1995, pps. 198–216.

———, Charles Jones, and Richard Little. *The Logic of Anarchy: Neorealism to Structural Realism.* New York: Columbia University Press, 1993.

———. *People, States and Fear.* Second Edition. London: Harvester Wheatsheaf, 1991.

———. "New Patterns of Global Security in the Twenty-first Century." *International Affairs.* Vol. 67, no. 3 (1991), p. 432.

Goldgeier, James M. and Michael McFaul. "A Tale of Two Worlds: Core and Periphery in the Post–Cold War Era." *International Organization.* Vol. 46, no. 2 (1992), pps. 467–91.

Gong, Gerrit W. *The Standard of "Civilisation" in International Society.* Oxford: Clarendon Press, 1984.

Hurrell, Andrew. "Explaining the Resurgence of Regionalism in World Politics." *Review of International Studies.* Vol. 21, no. 3 (1995), pps. 331–58.

Keohane, Robert O. and Joseph S. Nye. *Power and Interdependence.* Boston: Little Brown, 1977.

Jackson, Robert. *Quasi-States: Sovereignty, International Relations and the Third World.* Cambridge: Cambridge University Press, 1990.

Mouritzen, Hans. "Kenneth Waltz: With Karl Popper between International Politics and Foreign Policy." In *The Future of International Relations: Masters in the Making.* Eds., Iver Neumann and Ole Waever. London: Routledge, 1996, pps. 66–89.

———. "A Fallacy of IR Theory: Reflections on a Collective Repression." Unpublished manuscript. Copenhagen, Centre for Peace and Conflict Research, 1995.

Ruggie, John G. *International Transformations: Essays in Continuity and Change.* London: Routledge, 1998.

———. "Territoriality and Beyond: Problematizing Modernity in International Relations." *International Organization.* Vol. 47, no. 1 (1993), pps. 139–74.

———. "Continuity and Transformation in the World Polity: Towards a Neorealist Synthesis." *World Politics.* Vol. 35, no. 2 (1983), pps. 261–85.

Singer, David J. and Aaron Wildavsky. *The Real World Order: Zones of Peace/Zones of Turmoil.* Chatham: Chatham House Publishers, 1993.

———. "The Level of Analysis Problem in International Relations." In *The International System: Theoretical Essays.* Eds., Klaus Knorr and Sydney Verba. Princeton, NJ: Princeton University Press, 1961), pps. 77–92.

———. "International Conflict: Three Level of Analysis." *World Politics.* Vol. 12, no, 3 (1960), pps. 453–61.

Tilly, Charles. *Coercion, Capital and European States AD 990–1990.* Oxford: Basil Blackwell, 1990.

Walker, R. B. J. *Inside/Outside: International Relations as a Political Theory.* Cambridge: Cambridge University Press, 1993.

Waltz, Kenneth. *Man, the State and War.* New York: Columbia University Press, 1995.

———. *Theory of International Politics.* Reading, MA: Addison-Wesley, 1979.

Wendt, Alexander. "Anarchy Is What States Make of It: The Social Construction of Power Politics." *International Organization.* Vol. 46, no. 2 (1992), pps. 391–425.

About the Authors

STEPHANIE G. NEUMAN is the Director of the Comparative Defense Studies Program, a Senior Research Scholar and Adjunct Professor of Third World security studies at Columbia University. She has also taught at West Point and at the New School for Social Research. Dr. Neuman publishes widely in the fields of third world military affairs and the international arms trade. She is the author of *Military Assistance in Recent Wars* and a contributor to the editorial pages of major newspapers and journals. She is currently working on a book about Third World wars.

MOHAMMED AYOOB is University Distinguished Professor of International Relations at Michigan State University. He has earlier held faculty appointments at the Australian National University and Jawharlal Nehru University in India, and visiting appointments at Columbia, Oxford, Princeton, and Brown Universities. He has published extensively on Third World conflict and security issues in the form of conceptual essays as well as case studies dealing with discrete regions. His latest book, *The Third World Security Predicament: State Making, Regional Conflict, and the International System* was published in 1995. His articles have appeared, among other journals, in *World Politics, International Studies Quarterly, Foreign Policy, Global Governance,* and *Washington Quarterly.* He has been awarded fellowships to conduct research on international conflict and security by the Rockefeller, Ford, and MacArthur Foundations.

CARLOS ESCUDÉ holds a Ph.D. in Political Science from Yale University and is Professor of International Relations at T. Di Tella University (Buenos Aires) and at the Argentine Foreign Service Academy (ISEN). He was former advisor to the Argentine foreign minister on foreign policy strategy (1991–1992), Guggenheim Fellow (1984–1985), and author of *Foreign Policy Theory in Menem's Argentina.*

STEVEN R. DAVID is a Professor of International Relations at Johns Hopkins University where he directs the International Studies Program. He has written widely on issues relating to international security and the Third World. David is presently working on a book examining the impact of internal war on global security.

K. J. HOLSTI is University Killam Professor of Political Science at the University of British Columbia, Vancouver, Canada. He is the former president of the Canadian Political Science Association and the International Studies Association. His most recent book is *The State, War, and the State of War* (Cambridge University Press, 1996).

DONALD J. PUCHALA is the Charles L. Jacobson Professor of Public Affairs in the Department of Government and International Studies at the University of South Carolina. Puchala is also the director of the Walker Institute of International Studies and his research in recent years has focused on culture, history, and international relations, particularly the relevance of moral philosophy to international analysis. His most recent publications include, *The Ethics of Globalism* and *International Encounters of Another Kind*.

AMITAV ACHARYA is Associate Professor in the Department of Political Science at York University, Toronto, Canada. He specializes in Third World security issues and Asia Pacific regional security.

BARRY BUZAN is Research Professor of International Studies at the University of Westminster, and Project Director at the Copenhagen Peace Research Institute (COPRI). Until September 1995, he was Professor of International Studies at the University of Warwick, and in 1997–1998 he was Olof Palme Visiting Professor in Sweden.

Index